WILDLIFE
of
SCOTLAND

EDITED BY FRED HOLLIDAY

Publication of this book has been made possible by
Gulf Oil Corporation on behalf of
The Scottish Wildlife Trust

MACMILLAN LONDON

Designed by Simon Jennings & Company Ltd
Line drawings by Hilary Burn

First published 1979 by Macmillan London Limited
Reprinted 1980

Published 1983 by
PAPERMAC
a division of Macmillan Publishers Limited
4 Little Essex Street London WC2R 3LF
and Basingstoke

Associated companies in Auckland, Dallas,
Delhi, Dublin, Hong Kong, Johannesburg,
Lagos, Manzini, Melbourne, Nairobi,
New York, Singapore, Tokyo, Washington
and Zaria

ISBN 0 333 35148 7

Printed in Hong Kong

Contents

Acknowledgement

One of the most important roles of the Scottish Wildlife Trust is to promote understanding of Scotland's wildlife. Gulf Oil Corporation is pleased to sponsor this book on behalf of the Trust as one of its contributions to the cultural heritage of Scotland.

List of contributors

Professor F. G. T. Holliday   Professor of Zoology in the University of Aberdeen, Chairman of the Nature Conservancy Council.
Acknowledgement is made to Angela Dyer, Professor Charles Gimingham, Dr P. A. Orkin, Robert Wright and Sir Charles Connell.

Dr W. H. Murray   Mountaineer and author.
Acknowledgement is made to George Scott Johnstone.

Dr Adam Watson   Research scientist, mountain and moorland ecologist
Acknowledgement is made to Elizabeth Allan and Marion Forbes.

Gunnar Godwin   Forestry Consultant; formerly Conservator, Forestry Commission.

Dr Derek Mills   Senior Lecturer in Freshwater Ecology and Fisheries Management, Department of Forestry and Natural Resources, University of Edinburgh.
Acknowledgement is made to R. N. Campbell and A. R. Waterston.

J. McCarthy   Deputy Director (Scotland), Nature Conservancy Council.
Acknowledgement is made to C. O. Badenoch, Mrs Bette Weir, Mrs J. Gammie and Dr D. Jenkins.

Dr D. Jenkins   Research scientist, wetland and moorland ecologist.
Acknowledgement is made to Drs W. R. P. Bourne, L. H. Campbell, J. D. Goss-Custard, P. Marren, I. Newton, A. J. Prater, I. J. Patterson, and to the British Trust for Ornithology, the Royal Society for the Protection of Birds and the Nature Conservancy Council.

Tom Weir   Author, broadcaster, naturalist and photographer.

Dr J. Morton Boyd   Director (Scotland), Nature Conservancy Council.

David Stephen   Author and naturalist; Director, Palacerigg Country Park, Cumbernauld.
Acknowledgement is made to Drs J. D. Lockie, Ray Hewson, David Jenkins, J. Morton Boyd, and to E. A. Smith.

Dr Jean Balfour   Chairman, Countryside Commission for Scotland.
Acknowledgement is made to Dr W. J. Eggeling, T. Huxley, Jessica Balfour and Mrs Diana Gladstone of Capenoch.

Foreword

A combination of geography, geology and the Gulf Stream has given Scotland a particularly rich and varied wildlife. For generations it was taken for granted and exploited; only in quite recent times has the need for consideration and conservation become apparent to more than a few dedicated enthusiasts. For much of this growth in understanding and education of the public, the Scottish Wildlife Trust must take the credit.

I hope that this book will take the process of spreading knowledge and understanding a stage further. The successful conservation of wildlife cannot be achieved by conservationists alone, it depends as much on a sympathetic and practical comprehension of the situation by people in many other walks of life. Planners, developers, engineers, farmers, foresters, gamekeepers and many others are all consciously or unconsciously involved in deciding the future of Scotland's wildlife.

Perhaps the greatest value of this book is that it is full of useful information about the Scottish countryside and its wildlife, and the more you know about a subject the more pleasure you can derive from it.

A note on the maps

Satellite pictures have been chosen to illustrate the geography of Scotland not only because they are more striking than any map, but also to emphasize that recording and sensing from satellites offers exciting new opportunities to scientists and naturalists in their studies of landform and animal and plant communities.

In these pictures the satellite orbit was 915 kilometres (570 miles) above the earth, and the use of the near infra-red end of the light spectrum to record the images provides a very strong contrast between land and water.

There is a key to the maps on p. ix. Further maps on the geology, glaciation and climate of Scotland may be found on pages 187–9.

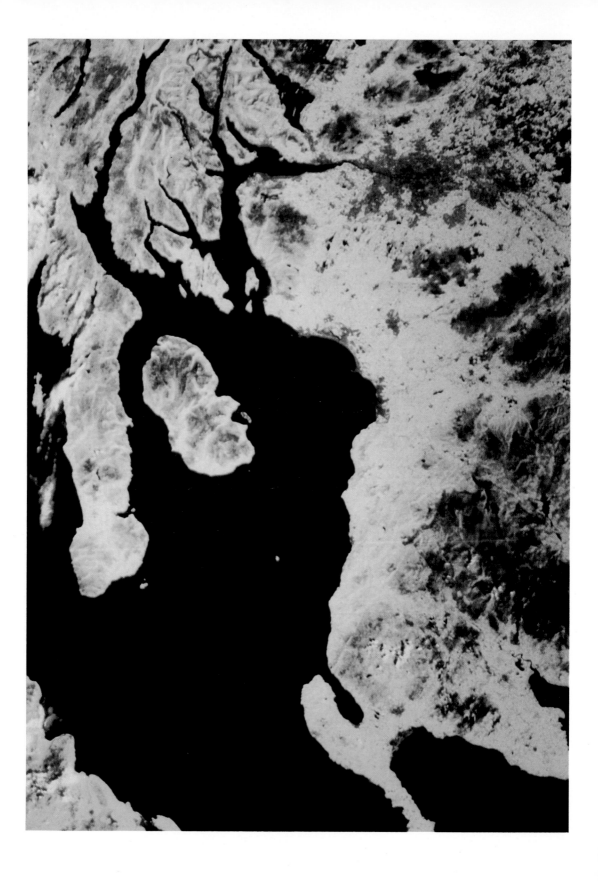

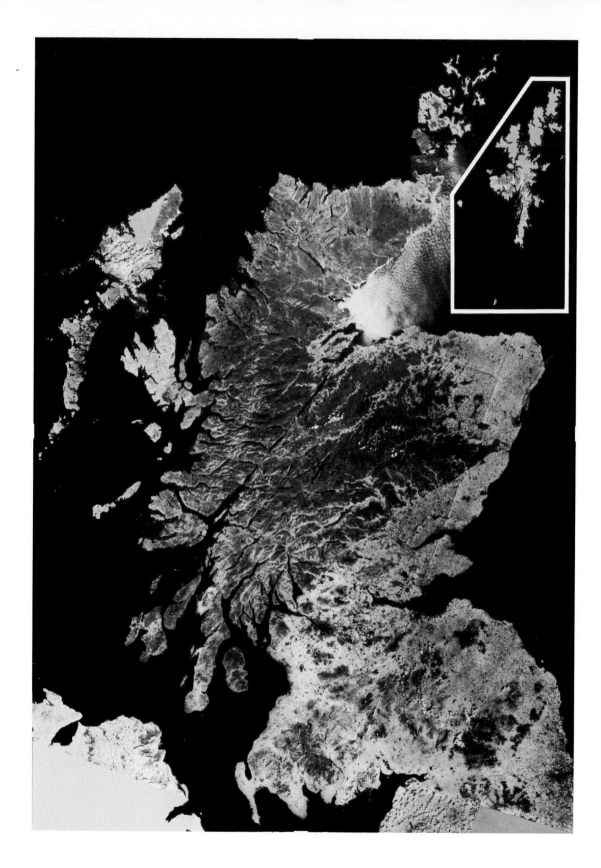

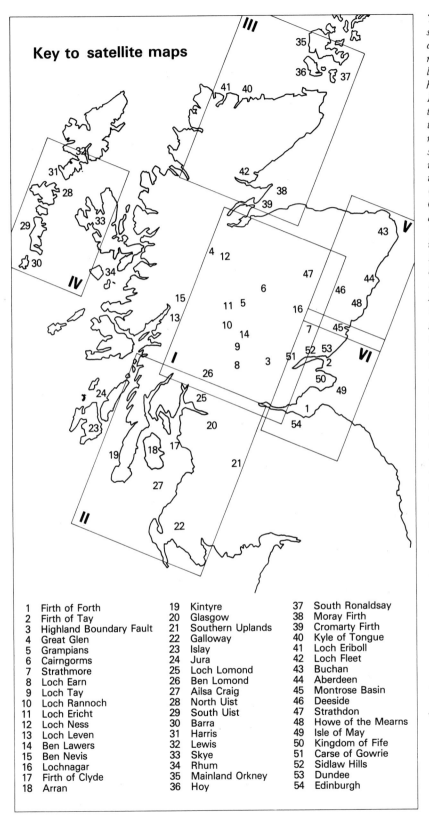

Key to satellite maps

1	Firth of Forth	19	Kintyre	37	South Ronaldsay
2	Firth of Tay	20	Glasgow	38	Moray Firth
3	Highland Boundary Fault	21	Southern Uplands	39	Cromarty Firth
4	Great Glen	22	Galloway	40	Kyle of Tongue
5	Grampians	23	Islay	41	Loch Eriboll
6	Cairngorms	24	Jura	42	Loch Fleet
7	Strathmore	25	Loch Lomond	43	Buchan
8	Loch Earn	26	Ben Lomond	44	Aberdeen
9	Loch Tay	27	Ailsa Craig	45	Montrose Basin
10	Loch Rannoch	28	North Uist	46	Deeside
11	Loch Ericht	29	South Uist	47	Strathdon
12	Loch Ness	30	Barra	48	Howe of the Mearns
13	Loch Leven	31	Harris	49	Isle of May
14	Ben Lawers	32	Lewis	50	Kingdom of Fife
15	Ben Nevis	33	Skye	51	Carse of Gowrie
16	Lochnagar	34	Rhum	52	Sidlaw Hills
17	Firth of Clyde	35	Mainland Orkney	53	Dundee
18	Arran	36	Hoy	54	Edinburgh

These satellite pictures should be studied alongside an atlas, for they contain a mass of information only a little of which can be highlighted here.

In the north-west (Map IV), the narrow channel between the Outer Hebrides and mainland Scotland offers a short-cut to shipping, and is therefore particularly vulnerable to oil pollution.

On Map II the city of Glasgow glows brightly, and below it the Southern Uplands lead south-west into Galloway.

Eastwards, on Map VI, lies the capital city of Edinburgh. The kingdom of Fife separates the Forth from the Tay, one of Europe's great rivers and largely unpolluted. Inland from Dundee are the fertile lands of the Carse of Gowrie.

Map I shows a number of the large lochs contained within the folds of the Grampian mountains. The Highland Boundary Fault can be clearly seen.

In Map V the elbow of Buchan juts out into the North Sea, home of herrings and reservoir of oil. Aberdeen and Deeside, Strathdon and the Howe of the Mearns are all visible.

Further north in Map III is the largest of the east coast inlets, the Moray Firth, with Mainland Orkney and the island of Hoy.

When looking at the composite map (opposite), remember that 80 per cent of Scotland's population is contained within roughly parallel lines running from Aberdeen to the Clyde and from Ayr to Dunbar.

Another feature that emerges with striking clarity is the interweaving of land and water – of enormous value to migratory birds.

Scottish Wildlife Trust Wildlife Reserves
(in order of acquisition)

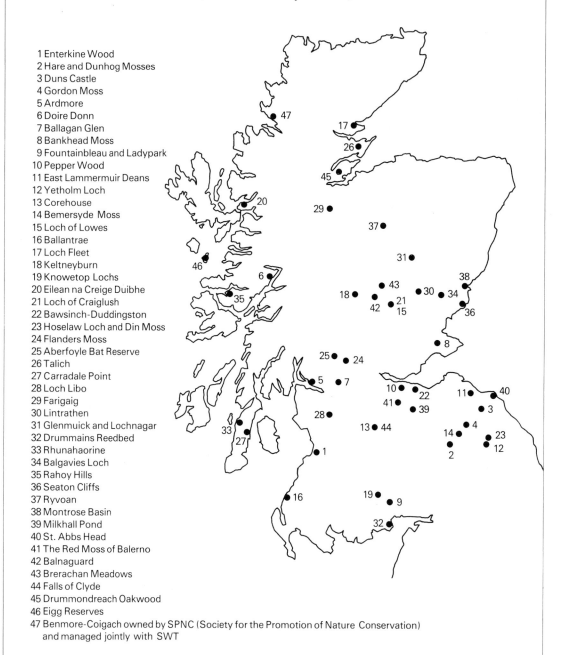

1 Enterkine Wood
2 Hare and Dunhog Mosses
3 Duns Castle
4 Gordon Moss
5 Ardmore
6 Doire Donn
7 Ballagan Glen
8 Bankhead Moss
9 Fountainbleau and Ladypark
10 Pepper Wood
11 East Lammermuir Deans
12 Yetholm Loch
13 Corehouse
14 Bemersyde Moss
15 Loch of Lowes
16 Ballantrae
17 Loch Fleet
18 Keltneyburn
19 Knowetop Lochs
20 Eilean na Creige Duibhe
21 Loch of Craiglush
22 Bawsinch-Duddingston
23 Hoselaw Loch and Din Moss
24 Flanders Moss
25 Aberfoyle Bat Reserve
26 Talich
27 Carradale Point
28 Loch Libo
29 Farigaig
30 Lintrathen
31 Glenmuick and Lochnagar
32 Drummains Reedbed
33 Rhunahaorine
34 Balgavies Loch
35 Rahoy Hills
36 Seaton Cliffs
37 Ryvoan
38 Montrose Basin
39 Milkhall Pond
40 St. Abbs Head
41 The Red Moss of Balerno
42 Balnaguard
43 Brerachan Meadows
44 Falls of Clyde
45 Drummondreach Oakwood
46 Eigg Reserves
47 Benmore-Coigach owned by SPNC (Society for the Promotion of Nature Conservation)
  and managed jointly with SWT

Introduction

Over the many millions of years of evolutionary time the land that is now called Scotland has passed through many transformations. Mountain ranges have been heaved up, only to be worn down under the influence of ice, wind and water. Rivers have changed direction or disappeared altogether; the sea level has risen and fallen, sometimes covering large areas of the land and sometimes receding from it. There have been vast changes brought about by earth movements, volcanoes, floods and glaciers.

Many of the plants and animals of these bygone ages of Scotland were very different from those of today, and they are known to us only by the fossilized remains of their bodies or the impressions they left in soft soils, now transformed into rock. Thousands of species had been lost from earth before man found any place on it, and the potential for man's existence was funnelled through the bodies of many of these early animals.

When man settled in Scotland he had already spread far from his origins in Africa. At his appearance on earth man was just another animal and apparently rather a puny one; no armoured skin, no poison fangs or powerful claws. But he had a large brain and hands capable of precise grip, and with these he made his presence felt. At first the powerful forces of his environment brought early death; most people probably died from disease or violence by the time they were thirty years old. Man's relationship with other organisms was that of hunter and scavenger – a relationship he often illustrated by means of cave paintings.

But as he cultivated plants and domesticated animals, man slowly progressed beyond this phase; he became a farmer. He began to differentiate between those animals that he could herd or keep in his home, such as cattle, goats and dogs, and those that although he might observe, capture and kill he could not control. He found plants that could be grown as crops, and recognized those that grew at the expense of his crops. And so a concept of 'wildlife' became apparent for the first time. This distinction between domestic and wild grew as the settlements of man became villages, towns and cities. People needed to be fed, crops needed protection and livestock needed to be guarded. Wolves would have been killed and weeds pulled up and burned. For man had fire and could burn forests to clear the ground. He built houses near rivers and into the rivers put his waste. He found that living in communities had advantages: some people were good at some things, some excelled at others. Some could grow food, others could build barns, and yet others had skills at tool-making. Division of labour and urbanization was established.

The cities and towns drew heavily on the surrounding countryside, and new laws changed old customs in the way the land was used. Man became skilled in the use of metal – copper, tin and iron – and needed fuel to smelt and work his furnaces. The timber of the forests, long used for building, now provided wood for burning and making charcoal; coal was discovered, and water and steam power added strength to man's arm. Urbanization became industrialization. Power and energy have been a feature of Scotland for centuries – from wood, wind, wave, water, coal, paraffin, oil and the atom, each source finding a place in the service of man and influencing the land.

This brief review of the progress of man brings to our attention two important points. First, that a great diversity of life has appeared on earth, flourished, died and left no living trace. Secondly that, with the appearance of man, a new evolutionary force came into being – one that discriminated between one animal or plant and another, favoured some species and acted against others, drastically altering old habitats and creating new ones. While change and adaptation to change has always been a constant feature of life on earth, man has recently introduced a rate of change too fast for the natural processes of animal and plant adjustment.

It is important for present-day man to recognize these two features of the evolutionary process, and to learn the appropriate lessons. Man should value variety, of both species and habitats, as sources of living material for the future. Once a species is extinct it cannot be recreated. Man too must recognize his place in the ecosystems of the world – it is a powerful place, from which he can understand and control much of the world about him. But the earth does not belong to this generation of man alone; for one or two generations to seize all the earth's non-renewable resources (living and dead) and mortgage the future would be an act of great irresponsibility.

The concept of 'wildlife' has developed from its early agricultural origins. As affluence brought leisure – at least to some – the beauty of fur, feather and flowers began to be recognized and exploited. The artist and poet found inspiration in the colour of flowers and the song of birds, and in the field sports of fishing, shooting, stalking and hunting, man matched his powers of reasoning, his senses and skill against the instinct and greater sensitivity of the quarry. Today we have a clearer perception of the values of wildlife than ever before.

Wildlife is often a marketable commodity – timber, venison and salmon all command good prices. The taking of a crop from our wild species carries with it an obligation to monitor the strength of the stocks, so that a yield is taken only when it can be made good by the reproductive rate of the species concerned. If an exploited species is in decline for any reason it should be protected until its numbers are once more restored. Indeed, as man gains greater control of all types of habitat, the concept of stock assessment and species management may need to be extended to many of our wildlife species in the future.

Many people gain great aesthetic pleasure from wildlife – the sight of a sheet of bluebells, for example, or *Primula scotica*, or leaping salmon, or a flock of geese overhead. Such sights have long been an inspiration to the artist and poet. Other people go further than 'looking for pleasure', and the study of nature becomes leisure-time education, an attempt to acquire knowledge for its own sake. Many television wildlife documentaries are based on this interest.

Finally, the study of wildlife has a crucial part to play in the advancement of science, not only so that we may find out more about how animals and plants 'work', but also that we may learn to use hitherto untapped resources. The most striking example of the latter is in the sphere of plant and animal breeding, where genetic raw material conferring resistance to disease or better growth rates may be bred into domestic species. In addition, studying wildlife can give man early warning of dangerous changes in the environment, such as the accumulation of toxic chemicals.

There is, of course, another side to the coin – the pest problem. Wildlife, however attractive it may be, does at times compete with man for his crops, and any conservation programme must include safeguards for agriculture, fisheries, forestry and other interests.

There is a new covenant to be made between modern man and wildlife. We have a duty to minimize the loss of plant and animal species in return for the pleasures and practical benefits that are to be derived from the great variety of animals, plants and micro-organisms. But if we are to have true reverence for life we must ensure that they have a place on this planet regardless of their use to man, for surely they deserve it.

Nature conservation has come a long way since the days when kings and nobles protected forests, deer and wildfowl in the interests of the hunt. Today in Britain there is a government agency, the Nature Conservancy Council, charged with acquiring and managing nature reserves, advising and teaching others about nature conservation, promoting research into the lives of plants and animals, recording and safeguarding the stories in the rocks. In Scotland the Council works alongside another government agency, the Countryside Commission for Scotland, in the important task of ensuring that the beauty and amenities of the Scottish countryside are conserved and interpreted for resident and visitor alike. In this work other agencies such as the Forestry Commission and local government authorities have key roles to play. The government's interest in nature conservation, however, was and still is prompted by the voluntary conservation movement, of which the Scottish Wildlife Trust is a vital part. It works closely with other voluntary bodies such as the National Trust for Scotland, the Royal Society for the Protection of Birds and the Society for the Promotion of Nature Conservation.

The Scottish Wildlife Trust was founded in 1964, since when it has grown steadily. It is a national body, with branches or representatives throughout Scotland and nature reserves in highlands and lowlands, cities and towns. Thousands of visitors visit these reserves each year to enjoy such sights as ospreys nesting beside Loch of the Lowes, red deer at Glen Muick, wildfowl on Duddingston Loch and seabirds and sea-pinks at St Abb's Head. The Trust keeps under review developments, plans and activities in the Scottish countryside, and promotes legislation for the protection of plants and animals. Most importantly, through its educational work it does much to ensure that the wildlife of Scotland will be valued and enjoyed by future generations.

Chapter 1
The High Tops

My first sight of Scotland's high tops came at an impressionable age, when I walked to the top of the Cobbler above Loch Long. Having no preconceived idea of what I should find, that first impression was etched sharp on my mind. It was a bright April morning with much snow on the tops. Seen from the lochside, the Cobbler's three rock peaks were blinding white upon blue sky, seeming remote from earthly life. Later in the day, when I had climbed into the corrie close under the summits, I entered this realm of rock, snow and glossy ice shining in the spring sun, and recognized it as true sanctuary.

I kicked a way up hard snow to the sun-washed rocks of the south peak. I had hitherto thought of rock as a dull inanimate mass, but this mountain was the living rock, clean as the air itself, pale grey with shiny streaks of mica and quartzite crystals. There was a curious joy in handling it and feeling the coarse grain under the fingers. At the platform on top the strangeness of the scene stopped thought: nothing but snow-bound rocks and boundless space, and circling round the horizon a white-topped host of mountains, rippling along the sky's edge like a storm-sea frozen. This arctic wilderness hung between heaven and earth, its beauty of form and colour, light and shade, not hostile to life but more simply incompatible with thought of it, a habitat too improbable.

This misconception was not to last long, although the awakening came not by dramatic encounter with eagle, wildcat, or monarch of the glen, but almost comically by a much more humble species. I had climbed in mid-April up Beinn a' Chroin (947 metres) above Glen Falloch, when I came on a little pool close under the summit. The day was perfect: the sun blazed from a cloudless sky. Suddenly I heard a loud purring, as if from some great cat. It seemed to come from the pool, and when I went to look I saw maybe fifty frogs, sunning themselves at the edge, croaking in chorus. I learned later that they mate and breed high on the hills, and leave the tadpole spawn in pools up to 915 metres and more; but the fact that frogs get there at all, that the pioneers are willing to hop that far uphill, gave me a new respect for frogs, and more besides. My wildlife eyes began to open.

I discovered that most four-legged animals seem prepared to go almost anywhere, whether amphibians, mammals, or reptiles – soon after finding frogs I watched lizards happily basking on rocks at 760 metres on Beinn Laoigh. I found snow the great revealer of the hidden, or at least not obvious, life. I have rarely seen a fox on a hill, yet the tracks go everywhere over the highest summits above 1220

The view from the north peak of the Cobbler shows the most southerly fjords in the Highlands. Loch Long runs obliquely to the Clyde estuary, with the Gare Loch on its left.

5

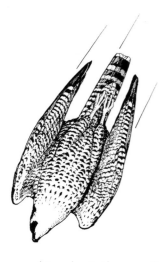

A peregrine stooping – one of the most exciting sights in the countryside.

metres, as do those of hares, stoats, weasels, rats and mice. When the old observatory was in use on the top of Ben Nevis, voles and shrews were regular visitors. Before I ever saw my first eagle at close quarters, I was thrilled by the scutch of its claws on a snow-capped boulder, followed ten feet lower by a deep imprint on the flank of the ridge, where the bird had taken a heavy hop before launching itself into space. On the summit ridge of An Teallach, I saw fox spoor that crossed the narrow crest and then traversed the east face at a high angle of 65 degrees above cliffs that dropped 520 metres to Toll an Lochain. A climber would not have dared to traverse that soft snow without a rope, but the fox must have scampered gaily, for there was no trace of hesitation.

The numerous, intriguing questions first posed by these and other animals were followed by others no less fascinating from the plant world. In April, when colour was scarce on the hills, the first sight of a dense clump of purple saxifrage in full flower, or in late May the pink cushions of moss campion edging the melting snows of Lochnagar, or creeping azaleas reddening the plateau in June, or in July some dark dripping cliff lit up by yellow mountain saxifrage spotted with red anthers – these and others, unsought because unexpected, gave continual delight. How did they all manage to survive, continue to germinate, and provide such fragile flowers despite droughts, long frosts and high scouring winds? The high tops were full of mysteries to be investigated.

The surprises in store seemed without end. I had thought of swifts only as birds of lowland country, until I saw one in the Cairngorms hawking flies along the lip of a high corrie. Its wild swoops and dives and upward surgings followed each other with such unbroken grace, bewildering in their speed, that the aerobatics I had so much admired in ravens seemed by comparison clumsy. The most dramatic sight I had hitherto seen on hills was a peregrine's thunderbolt stoop near the Saddle in Kintail when it struck a small flock of birds, but not even that matched the swift in spectacular quality. The winged insects surprised me in a different way. I had imagined moths and butterflies to be lovers of low sheltered ground, too fragile for rough hill country in Scotland, only to find them apparently more numerous among the hills than anywhere else – so numerous in fact that no full account of them in the Highlands has yet been given. In 1976, when the Nature Conservancy engaged Euan MacAlpine to investigate moths in their Cairngorm reserve, only 115 species had been recorded; in two years' summer work he added some 250 species. The hills are richer in life than men ever imagine, for bare and high as the ground might seem, its complex structure offers a huge variety of habitats.

Landform

Scotland's gestation period might be said to have begun 200 million years ago with the first movements of the continental drift that led in the end to separation from her parent bodies of North America and Eurasia, but the conception is unsatisfactory, for her oldest rocks had birth much more than 2000 million years earlier. On the other hand, no shape foretelling that of today began to emerge until recently, when 20–30 million years ago the Scottish Highlands were lifted up as a plateau linked to Scandinavia. Rainfall and rivers cut the plateau into

A fine gorge at Glen Nevis, gouged out by moving ice.

many hundreds of hill shapes, which stood far higher than now and spread 195 kilometres further west. About 10 million years ago, when the western borders of Eurasia subsided, the Atlantic flooded the plain between Scotland and Norway, as also the western half of the Highlands, where many westward-running glens became fiords and high tops islands. Not until then had the dominant structural features of the Highlands been formed.

The first main feature is the tableland, from which hills and glens have been cut; its uniform height can been seen at once from any of its mountain tops, with only occasional rollers topping the others. The second is the crisscross graining. One set of folds and faults runs diagonally north-east to south-west, and this was formed between 400 and 500 million years ago during the upthrust of the Caledonian orogeny. The transverse grain is the more recent, when the tableland rose with a south-east tilt, causing new rivers to run down the slope and to carve innumerable glens such as Glen Spean and the Lairig Ghru. Where these crossed rivers of the older Caledonian grain, some extraordinary diversions were caused if the older rivers lay in faults that allowed them to erode their beds faster than the new rivers. An example is the river Coe, which originally flowed east across Rannoch Moor to the North Sea plain from a source in Ardnamurchan – until it was intercepted by a river running south-west in the Great Glen fault line. The Coe section, deprived of water, finally reversed its flow when silt blocked its passage to Rannoch. Similar examples can be found all over the country. The result was the close-carved chop of Highland topography, which looks bewildering on a map until, knowing the cause, one can pick out the pattern. The clearest examples of the old grain lines are the Great Glen (a fault), Loch Tay (a fold), and the big sea lochs of Argyll; the clearest of the transverse plateau grains is the valley of the Garry and the Tay.

A third feature, a result of the basic structure and subsidence, is the wild indentation of the west coast. The sea lochs which run 50 to 60 kilometres into the hills channel some warmth from the North Atlantic drift and west winds far into the mountains rising directly from sea-level; this provides both a rich variety of vegetational colour, and the juxtaposition of mountains, lochs and woodlands, blending in a beauty of landscape peculiar to the west Highlands. Their variety of colour and form is due in part to the varieties of underlying rock, but a main ingredient is also this Atlantic atmosphere, for which penalties are paid in rainfall and storm. Eastward, the land dries.

South of the Great Glen, the main body of the Highlands is built up of two broad parallel belts of crystalline schists, running parallel to the Great Glen and the Highland–Lowland line. The belts are of much the same kind of metamorphic rocks, but of different age, and intruding into both are large scattered bulks of granite, which form the higher Cairngorms, Rannoch Moor, and the hills of the Black Mount and Loch Etive. The detail of structure is complex, but the higher hills are mostly of mica-schist, quartzite, granite, gneisses, lavas and volcanic ashes. The mountain shapes sliced out between the glens are long broad ridges and massive humps, and these again have huge rock corries plucked out of north and east faces – seen most splendidly in the Cairngorms, and in the central Highlands on Ben Nevis, Creag Meaghaidh, and Bidean nam Bian of Glencoe. Where the tops have been capped by quartzite they have taken a peaked form, as on the Mamore range of Lochaber.

Top: Frogs can be found even at 600 metres, like this one pictured in the Tarmachans. Bottom: A fox makes its marks in the snow.

7

South of Rannoch, the southern Highlands consist of more rounded, grassy hills, craggy on the flanks but without big cliffs at the backs of their corries. They have a west seaboard more lengthily fretted by peninsulas than any part of the coast north of the Great Glen. The varieties of hill shapes shared by the south and central Highlands and the Cairngorms are matched by their glens: the barren sweeps of the Lairig Ghru, the rock canyon of Glen Coe, the wooded river gorge of Himalayan type in upper Glen Nevis, the 40-kilometre defile of Glen Lyon winding through changing scenes of mountain, woodland, river and farmland meadow are without rival of their own kind north of the Great Glen. But they are widely spread, separated by great hinterlands of moor and hill, and have to be searched out.

North of the Great Glen the scene is quite different. The land of highest scenic quality is concentrated down the west coast; here one is brought back to the Atlantic. The Outer Hebrides are clearly visible from great numbers of hilltops along the main spine, which runs 240 kilometres from near Loch Eriboll to the island of Mull, without including offshoots like the Cuillin of Skye, formerly a mainland peninsula. The whole north-west region falls naturally into two parts: the west district between the Great Glen and Strath Bran (the latter giving the pass over the spine between Cromarty Firth and Loch Carron), and the north district between Strath Bran and the north coast of Sutherland.

The distinctive landscape features of the west Highlands are first the dense pack of 120 tops above 915 metres, with still more just below

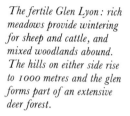

The fertile Glen Lyon: rich meadows provide wintering for sheep and cattle, and mixed woodlands abound. The hills on either side rise to 1000 metres and the glen forms part of an extensive deer forest.

that height, closely trenched by a maze of glens. Short cuts through the maze are happily given by a series of parallel glens running east to west and linking the Great Glen to the Atlantic coast; the more important of these are Strath Bran, Glen Moriston and Glen Shiel, Glen Garry, Loch Arkaig and the Loch Eil pass to Arisaig. From the low hills of Morvern in the south, the mountains rise northwards in growing waves until they top 1160 metres above Glen Affric. They attract a huge rainfall of 300–500 centimetres. (By contrast, only 100 centimetres is recorded at the tips of seaward peninsulas like Ardnamurchan, Morar and Knoydart.)

The district's second feature is deep penetration by the sea at Loch Carron, Loch Alsh, Loch Hourn, Loch Nevis and Loch Sunart. The coastline is too heavily riven to carry a road from north to south. Eighty islands lie off its shore. The hills of Skye, Rhum and Mull are unique to the district, for they are mostly basalt with gabbro and granite intrusions, whereas the mainland hills are Moine schists. They are as a general rule steeper than ranges south of the Great Glen, and much more pointed. The spine lies very close to the heads of the sea lochs, giving short steep rivers westwards and long ones to the east. Most of the land is bare of trees and given over to sheep and deer, but Glen Affric and the lower reaches of Glen Garry have splendid woodlands set among rivers and lochs that rank among Scotland's finest scenery.

North of Loch Carron the landscape changes abruptly. The seaboard mountains from Applecross to Loch Eriboll – a distance of 140 kilometres – are mainly of Torridon sandstone, with outcrops of gneiss as far as Assynt (90 kilometres), then of sandstone and Cambrian quartzite projecting sometimes in monolithic shape from a groundswell of gneiss. All this rock yields a poor soil; the hills have little of the west Highlands' grassiness – sparse heather clings to the flanks, but the tops seem as bare as the face of the moon. In the Wester Ross glens the change is less sudden, for they are grassed and partially wooded, but north of Loch Maree the land hardens to an elemental simplicity of rock, bog and water. The mountains that rise from this land take the shape of plum puddings in Applecross; in Torridon, Maree and Loch Broom, of swinging ridges, some with cockscomb crests; in Assynt, of towers; in Reay Forest, of twisting ridges of quartzite. The variety is enthralling, and it is enhanced when seen from the hills by the gneiss moorlands which, for all their seeming barrenness, are alight with countless hundreds of lochans that change colour and brilliancy with the sky. Hidden among the ranges, invisible from the roads that ring their perimeters, are two of Scotland's best wildernness areas: Achaniasgair between Loch Maree and Little Loch Broom, and the forests of Inverpolly and Glen Canisp in Coigach and Assynt.

East of the coastal spine, the hills of Easter Ross, Sutherland and Caithness are Moine schists of uniform structure, spreading away in a monotonous swell of desolate moorlands that rarely lift above 300 metres. Where mountains do prick out, such as Beinn Laoghal and Ben Hope, they look all the more distinctive.

Whatever the scene, everyone travelling into the north-west Highlands is quickly aware of the feel of the sea. Even when out of sight it gives an ambience quite unlike that of hill country to the south-east – a more bracing air, perhaps, and a sense of oceanic light and freshness. The coasts are the windiest of Britain's mainland.

Weather

Highland weather has been notorious since long before records began, and the west coast spine must carry part of the blame. Sited between the Pole and the tropics, and between the Eurasian continent and a wide ocean, all exchanging double airstreams, the Highlands are plagued by the consequent overhead passage of fronts and depressions. Their succession is incessant and mercurial. The damp winds of the prevailing westerlies have to take a sudden rise over the hill barrier, which makes the west Highlands the wettest part of Europe. The annual rainfall is 152 cm on the coast, but down the long Highland spine it is as much as 305 cm, rising at its worst to more than 500 cm near the head of Glen Garry. The corresponding figures for the east coast and Cairngorms are cut by half. Cairngorm weather is typical of the east coast, where a wind that backs south-east has been known for centuries back as the *gaoth na Maoirn*, or the wind from the Mearns, denoting the onset of cyclonic storm.

Summer sea-level temperatures show almost no difference between east and west, and are barely 1.66°C higher south than north. In winter, the west is only 1°C warmer than the east. The real differences are in height above sea-level. Temperatures normally drop 1.66°C to 2.8°C at each rise of 300 metres. Rainfall increases likewise with height, and wind at 915 metres is usually double its low ground velocity. Thus rainfall near the base of a mountain like Ben Nevis may be less than half that of the summit. It follows that mountain trees are stunted according to altitude, both because their season of growth is shortened by the cold, and their leaves are either over-ventilated by wind and, becoming parched, fall early, or else are over-worked in the transpiration required to shed excess water where rain has water-logged the ground. The same stunting occurs on low ground in the Hebrides unless at sheltered sites, and on all exposed west coasts, especially in Sutherland.

The driest time of the year is from March to June with a change of prevailing wind from westerly to easterly, and with sunshine and daylight hours reaching their maximum together. This optimum period is interrupted early in May by cold weather with new snowfalls on the hills, so long established in the west that they are known as 'the lambing snows'. The greater warmth of July and August often comes with a rise in rainfall, which tends to die away with the cooler weather of September and October.

The outstanding climatic feature of the Scottish hills is wind, strong and persistent, blowing with a violence of which lowlanders have usually little conception. Storms blow every year over the highest Lochaber tops, often at velocities of 160–240 kph in winter, although not in summer. The abrupt drop in temperature at heights above sea-level gives a good snow cover on upper hill flanks and summits, and can bring snowfall there on any summer's day – Ben Nevis has a mean annual temperature below freezing point. The Cairngorms, with smaller rainfall than the west Highlands, experience heavier snowfalls brought in by the winds from the Mearns.

Every form of life that climbs into the hills, plant or animal, has to find ways of adapting to extremes of cold, wet, wind, frost and drought. While the animals of hair and fur may thicken their coats, and birds their down, or frogs and lizards hibernate in holes, the most striking devices employed to beat high top weather and ground are those of the arctic-alpine plants. Some examples of this adaptation are the huge disproportion between root and shoot, as in moss campion, where the root is several feet long and the shoot a low cushion; the prone growth of azalea and juniper creeping close to the ground; the small, fleshy, waxy leaves grown by stonecrops and roseroot; and the woolly leaves of alpine mouse-ear.

The drier weather and better drainage of the east Highlands produces marked differences from the west in vegetation, especially in the stature of the native trees in the valleys and the denser heather of moors and hills. The forests of Deeside and the Spey are renowned for their Scots pines, whose dark green crowns lofted above red branches contrast so well with the lighter birches. Eastern landowners planted freely, so that native and exotic species are richly mixed in some Atholl glens – the Tummell, for example, wooded in larch, pine, oak, holly, birch, cypress, ash, chestnut, alder and many more besides. Western weather tends to restrict growth rather than variety, but during the days of the old Caledonian forest sheltered straths away from the coast, like those of mid-Argyll and the south Highlands generally, grew far-spreading oakwoods, mixed with pine and birch. Since the felling of the forest over the last thousand years, the native hardwoods of the west have been largely replaced by the Forestry Commission with Sitka spruce.

The greatest blessing brought by bad weather to the west, as also by geological accident, is an abundance of freshwater lochs, which are

A glacial moraine dam contains Loch Toll an Lochain of An Teallach, a classic cirque in Torridonian sandstone, near Dundonnell. The banded rocks rise in a crescent-shaped backbone extending for five kilometres, with eleven tops over 1000 metres.

largely absent east of a line drawn from Inverness to the Tay estuary. They are an asset of the first order to landscape and wildlife. Their presence, shape, size and huge number are mainly a result of ice action; even during the last glaciation the heaviest snowfall and greatest thickness of ice lay well to the west of centre. The bigger lochs lie in the long rock basins, where geological faults and folds had been first deepened by rivers, then largely filled in by silt and debris, and finally excavated by glaciers, sometimes to great depth near their heads. Abundant though they are, they are few compared to the many thousands of rock lochans and moraine lochans. The rock lochans fill hollows gouged by glaciers out of resistant rocks, seen at their best on the gneiss moorlands of west Sutherland, in corries close under the summits of Wester Ross, and on hill ridges and moorlands everywhere – although never on the splendid scale of the north-west. The moraine lochans are in hollows dammed by the rubble of retreating glaciers. They are found anywhere between the glens and hill corries: Loch an Eilein is an example in the Cairngorms. Rock and glen lochans may often be dammed by old moraines to give greater depth, like Loch Coruisk and Loch Lomond. But first and foremost, it is the glen lochs with woodlands and rivers that combine with hill shapes to give the finest Highland scenes and the richest wildlife.

The rock skeleton

When I first walked through the Highlands, and by knowing them began to enter into possession, I was struck by how lean the land was – everywhere the bare bones broke surface, outcropping in crags, exposed in slabs, prominent in ribs, lifting up in mountains. Being in such constant company with the rock and water basic to life around, I felt a need to know how the rocks came to be there, and why in such varied kind and shape.

The building of the skeleton has been a story of construction, demolition and renewal, repeated in cycles through several thousand million years. The oldest Highland rocks now datable by radiometric methods are the Scourian gneisses of west Sutherland, named after the village of Scourie and aged 2200–2600 million years, and the Laxfordian gneisses, named from the Laxford river and aged 1600 million years. Such gneiss, a pink or grey rock of both sedimentary and igneous origins, has been metamorphosed and toughened by heat and pressure deep in the earth. It extends from the Urals west through Greenland across northern Canada (of which Scotland was once part), and most likely underlies all later Highland rocks.

Vast quantities of gneiss sands were eroded off that old northern continent and deposited in the estuaries, deltas and lakes of its south-east seaboard, which then sank as nearly 5000 metres of strata accumulated on top. Red Torridon sandstone was thus formed around 900 million years ago, and then by warping of the crust it was raised into mountain ranges.

At this same time the gneiss sediments were also laid down nearly 6100 metres thick across a huge area of the neighbouring sea-floor, and were then metamorphosed around 740 million years ago by heat and pressure to form the Moine schists, which later were folded as a high mountain range (the Torridon rocks had not been folded). This Moine–Torridon rock mass covered lands vastly greater than now, but so vigorous was erosion during the next few hundred million years that the mountains were swept away, the whole reduced to a plain, and the old gneiss partly exposed once more. A slow downwarping caused a Cambrian sea to cover much of the Highlands, but the old gneiss continent still stood to the north, and during the course of another hundred million years this supplied to the sea-floor sandy sediments 5 kilometres thick.

This mud and sand became metamorphosed into the crystalline schists and quartzites named Dalradian (after the first Scots kingdom of Dalriada) which still cover most of the south, central and north-east Highlands. They and underlying Moine rocks were raised to a mountain range of possibly Himalayan scale. The building process, lasting nearly 130 million years, has been named the Caledonian orogeny since it included all Scotland from the Southern Uplands northwards, but the continent then built also comprised Scandinavia and Greenland, from which the range can still be traced through Newfoundland south into New York State. The formerly flat beds of schist were heaved into mountainous overfolds while magma from under the crust burst through into the upper rock to crystallize as granite, now exposed by denudation of the schist to form the Cairngorms and the hills of Loch Etive and Rannoch, and smaller intrusions. The succession of fold movements laid down the north-east to south-west grain of the Highlands.

The horizontal pressure from east-south-east generated by the orogeny caused phenomena still visible in the north Highlands along a hundred-mile line between Loch Eriboll and the Sleat peninsula of

Volcanic basalt scenery on Skye; on the left is the pinnacle known as The Old Man of Storr, and Raasay is seen through the gap across the water.

Skye. This line, the Moine thrust plane, marks the edge of a great mass of Moine schist thrust forward to override or displace the gneiss, Torridon sandstone, and Cambrian quartzite-limestone to its north-west. A good example of displacement is seen near Kylesku, where chunks of gneiss 460 metres thick have been carried forward over Cambrian quartzite resting on gneiss. Another surprising illustration can be seen on the east of the pass through Assynt, beside Loch Awe. A slice of limestone plateau, topped by two 460-metre hills, has been carried forward bodily on the back of the advancing schist.

The Caledonian range on its rising was unclothed by vegetation, for the plants then evolving from the sea were unable to invade such arid land. The bare mountains were stripped down by rain and flood, depositing Old Red sandstone in shallow seas, basins and estuaries during the Devonian period, when Scotland lay near the equator. The Old Red built up to a depth of 915 metres in Caithness and nearly 6000 metres in Kincardineshire. It lies too in a broad belt down the Highland fault line between Stonehaven and the Clyde estuary.

During the last phase of the Old Red sandstone period, volcanic outbursts poured lavas across much of Scotland and, together with intrusive granites, built up the hills that now by erosion of top cover form the Cheviots, the Pentlands, the Ochils, the Sidlaws, the Lorn plateaus, and the mountains of Glencoe and Ben Nevis. The rocks of the two latter were made by volcanoes of cauldron subsidence after the lavas had piled up over the land. In Glencoe, a circular column 8–14·5 kilometres wide sank down 1200–1500 metres; the lavas inside being thus shielded from erosion were left as a plug, the relics of which form the present hills, while the upper lavas that covered the country above and around were completely stripped away. On Ben Nevis, the circular plug did not sink immediately. First a chasm opened below, deeply subterranean, and was intruded by magma crystallizing as granite in several phases; only then did the centre of its subterranean ring subside, so that the roof of schist topped by lava sank down into the magma that filled the cauldron. This central lava core is now the summit cliff, baked to form andesite 600 metres thick. The lower slopes and neighbouring mountains are the once deep-buried granite, exposed by the denudation of thousands of metres of their lava and schist top-cover.

The story of the Highlands' crustal folding had ended, but during the Devonian period and lasting until late in the Carboniferous, crustal pressures caused by mountain building in Europe, Africa and America were opening a wrench-tear now shaped as the Great Glen. Many geologists believe that in the course of 100 million years the northern block of Scotland moved 105 kilometres south-west. The deep split in the crust still subjects the glen to local tremors.

During the 300 million years following the Devonian period, little new rock was formed compared with the huge denudations by weather. In the first, Carboniferous period the land was reduced to a plain, while tropical jungles flourished in the Lowlands and volcanoes erupted lavas – of which Arthur's Seat and the Campsie Hills are mementoes. Crustal drift had meanwhile brought Scotland to a point 20 degrees north of the equator (drift was latitudinal as well as longitudinal). In the Highland area, warm shallow seas flooded over downwarped lands in the west, depositing the Triassic, Jurassic and Cretaceous sediments, of which only vestiges now remain on the Inner Hebrides between Mull and Skye. Flashfloods and denudation caused

Liathach (1053 metres) in Glen Torridon, Western Highlands.

Above : Snow buntings are gregarious birds — flocks are aptly known as 'snowflakes'.
Right : A male snow bunting in winter plumage.

Top left : A ptarmigan in summer plumage matches the lichen-covered rocks.
Far left : Ptarmigan eggs.
Left : A dotterel on its nest in the heather.

vast accumulations of New Red sandstone, which still form the hill-land of most of Arran.

In this Mesozoic era the continental plates had begun to drift apart, approximately 200 million years ago in the Triassic period. Near the start of the Tertiary era, Greenland split off from Scandinavia (of which Scotland remained part), and the start of that particular drift has been dated to 60 million years ago. It was followed by prolonged volcanic eruptions on a line between Iceland and Ireland. These continued off and on for ten million years and gave the Highlands and Islands their last contribution of new rocks. Volcanoes on St Kilda, Skye, Rhum, Ardnamurchan, Mull and Arran, and probably others now submerged, erupted lavas that built up a tableland some thousands of feet taller than their 915-metres remnant of Ben More on Mull. Crustal tension-cracks following the drift swarmed out from the volcanic centres as far as north England, but came too late to feed the plateau with lava flows. Magma rose under the volcanoes to crystallize subterraneously as plutonic granites and gabbros. By the time the Tertiary era had half run its course, most of the great plateau had again been denuded to near sea-level. Its ruin was so complete that the plutonic rocks once so deeply buried under the old volcanoes were exposed as masses of granite and gabbro, now further broken up into the hills of the Red and Black Cuillin, Rhum, St Kilda and north Arran. The only substantial fragments left from the basalt of the old plateau are Mull and Skye.

Thus far, the portion of crust occupied by Scotland had at no time borne any shape remotely resembling that of today; but now that first shaping began. Scotland's climate had become subtropical and was still cooling during the middle Tertiary era when new movements of the crust raised a tableland. It became jacked up as one block without any folding in a series of pulses that came off centre to the west. They lasted from 30 to 20 million years ago, occurring around the time of the crumpling up of the Alps. The plateau having taken its south-east tilt, the rivers flowing down east and west cut the rock at right-angles to the old Caledonian grain, whereupon the rivers of both sliced through even the hard crystalline schists of the Moine and Dalradian series, eroding glens 760 metres deep, isolating long hill ridges and breaking the land into hundreds of mountain tops. Two final events gave the landform of present-day Scotland. These were the downwarping of Europe's west seaboard, which flooded the North Sea basin and Hebrides, and the Ice Age.

Drift having brought the continental plates and their ocean basins to their present positions (the rate of drift between Europe and North America in recent millennia has been half an inch a year), an apparent consequence was the southward advance of north polar ice, which has recurred three times since the first of 600,000 years ago. In Scotland, no trace remains of any but the last, which came to two maxima of glaciation in 55,000 B.P. (before present), and 20,000–17,000 B.P. Each advance has been followed by warm interglacials, in one of which we appear to be at present.

During the first phase, Scandinavia and Scotland were buried under an ice cap 1525 metres deep. Only St Kilda lay beyond the western edge, which ran from south Ireland towards Norway's North Cape. The cap lay 610 metres thick over the Outer Hebrides, from which the only projecting nunatak was Clisham (798 metres). A recession of ice lasting many millennia then occurred as temperatures

Top: A spray of the common juniper, thick with berries.
Bottom left: The Scotch argus butterfly, Erebia aethiops.
Bottom right: The mountain azalea forms a dense mass of flowers.

rose sufficiently to allow recolonization of the land by arctic plant and animal life. The mammals included woolly rhinoceros, hairy mammoth, bear, northern lynx, lemming, reindeer and elk. The North Sea basin grew woodland, for much of its southern plain had dried out by withdrawal of sea into polar ice. The mammals held out in Scotland at least until 27,500 B.P. (carbon date for rhinoceros). Two thousand years later, the second phase was under way.

At the second maximum, the Highlands had two glacial centres: one was on the Grampian spine, where the cap was 868 metres thick on the Cairngorms and 915 metres at Schiehallion, maintaining this depth southward to the Highland line; the other was on the western spine, where the cap was 1070 metres over the Northern Highlands and 1100 metres over Rannoch Moor, falling westward to 490 metres over the Hebrides. The heavier snowfalls and ice of the western spine caused more powerful ice action on steeper hillsides than occurred in the Cairngorms, with consequent deepening of rock basins both in glens and the later sea-channels. Thus the head of Loch Lomond was gouged to 200 metres, Loch Morar and the Sound of Raasay to 300 metres and more, and Skye, Mull and Arran were ploughed off from the mainland, to become islands when the sea rose. (This over-deepening of sea-channels and lochs made them desirable sites for construction of oil-production platforms in the 1970s.) In gouging out the floors of the lochs, the glaciers pushed forward debris which was sometimes deposited as an outer dam, divorcing the loch from the sea as at Loch Awe, Loch Shiel, Loch Lomond and several others, or else creating narrows that linked an inner loch with an outer. By similar action of the ice on a smaller scale, the corries on the high tops were carved out of former hollows, with outer lips that often retained lochans when the ice had melted.

Even at maximum glaciation a host of nunataks thrust clear of the ice-sheet – notably the tops of the Cairngorms, Ben Lawers and Ben Nevis. It seems possible that some species of arctic-alpine plants survived there, as they do now within the Arctic Circle.

After 17,000 B.P., warmer summers brought a gradual rise in snow levels and a slow dissolution of the two ice-sheds, which broke up into independent glacial centres. The retreat of the ice was no steady progression, for three readvances occurred, briefly halting the general ebb. The final shaping of the hills began when the ice cap diminished to form glaciers still thick enough to flow in several directions at once over the ridges between glens, where they left moraines either on their backs or upper flanks, and shaped saddles.

When the tops and plateaux and summit ridges came clear of ice, and their upper corries were exposed, the cliffs already plucked out from under them at the backs of corries by the former weight of moving ice were attacked anew by frosts, which further sharpened peaks and sculpted cliff-faces into protuberant ridges, buttresses and pinnacles. While the glaciers shrank down into single valleys they widened and straightened the walls, truncated spurs, left hanging valleys on flanks (with later waterfalls), ground ravines into U-shape, and everywhere scored rocks with striae or sometimes polished them like boiler-plates.

At their last stage, after 13,000 B.P., the wasting glaciers deposited much more drift among eastern hills than western. The shorter western glaciers lived longer but ran faster into seaward graves, and if they died on land died in haste, leaving no monument in marshalled stone. The Cairngorms fared better, especially where the

Glen More glacier, on dying back to its parent body the Spey glacier, buried the Moine schists under beneficial deposits of clay, sand and gravel. The forests of Abernethy and Rothiemurchus owe good growth to the soil thus given.

Near the end of the Ice Age, around 11,000 B.P., a millennium of renewed cold again filled the glens with ice, which in Lochaber grew great enough to block the mouth of Glen Spean to a height of more than 300 metres, so that a great lake dammed behind left beaches known as the Parallel Roads, best seen in Glen Roy. A thousand years later the Scottish Ice Age ended with a slow withdrawal of glaciers into high mountain corries. Fed by polar ice-melt, the world sea had been rising since 17,000 B.P.; it had flooded over the land bridge to Ireland, and through the Hebridean channels and Great Glen, until the land, relieved of the enormous load of ice, rose up too. Raised beaches were left in the Great Glen as evidence, and the Loch Ness 'monsters' – if such there be – could thus have been trapped.

The recolonization by plant and animal life had long since begun. A new Highland country with a wealth of potential habitats had been prepared. The land had been many times stripped and rebuilt, submerged under seas or lava flows, crumpled up and planed down. Entire rock overlays thousands of metres deep had been removed in long, slow processes while life adapted at leisure. The new Miocene plateau had been chiselled into hills, glens and islands far more searchingly by falling and flowing water than by glacial action. Invasion by ice a mile thick had not given the land its basic

As the land rose when it was freed from its load of ice, the changing sea-level resulted in spectacular raised beaches. Here, near Gairloch, is an excellent example of such beaches.

topography, it had merely deepened, rounded and shaped more finely the forms already given. But for life-forms it was cataclysmic. Nothing in the Highland story is more astonishing than the speed with which wildlife moved into the emptied land at least 4000 years before the close of the Ice Age, and despite the withering cold of winters longer than now, held its ground.

Colonization

The land emerged from the ice flayed. In grinding the rocks the ice had freed life-enhancing minerals, and as soon as summer temperatures reached 6°C, plant life seeded itself north from England, which had not been glaciated south of the Thames. The English tundra (radiocarbon dated from 30,000 B.P.) spread north behind the wasting ice, leapfrogging glacier-arms, until by 14,000 B.P. at latest the Scottish lowlands had tundra enough to feed mammoth. The plants were mosses, lichens, sedges and a variety of arctic-alpines now common on the mountains. There were no trees at first, but as soil developed on glacial deposits and temperatures rose a little, dwarf birch and willow were followed by juniper.

As early as 12,800 B.P. the west spine of Ross-shire, during the valley glacier period, had grown a plant cover of the crowberry–heath type, with birch copses around 275 metres. This birch would still be small and scrubby. By 12,000 B.P. summer temperatures had risen to 10°C, and winter to minus 7°C. The open tundra was predominantly heather and crowberry, and three brown butterflies had arrived: the Scots argus, marked by red eye-spots with metallic blue centres, the mountain ringlet, and the large heath, paler than the others. The pioneering mammals were reindeer, giant elk bearing 40-kg antlers, aurochs or wild ox with a 1.2-metre horn span, standing 1.8 metres at the shoulder, red deer, blue hares, stoats, brown bears, lemmings and voles, followed by northern lynx, otters, foxes, wolves, weasels, badgers, brown hares, hedgehogs and horses. The birds able to tolerate sub-arctic weather and closely follow the retreating snow were willow grouse, ptarmigan, snow-buntings, dotterels, golden plovers, and black- and red-throated divers. The geese and swans that now fly north from Scotland to breed in the Arctic lands in summer would then have flown into Scotland instead from further south. Arctic birds resident and breeding would include gyr falcons and snowy owls, among others.

After 10,000 B.P. the warmer climate caused the initial invasion by juniper and birch to be followed by forests of birch and pine, with much oak in the southern Highlands. Its canopy was open enough for an abundant growth of hazel-scrub to exclude heath. The plants of the tundra, unable to grow in the shade of the trees, had long since begun their retreat into the mountains. This Boreal period of 3000 years caused the extinction of the giant elk, which required the rich open pasture now gone. Woodland mammals such as roe deer, wildcat, squirrel, beaver and pine marten had now arrived in the Highlands together with ospreys, capercailzies and crossbills, and nearly all the small song birds. From 9500 B.P. peat began to form on the moors, through deposits of withered vegetation failing to decay on cold, wet, acid ground. The opening of the Dover Strait around 8000 B.P. halted the intake of many flowering plants and of all mammals except man –

An immature white-tailed sea eagle soars over Fair Isle. These birds ceased to breed in Britain early in the present century, but the NCC have recently reintroduced them to Rhum in the hope that they will breed once more.

an immigrant significant later for his baleful effect on Highland landscape and wildlife. According to carbon dating, man first appeared in Fife around 8000 B.P.

After 7000 B.P. came two thousand years of warm wet weather, when temperatures rose higher than now by 2°C. The tree line rose to 610 metres – today's limit – and the forest grew dense; but with leaching of the soil and the spread of sphagnum moss, peat and heather, the hazel was devastated, the alder invading the Lowlands failed to develop in the Highlands, and the tree line was again cut back. The lemmings and northern rat-voles could not survive. On the mountains, some arctic-alpine plants that needed base-rich soils found good supplies of nutrients on screes and gravels and crags.

After 4500 B.P. the weather dried for some 1500 years and the Highland forest, regaining the ground lost to bog, mounted to a record level of 1000 metres. Even St Kilda carried birch and hazel scrub. The forest was predominantly pine and birch in the central and east Highlands, oak and birch in the west, and birch in the north. Mixed in with this were variable amounts of hazel, elm, rowan, aspen, willow, holly and alder. Land birds achieved a density never equalled before or since, and the woodland species became so well established that even when man deprived them of tree cover in later millennia they held their ground.

Around 2450 B.P., in the last century of the Bronze Age, the dry sunny weather reverted to the cool and wet climate that has since persisted. The tree line fell back to 610 metres, and moorland birds spread as heather and peat advanced.

Almost all destruction of wildlife was henceforth at the hand of man. Three species of mammal had been lost by natural change, and Neolithic man had killed the northern lynx. The further extinctions by man's hunting and destruction of forest were brown bear in the tenth century, reindeer in the twelfth, elk and aurochs in the fourteenth, beaver in the sixteenth, boar in the seventeenth and wolf in the eighteenth. Two others have escaped the gun and gin-trap most narrowly: one is the polecat, now rarely seen – most alleged sightings turn out to be feral ferrets – and the other the pine marten, a woodland mammal expert at catching birds and squirrels. It escaped last century by retreating to the mountain screes of Ross and Sutherland, and there took refuge until recent years, when it has been able to spread south of the Great Glen. The wild mammals introduced by man have been fallow deer and sika, reindeer, mink, grey squirrels, musk rats and rabbits. The improvement of firearms brought the extinction of crane and bittern in the eighteenth century, the great auk and white-tailed sea-eagle in the nineteenth, and the kite, goshawk and osprey in the twentieth century. The osprey has made a successful return since the 1950s, thanks to the Royal Society for the Protection of Birds. Some extinction of arctic-alpine species has occurred through collections made by botanists, and many others reduced to rarity by the grazing of deer and sheep. But the greatest loss of all was that of the Caledonian forest, which in the Middle Ages extended at least from Strath Earn to Strath Farrar, and from Appin to Deeside.

The Lowlands and Southern Uplands had lost their forests early, beginning when Bronze Age man cleared them for grazing and cultivation around 3000 B.P., and continuing through the Iron Age when the Celts brought in big herds, until by the fifteenth century A.D. the demands of a growing population had destroyed virtually all the

Pioneer butterflies: the large heath (above) and mountain ringlet.

trees. The Highland forest had thus far escaped serious inroads. The northern woodland of Ross and Sutherland, mainly birch with oak on the lower ground, was burned and felled by the Vikings from A.D. 800, but not beyond hope of regeneration. The Caledonian forest stayed largely intact until the end of the Middle Ages, by which time it was nearly 9000 years old. In 500 years more it was destroyed by man, at first for expedient motives, then mainly by uncontrolled exploitation.

The assault on it began with the firing of local woods by men of the townships to deny refuge to wolves, which had become a great nuisance. The same course was followed by chiefs, barons and generals to oust rebels and outlaws in the civil wars, feuds and revolts of the sixteenth and seventeenth centuries. Large bands of men at the seasonal break-up of armies and smaller marauding bands would occupy the woods while plundering the countryside for winter stores before returning home. In the late sixteenth century the first iron smelters moved into the Highlands from England, and then from the Lowlands too. Their fellings greatly increased in the eighteenth century, when estates were forfeited after the Jacobite risings or sold by landowners to get money for town life. When the fellings ended around 1813, through replacement of charcoal by coke, the great forest had already been broken up and was widely interspersed with moorland. Unluckily it was given no chance of regeneration. The iron smelters were succeeded first by flockmasters, who ousted the cattle farmers and fired the woodlands, whole glens at a time, to extend their sheep ranches; by tanners who skinned birch trees; and finally by deerstalkers. Sheep and deer ended regeneration, and the remnants were decimated by emergency fellings for the world wars.

Despite partial reafforestations with conifer plantations, the Highlands could not take loss of the native trees on so great a scale without dire consequences. The increase of flooding, erosion and leaching of soils reduced fertility. The deforested Highlands represent devastated country, shorn of its natural complement of wildlife, and made less productive for man. The process is not irreversible – the Scottish Highlands compared with others of Europe are still well stocked – but the reafforestation most helpful in providing varied habitats is not the monoculture of Sitka spruce.

The only true wilderness areas of the Highlands, unchanged by man or his domestic animals, are the hill tops above 915 metres. Individual sheep stray there rarely and then only in summer and by chance, for the grazing is never so good as lower down. The tops are islands of the skies. Stony or grassy, they are permanently inhabited. Plant life, whether lichens, mosses, grasses, heaths or flowering arctic-alpines, depends on the kind of rock and its weathered shape from the extremes of Sutherland quartzite to Ben Lawer's calcareous schist, and from gabbro and sandstone pinnacles to the granite and schist plateaux – and depends too on the micro-habitats and micro-climates that these give in endless diversity. Numerous invertebrates are able to find a home on the tops – more than fifty species were counted on the summit of Ben Nevis – and to adapt to the special conditions. Such a one is the webless spider, which lives beneath stones and snow. The larvae of several moths feed on moss, or moss campion, or the leaves of shrub heaths according to their kind. One, the northern dart, spends two years high in the caterpillar stage. Ptarmigan, dotterels and snow-buntings all nest on the high tops between 820 metres and 1220 metres. The mammals that can stay high are naturally the smaller ones, common and pygmy shrews, and mice whose maze of runnels are exposed in spring when their snow-roof melts. Mountain hares, although they are moorland feeders, stay mainly above 600 metres. Most birds and mammals visit the tops only briefly or incidentally, but are sufficient in number to give hill-walkers the constant chance of a sighting. The larger mammals are occasionally seen crossing ridges but almost never on summits – not even red deer.

The high tops near 915 metres provide a habitat unique for the severe conditions imposed: prolonged high winds and frequent storms, months of snow cover, rocky soil deficient in humus, the constant alternation of humid air with frost and of heavy rainfall with drought – the latter especially from April to June – and throughout the year low ground temperatures occasionally rising unduly high on south slopes. The few plants and animals able to survive in these extreme conditions must be the toughest of the tough, one would think, yet by an extraordinary paradox their endurance and strength is hidden behind soft, delicate and fragile outer forms, all small and easily crushed.

Appreciation of wild countryside and wildlife over the last thirty years has brought new dangers to both from human pressures, for much of that appreciation is still at a level of ignorance, the more damaging as access is made ever easier. Ease of access has given scope to a pernicious conception that the wildlands and wildlife are there to minister to man's need for recreation, and that that is the prime purpose of sparing them some protection. The fact is that they have being in their own right, and that man's life and health are inseparably bound up with theirs. His recreation is an incidental gain, not an end to be reached by exploiting land, where that means degrading it.

The Highlands were so degraded for quick commercial ends when man lacked knowledge. He has that excuse no longer. The understanding is there, held· by a growing number of men but still needing wider dissemination and assent. Care for the countryside and man's fellow creatures now and in the future has become his responsibility.

Among the mammals introduced to Scotland by man is the sika deer, similar to the red deer but smaller. Here two bucks gallop off through powdery snow.

Chapter 2
Wildlife on the Hill

As hill ground covers about 75 per cent of Scotland, it would take most of this book to do justice to the wealth of wildlife in such a vast area. There is space here for only a brief introduction, which I hope will at least whet your appetite. I shall write not just about the wildlife that occurs on our hills, but also about how it comes to be there, how it is changing, and what we must do to safeguard it. So, when you go to the hills in future, I hope you will see them and their wildlife with a new eye – an eye both more understanding and more appreciative.

The hill lands are one of Scotland's most precious features. The very names of the hills are part of the spirit which is Scotland and which makes a Scot feel Scottish; from all over the world visitors come to see their magnificent scenery. The wildlife is an important part of this richness. Imagine how bleak our hills would be if no golden eagles swept over the ridges, no arctic-alpine flowers shone like jewels on the dark rocks, and no heather or thistles bloomed on the moors.

In local speech there are no mountains in Scotland. Instead, everything from Ben Nevis down to a coastal moor is fondly called 'the hill', or in Gaelic *am monadh*. Phrases such as 'Have you been on the hill today?' or 'It's not a good day for the hill' display your experience of the Scottish hill country better than naming all the peaks. The 'hill' is a useful word, as it covers all moorland and hill land irrespective of altitude. Classifications based on altitude are misleading anyway; ground at 460 metres in Angus has very different wildlife from ground at 460 metres in west Sutherland. The only feature common to all the hill is open treeless terrain with short vegetation, mostly containing some heather or other dwarf shrubs, and this occurs from sea-level to 1340 metres.

The variety of habitats

Compared with most parts of the world, Scotland offers an astonishing variety of landscape, vegetation and animal life within a very small area: you will seldom go five miles on the hill and still be in the same kind of country. The main cause of this is the great variety of rocks. Frost, rain and wind break down soft, lime-rich rocks such as limestone and basalt fairly quickly into a deep, fertile soil, whereas the hard, more acid granite weathers slowly into a poor, shallow, gravelly soil. Heather thrives on the acid soils, whereas limestone carries a grassland rich in flowering plants, and many of the sudden, striking contrasts in

The moraine dammed Loch Avon, in the Cairngorms.

vegetation and scenery typical of Scotland – such as the bright green slopes on limestone at Blair Atholl and on epidiorite at Morven near Dinnet – are due to this. Even on the acid ground which occupies most of the Scottish hill you will often come across lime-rich patches supporting plant-rich pockets like little gardens. On sunny days the fragrance of these scented braes rises in sudden hot waves off the ground – a memory to sustain you through the long cold months of winter.

Springs are always worth visiting for their beautiful soft mosses and the taste of their fine cold water. Springs seeping from rich rocks carry more plant nutrients than from poor rocks, and this affects plants growing in the stream. The presence of yellow saxifrage for instance indicates water fairly rich in lime. Springs from a rich rock also convey nutrients to poor ground downstream, thus making it more fertile. Where peat forms such a deep barrier that plant roots cannot reach the soil or rock below, only a mixture of sparse heather and other unpalatable plants can grow, but where water seeps out of the peat from rich rock underneath, you will see a fertile pocket with grasses, flowers and more animals.

The Scottish hill landscape so familiar today looked very different in the past. What we now see is mainly a result of the vast glaciers that once covered all of Scotland, and more recently much of the Highlands, in successive waves of ice. The slow-moving glaciers scraping their way downhill scooped out colossal quarries that we now call corries and glens, and dumped the gravel and boulders in huge heaps on lower ground. Torrents roaring off the melting ice cut out spectacular, now-dry ravines on otherwise smooth hills, and washed more gravel into ridges lower down. This gravel is known as glacial drift – and infertile stuff it is; ridges of it dammed up water, and so formed many of Scotland's hill bogs and lochs.

Glacial drift gouged out from poor rocks can be moved down by glaciers or glacial rivers, and dumped miles away on top of rich rocks. Plants growing on this poor drift cannot reach the rich ground below, so you will often see an infertile area even though the geological map (which shows the underlying rocks) would indicate that it should be fertile. Conversely, other places are richer than you might expect from the poor rock below, through fertile drift having been moved there from lime-rich rocks. You can see this fascinating variation by looking at loose stones and rocks. If these are mostly granite, on ground lying over limestone, you may expect the place to be infertile, and vice versa.

The Scottish climate, one of the most fickle in the world, adds further variation to hill soils and wildlife. In areas of high rainfall, plant leaves that fall off in autumn remain sodden, airless and cold. The bacteria, fungi and tiny invertebrate animals that decompose plant leaves cannot thrive in such conditions, so the plant remains do not rot into soil but build up as a layer of undecomposed peat. Plants need phosphorus and other nutrients which they usually get from the soil, but deep peat forms a barrier that seals off plant roots from these nutrients in the rocks or soil underneath. Plants on deep peat have to live on the low supplies of phosphorus and other nutrients in rain and atmospheric dust – and they cannot depend on them for long, as heavy rain will soon wash the nutrients away. So vegetation on peat grows poorly, even over rich rocks such as limestone. The only plants that abound there are species such as bog asphodel, deer sedge and sphagnum moss, which can tolerate waterlogging, acid ground and

Top: The greenshank, seen here on heather, needs a habitat of short vegetation with frequent shallow pools. Bottom: Remnant birch at Inverpolly, a National Nature Reserve.

scarce nutrients. But where the climate is dry, as in eastern Scotland, you can walk on moors almost completely covered by heather, a plant that thrives best on dry, gravelly ground without deep peat. As you go west and into a wetter climate, look out for the ground becoming wetter, the peat thicker and more extensive, and the vegetation less heathery but more grassy and mossy. The effect of climate on habitats also depends on aspect; for instance, farmland extends higher on sunny, south-facing slopes than on north-facing ones. Wind and snow also cause habitat variety, as we shall read later.

Much of the variety of our habitat in Scotland depends on drainage. Steep slopes support plants that prefer dry ground, such as heather. Being well drained, stream banks have more fertile soils than the wetter, peaty ground nearby. They carry a rich grassland attractive to grazing deer and sheep. Most of the well-drained valley grasslands were cultivated up to the nineteenth century, but now the inhabitants have gone, some in forced clearances and most in later voluntary emigrations. The many ruins of farms in empty glens are a sad reminder of the extinct communities that once worked these uplands. In the very highest glens you may see the ruins of shielings on small grassy spots, where farmers once summered with their cattle, using the upper grazings and so resting their cultivated land lower down. When you walk the many cross-country paths over the hills, remember that most were once important local transport routes.

Man has had the most profound effect of all on the habitats of the hill. When the Romans invaded Scotland, they described Caledonia as a land of bogs and great forests. In later years man cleared much of the lower forests for agriculture, and after centuries of grazing and burning in the higher forests all that remains today of this once-grand old Caledonian forest is small patches of Scots pine and birch in some remote glens. In a few places these grow up to 600 metres. This shows that much of our hill ground, which many people regard as natural, is really man-made and man-maintained. It soon reverts to forest if sheep and deer are kept out. These high tree lines at 600 metres occur only in a few sheltered valleys far inland, such as upper Deeside and Strath Spey. Near the coast, trees seldom grow above 300 metres, and on exposed coasts and islands not even at sea-level. In other northern countries such as Norway and Alaska, a scrub of willow, birch and dwarf birch stretches above the tree line, but in Scotland this has been virtually wiped out by grazing and burning. Only scattered bushes remain, on bogs and cliffs out of reach of sheep and deer. If no grazing and deliberate burning took place, the only open hill would be on coastal moors, lowland peat bogs, woodland turned temporarily into moorland by accidental fires, and the high tops.

The high tops are the only part of the hill that has remained relatively unaffected by man. Here the climate is too severe, and the vegetation usually too scanty, to support many sheep. Because it is unprofitable, sheep are not run at all on the most infertile high tops such as the Cairngorms, Lochnagar and the Reay Forest, and vegetation grows so sparsely that it does not burn. The high tops, along with the coast, are therefore the most natural kinds of land in Scotland.

In the early nineteenth century landowners cleared many people and their cattle from parts of the Highlands to make way for vast flocks of sheep, which were more profitable. But sheep are such selective grazers that the quality of the pasture deteriorated and the land became less able to support them. At much the same time landowners fostered red deer greatly, turning arable farmers out of some glens that became prime winter grazing for deer, and taking stern measures against local poachers. The bigger deer stocks have since completely prevented regeneration or extension of most old woodlands, and the rise of grouse shooting in the nineteenth century also helped maintain moorland. The advent of large numbers of sheep brought an increase in the ticks which they carry and consequently in the virus disease of louping ill carried by the ticks. Louping ill now kills many red grouse, which have not yet evolved much resistance to the disease.

On moors and lower hills, heather and other plants grow faster than animals can graze them, and so become taller each year. Eventually the rank vegetation has to be burned to produce a young, more nutritious sward again. Gamekeepers, deer stalkers and shepherds do this, as grouse, red deer and sheep all benefit. Although grasses, blaeberry, bell heather and cross-leaved heath thrive better than heather in the first few years after a fire, heather usually crowds them out later. Each cock grouse defends its own area of heather, but sheep and red deer graze in groups. Fires for grouse are therefore small, whereas shepherds and deer stalkers generally burn big tracts, often 20–40 hectares at a time.

If you travel across the Highlands from east to west, you will see three major kinds of land-use and management, depending mainly on climate. On three million acres of heather-dominated low ground in the east, the top value lies in red grouse. Further west and at high altitudes in the east, where the climate is wetter and the vegetation

The bristling peak of Stac Polly, carved from Torridonian sandstone, is part of the Inverpolly National Nature Reserve. Erosion by the feet of visitors adds to the already denuded state of this hill.

more grassy, red deer are of greatest value. Sheep graze nearly all ground of both types. In the wettest and least heathery parts of the west, sheep take over the main economic role from deer. In the Southern Uplands sheep are most valuable, except on some heathery moors, mainly in the east, where grouse are more important. In recent decades the heather on many southern moors was so badly burned that grouse became scarce and shooting uneconomic. As a result, moorland has been turned over to afforestation. Dense woods now cover so much of the Galloway hill that some moorland birds such as raven and golden eagle have become scarce.

Over much of the west Highlands, farmers give little or no supplementary food to their sheep because of the shortage of arable land for crops. The sheep live free on the hill almost like wild animals, except that they are rounded up twice a year. Many die, and the abundance of carcases props up numerous carrion-eaters such as eagles, ravens, crows and foxes. These would decrease greatly if sheep farming were to decline, or if it became more intensive as on hill farms in north-east Scotland. As winters in the north-east are too snowy for sheep to be left free on the hill, farmers there must feed them and give other intensive care. Thus very few die on the hill, and carrion-eaters are scarcer than in the west.

Continuous grazing for many decades by numerous sheep, deer and cattle has changed the heather-dominated vegetation on many hills to more grassy swards. These consist mainly of mat grass in the east, and purple moor grass and deer sedge in the west. These grazing-induced changes are common in the Southern Uplands and the west Highlands, where you may see a sudden change in the vegetation along the line of a fence, with heather on one side and unpalatable grass on the other. This indicates heavier grazing on the grassy side. When foresters fence out sheep and deer on these grassy moors, heather comes back quickly.

So, although many people think of our moors and hills as enduring and unchanging, they are really in constant change. The vegetation is continually altering as it grows after fire, or becomes grazed, or invaded by trees. Heavy rain often washes out soil from the bare slopes, and sometimes this erosion cuts huge gullies. The bare and infertile countryside that man has created in the west Highlands has aptly been called a 'wet desert'; today it has its own stark beauty, and gives a sense of grand space and wilderness that is deeply attractive to modern city-dwellers on holiday. But let us also remember it as the wet desert and as the countryside where many Gaelic hill folk once made a living. We will not understand the present wildlife unless we remember these things.

The main kinds of vegetation

The heather or ling for which Scotland is so famed is the main plant on our lower hills and moors. In the east Highlands entire hillsides support an almost pure stand of it: during a good year for heather bloom, you can see hills several miles away glowing a warm pink in late August. The air is heavy with the pungent scent of the flowers, and throbs with the buzzing of bees working on the masses of bloom. As you walk across the moor, every step throws up a tiny cloud of yellow pollen. But even these ling-dominated hills have much variety if you

Bell heather

look closely. On the best-drained and south-facing sunny braes on east Scottish moors, you will see bell heather in abundance. It has leaves of a darker green than the ling, and a darker red flower which stays in bloom for several months. On the slightly richer of the dry gravelly soils, the dark green leathery leaves of bearberry cover much of the driest ground in a low carpet, and the petty whin shows its bright yellow flowers in June. Blaeberry also grows commonly on well-drained ground, especially on the higher moors in east Scotland; you can easily recognize its pale green woody stalks. Along with it you will often see the cowberry, known locally as cranberry.

In damp places you will find the delicate, pale pink blooms of cross-leaved heath. Wet ground with slow seepages of water supports dense patches of rushes, and at low altitudes also the woody shrubs of bog myrtle. The slowly seeping water contains more nutrients, which both species require. Also, bog myrtle can fix atmospheric nitrogen and turn it into nitrate, thus probably adding to soil fertility. Bog myrtle gives a grand touch of colour when its yellow catkins open in May, and on hot summer days you will enjoy the delightful aromatic scent from its leaves. The worst-drained ground in extensive basins carries deep peat, with a vegetation mainly of cotton grass, cross-leaved heath and a little heather. Being tussocky, it makes heavy going for the walker. As cotton grass starts growing early in spring, it has a higher nutrient content then than other plants. Deer, hares and grouse seek out the yellow flowers in March or April, and so you seldom see dense masses of the later white cottony heads, except inside a fence.

A similar vegetation typical of deep peat covers a vast area of high moorland plateau in the central and east Highlands. It becomes especially extensive on Am Monadh or The Mounth, the hill range from Drumochter eastwards almost to Stonehaven, and also on the Monadh Liath east of Loch Ness. Much of the peat blanket has eroded into a maze of peat hags. There, stretches of flat bare peat and gullies of bare peat surround vegetated islands and tongues of deep, uneroded peat. As the tops of the islands are well drained, plants grow better there. Where erosion has cut down to the well-drained and richer soil below the peat, plants also flourish, and you may even see high-quality, lawn-like grassland. The hags are therefore more fertile than undissected peat bogs, and support more grouse, hares, deer and golden plovers.

Cross-leaved heath

Less nutritious grasses and sedges such as purple moor grass and deer sedge form the main vegetation on wet valley bottoms and gentle slopes, especially in central and western Scotland. Unpalatable and therefore little grazed, they grow tall and fibrous in summer, and die in autumn to a pale yellow, straw-like colour. Even a mile away, the colour of a hillside can tell you much about the vegetation there and the extent of grazing.

Highly fertile black or brown earth such as you have in your garden seldom occurs on the moors, but may be found in small patches in well-drained areas. It carries a nutritious vegetation that botanists call an *Agrostis–Festuca* (bent grass and fescue) grassland. Often this is 'herb-rich' because of the thyme, violets and other flowering plants growing through the grass. It stays bright green throughout the year because grazing animals crop it like a lawn. Earthworms and numerous insects live in this fertile earth, and mole hills are much in evidence. The more extensive tracts of rich alluvial earth washed into the glen bottoms once supported arable farmlands, but most are now home for sheep, red deer and in some places hill cattle, grazing among the ruined farms.

Bracken grows on some of these patches of good, well-drained soil, often with high-quality grassland underneath it. Formerly kept down by people cutting it for bedding and by the trampling of cattle, it has now become an agricultural pest over large areas. Sheep do not like going into it, and it is poisonous to cattle that eat it. Its abundance indicates mismanagement: having too many sheep relative to cattle, and letting heather get so senile that it cannot compete with bracken after a fire.

The moors and lower hills of the far west carry their own kinds of vegetation. You will see rough, unpalatable grassland on most ground, and usually little heather except on steep slopes. The heaviest rain falls on high hills miles inland, for instance in Knoydart and near Tyndrum. There, even steep slopes carry rough grassland. Deep peat bog covers vast stretches of flat or gently sloping low ground in Caithness, Sutherland, and at Rannoch Moor. As hills in the west rise steeply, with a few plateaux, you will find less peat hags than on the extensive plateaux of the east Scottish moors. The only flat, heather-dominated moorland lies at low altitudes near the coast, where rainfall is lightest, as at Kinlochbervie, Islay and south of Oban. But even in the west you will see fertile grasslands on low hills where rich rocks crop out, for instance on the beautiful greens over limestone at Elphin, north of Ullapool.

Water vegetation grows in the many pools and tarns so characteristic of our peat bogs. You will enjoy the sight of bogbean in the pools and water lilies in the sheltered lochans. Uncommon on the dry, smooth Southern Uplands and north-east Highlands, these pools and tarns become more frequent in rough, wet, peaty terrain, as in the Cairngorms and central Perthshire. In the even rougher ground of the far west mainland and the islands, they abound. There, from hill tops on the edge of the bogs, you may see the dark face of the land transformed as hundreds of pools and lochans flash brighter than silver in the sun.

Willow scrub on bogland and birch scrub on drier ground are interesting kinds of vegetation, but grazing and burning have exterminated them in most places. Juniper scrub on dry ground has also largely gone. Fortunately it still thrives on the hill in a few places over rich rocks in the north-east Highlands, especially near Ballater and Tomintoul. But its hold is precarious.

A clear boundary runs between moorland, where some tall heather nearly always occurs, and the arctic-alpine zone above. A dwarf type of heather does grow in the lower part of the arctic-alpine zone, but usually along with more blaeberry, crowberry and mosses than lower down. You will also see more of the grey and yellow 'reindeer-moss' lichens, and many other plants common in the Arctic. Near Ballater the zone begins at 840 metres, in the Cairngorms 760 metres, in Wester Ross 600 metres, in north-west Sutherland 430–60 metres, and near Cape Wrath 190–300 metres. The windier the place, the lower the arctic-alpine zone goes.

In this zone, severe weather keeps the vegetation short, despite little grazing and no burning. Plants creep low over the ground. Dry cold winds turn green leaves brown during snow-free periods, and snow moulds kill other leaves in hollows where snow lies long. Gales are so strong that they often tear out vegetation, and sometimes throw gravel on to plants several metres away. You will see much more bare ground – sand, gravel and rocks – than on moorland. On the most exposed summits, hardly any vegetation exists. As the plants grow so little, their annual accumulation of dead leaves is much smaller than on lower hills, and so there is little or no peat. Soil, gravel and stones are unstable, continually moving because of freezing, thawing and water movements. Streams on the high plateaux often spread up to ten metres wide, with little channels weaving in and out of the gravel like braided hair. Look out for the beautiful red, green and blackish mosses in the water. These streams are important for wildlife, as many pools dry up in late summer heat-waves, when much of the hot sandy ground resembles a desert.

Snow is of key importance for vegetation on the high tops. It protects plants from desiccating winds, provides water for the summer, and so leads to better plant growth and in turn deeper soils. On the upper moors and the lower part of the arctic-alpine zone, areas under prolonged snow are bright green because heather does not like shade and the paler green blaeberry takes its place, along with some mat grass. Above 900 metres, you can spot the location of big snow fields by the predominant mat grass. In autumn it fades to pale yellow, contrasting with the gold of the deer sedge.

Many deep hollows hold snow so long that plants grow for only a few weeks in August and September, and so vegetation and soil are sparse. In a deep pocket on Brae Riach, one snow patch that melted only twice this century had no vegetation underneath. You will see only a few species that withstand prolonged shade, such as dwarf cudweed and the blackish mosses *Dicranum starkei* and *Polytrichum norvegicum*. Our biggest alpine grasslands, with much mat grass, lie in larger and less sheltered hollows where the snow fields usually melt by July; there, the sward is continuous and bare ground scarce. As gentle slopes and plateaux are more windswept and hold little snow, more bare ground occurs there. They carry a vegetation mainly of woolly hair moss and stiff sedge, but at higher altitudes you will also see the beautiful pink-flowered cushions of moss campion, least willow, and occasionally thrift. On more exposed ridges and plateaux, where gales blow most of the snow away, bare gravel and stones cover the ground, with only scattered clumps of woolly hair moss and spiky tufts of three-leaved rush. On the very top of Ben Nevis and Ben Macdui nearly all the surface is stone and gravel. As the prevailing winds in Scotland blow from the south-west, slopes facing westwards are less snowy, drier and more barren than east-facing slopes.

Many beautiful lichens grow on boulders, such as the lemon-yellow *Rhizocarpon geographicum*. (Their growth patterns have been

Blackcocks confront each other on the trampled vegetation of the lek.

used by geographers for estimating when last our hills held glaciers.) Cliffs are even more important for vegetation, as they provide ledges free from the ubiquitous mouths of sheep and deer. In the Highlands we have the best variety and greatest abundance of rare arctic-alpine plants in the British Isles, especially on the lime-rich rocks of Ben Lawers, Caenlochan and Glen Clova. Although they have been considerably depleted by collectors and gardeners, they are still magnificent. Many species have demanding requirements – for instance, mountain avens and purple saxifrage need lime-rich conditions, whereas the tufted saxifrage prefers cold, damp, north-facing crags. Arctic-alpine plants produce some of the most beautiful flowers in Scotland; their blooms light up the bare gravel and rocks, and are brighter-coloured and more precious than any gemstone found here.

The main animals

What animals you see on the hill will depend chiefly on the kinds of vegetation there. The bulk of the animal life anywhere in the country, however, consists of tiny soil invertebrates. Along with bacteria, these are of crucial importance for maintaining soil fertility and thus for the existence of all land vertebrates, including mankind.

The Highlands are of great interest to entomologists, containing as they do a wealth of rare northern and arctic insects and other invertebrates, including some species completely new to science. The main moorland insects above ground level are small flies such as midges, but there is a great variety of others including dung beetles, big ground beetles, and larger flies such as the St Mark's fly with its characteristic hanging flight and dangling legs. In wet patches with rushes, the tiny crane fly *Molophilus ater* is particularly abundant, and forms one of the main insect foods for grouse chicks. Many species of small moths live on the heather moors, as well as some spectacular large ones such as the oak eggar and emperor moth, whose caterpillars eat shoots of heather and blaeberry. Other striking insects are the plant bugs whose capsules of 'spittle' dot the heather like snowflakes. The caterpillars of the heather beetle eat heather on damp ground at low altitudes. In bad outbreaks they turn the greensward ragged and brown within a few weeks, but a parasitic wasp can reduce their numbers greatly by depositing its eggs inside the caterpillars. Spiders are common on all hill ground; on moorland in summer you will often see their nests spun round heather shoots, and sometimes scores of tiny young spiders crawling out of the nests. Dragonflies, among the most beautiful of all our insects, occur on ground with lochsides, slow-flowing streams and pools. Look out for pond skaters on the surface of small, fertile puddles, and for water beetles swimming in deeper pools.

The insects most obvious to the average tourist are those that annoy him. On the dry, lower moors of eastern Scotland, the abundant houseflies irritate with their buzzing. Midges occur infrequently there, and horseflies – 'clegs' in Scotland – rarely. You will find mosquitoes only locally, near low-lying bogs, lakes and woods in sheltered valleys far inland. West of upper Deeside, clegs and midges become more common. They abound in the far west, where damp ground and innumerable pools offer good places for breeding. Other northern countries such as Sweden and Canada also have hordes of biting insects

Top: A lizard suns itself on a lichen-covered rock.
Bottom: An adder moves down a watery path in Glen Rosa, Isle of Arran.

Right : Red grouse come to the roadside to fill their gizzards with grit, which grinds the food — heather shoots — before it is digested.

Left : Grouse chicks rely on disruptive coloration for concealment.
Below : A grouse crouches in the heather, well camouflaged against predators.

in summer, but there the mosquito is the most abundant. Our treeless Scottish uplands are too windy for it, but we may expect a change as the new woodlands become more extensive on the moors.

Many arctic insects live on our high tops. You will also see invertebrate species common at low altitudes, such as the housefly, the harvestman *Mitopus morio*, and the ground beetles *Carabus glabratus* and *problematicus*. On the high snow fields in summer you can usually find many insects stranded and comatose, unable to get off because they have been immobilized by cold. Sometimes you will see various lowland insects such as ants and woodland weevils on the snow, presumably blown there by strong air currents. The damp ground under stones holds many insects and spiders, and you will find bumblebees working on the hill flowers. Crane flies are common on all hill ground, even on the most barren places. They form an important food for small songbirds such as wheatear and snow bunting. On moorland they tend to be more numerous on wet moors, and on the high tops they abound on wet moss in the streams.

Many frogs and newts still thrive on the hill, unlike most parts of Britain where they have become much scarcer following the drainage of farmland. Frogs breed even in the lower part of the arctic-alpine zone. Adders and lizards are also widespread on lower hills and moors, reaching greatest abundance on the dry moors of east Scotland.

Our moors and lower hills support many birds. Some of them, such as red grouse, have a strong influence on land-use and management, which in their turn profoundly affect vegetation and animal life over huge areas.

Red grouse feed mainly on heather shoots. On the heather-dominated moors of eastern Scotland they abound, with up to one breeding pair per hectare in good years. Grouse numbers fluctuate fairly regularly over a period of years: the red grouse is one of several northern species, such as lemming, short-tailed vole and snowshoe hare, that show these periodic cycles.

Some moors have more grouse than others. Ground over lime-rich rocks carries more pairs in spring, and on average these rear bigger broods than on moors over granite and other poor rocks. Heather shoots on rich moors contain more phosphorus than on poor moors. Also, rich moors support a wider range of other species of plants which grouse will eat and which give better nutrition than heather. Even on ground over the same rock, some places hold higher stocks than others. Tracts of rank unburned heather have few grouse. Other areas, with heather too short because of big fires or heavy grazing, support few or no grouse because the birds cannot get enough cover. On the best places you will see a patchwork of different heights, offering within a small area some short heather for good food and some tall heather for cover. This can be achieved by burning long strips not more than thirty metres wide, but on most grouse moors in Scotland the burned patches are too big, or there is too little tall heather, or too little short heather. Only on a few moors has management been improved greatly in recent years, producing large increases in stocks and bags.

Further west, grouse stocks decrease as heather becomes sparser and burned patches larger. On the poorest parts of the Cairngorms and in the far west, you will find only about one breeding pair per 20–40 hectares. On this ground, fires burn out big areas, often several hundred hectares at a time.

Traditionally, many gamekeepers on grouse moors have

Top: Heather-burning on Rannoch moor. Regular patch or strip burning encourages new growth, which provides food for grouse.
Bottom: A female hen harrier incubates her eggs.

31

persecuted hen harriers, golden eagles, crows and other species that kill grouse or eat their eggs. They thought that one grouse more to a predator meant one less to the guns in August. But in wild populations one animal more to a predator often means that one less will die of starvation. Apart from shooting, most grouse deaths are due to predators in winter. If you walk the moors in late winter and spring you will see many carcases or piles of feathers where grouse have been killed. This looks bad to a keeper, but research shows that most of these grouse have been excluded from land-holdings on the heather by the aggressive behaviour of their fellows. Such homeless birds die in any case before the breeding season, even if they escape predation in winter. Although crows may take so many grouse eggs that few are left for hatching, this indicates inefficient keepering: it is not difficult to eliminate crows during the grouse-nesting time by a short concentrated campaign, and crow numbers are kept high artificially by waste cattle food and dead sheep.

Black grouse have declined greatly in west Scotland, and thrive now only on moors and lower hills in the east. You will find the best stocks in places with a mixture of scrub, tall heather, bogs, shorter vegetation and farmland. The hen chooses thick heather for her nest, and then takes her chicks to damp ground with rushes, tall heather, bog myrtle and scrub. Heavy grazing, burning and draining have destroyed this mixture over big areas. But the black grouse thrives again when the afforestation of open moorland artificially provides the preferred mixture of rank heather, dry and wet ground, and scrub. High numbers last some years until growing trees crowd out the moorland vegetation, when once again the local population dies out. In spring, blackcocks display communally at a 'lek' or display ground on short vegetation, where the hens come to be mated by the most vigorous cock. The blackcocks' display is one of the most spectacular wildlife sights in the world.

A short-eared owl rests on a roadside post in Orkney.

Thick heather offers the preferred habitat for meadow pipits, and bog myrtle and tall heather hold a few stonechats and whinchats on the lower moors. Skylarks like more heavily grazed, shorter vegetation, and wheatears prefer ground with some rocks. Ring ousels have a widespread distribution, but few are found at any one place; they prefer well-drained slopes with screes and rocks, especially with juniper scrub. Twites are most common near old croft lands, and linnets and yellowhammers at the moor edge amongst whins and broom next to the fields. Well-burned grouse moors have a bigger variety of vegetation height and vegetation type within a small area than the more uniform moors further west, and because of this you will find more species and bigger numbers of small songbirds there.

Some of the most interesting birds of our moors are the waders. Snipe may be found in wet bogs, and curlews in wet rough grassland. Golden plovers like peaty ground and heavily grazed or burned patches. Lapwings and oystercatchers also occur on patches kept open by burning and grazing, and the more fertile wet bogs are the home of the redshank. Dunlins live on peat bogs. One of the most delightful experiences on the hill is to listen to the wader song at its height on a warm spring morning or evening. The bubbling song of the curlew has a special wild magic. On the lower moors many of the curlews, redshanks, golden plovers and oystercatchers that nest on the hill do much of their feeding on nearby farmland when they first arrive, and often all summer as well. This explains why they abound on moorland lying next to the richer soils of the farmland rather than in the middle of continuous moorland. Farms below extensive moorland, such as in upper Strathdon, attract extra concentrations of waders after heavy snowstorms in spring, until the snow thaws again on the hill. In a snowy April you may see scores or even hundreds of golden plovers in one field. Nearly all species of waders are much more abundant on the more fertile soils of the east Highland moors than in the wetter west. But even in the east the poorer ground with deep peat supports few or no curlews, redshanks, lapwings and oystercatchers.

By contrast, you will see more greenshanks on the infertile western bogs than in the more fertile east. They feed in shallow pools and tarns, which abound in the west. The greenshank is one of our most beautiful waders. In Scotland it lives mainly on open, short, heavily grazed or burned vegetation with permanent shallow pools and tarns, and so it depends on man's artificial maintenance of open ground. In the rest of Europe it breeds only on forest bogs. Although we have a few greenshanks on forest bogs in Strath Spey and elsewhere, little of this habitat remains in Scotland.

In recent decades Scandinavian waders such as Temminck's stint, wood sandpiper and others have bred on Scottish bogs, possibly due to a change in climate. But because many more skilled bird watchers now search for rare birds, we cannot tell whether these species really are new breeders or whether they occurred previously but were overlooked.

Among the finest birds of the hill are our birds of prey. Scotland now has some of the best populations of golden eagles and peregrines in the world. Insecticides and other toxic chemicals in the prey have contaminated peregrines and eagles in most countries, and in many places no peregrines are left. In west Scotland, where few grouse and other live prey occur, the eagles feed chiefly on sheep carrion in winter, and most peregrines have to go to the coast in winter to find enough live prey. From sheep wool the eagles picked up dieldrin and other pesticides present in the sheep dip, and the peregrines at the coast ate sea birds contaminated with toxic chemicals. In the early 1960s in the west, the result of this pollution was that the shells of their eggs became thin, many eggs broke, fewer young were reared, and the peregrines' breeding stock also decreased. After dieldrin was banned, the eagles began to breed successfully again in the west. As the north-east Highlands hold many grouse, ptarmigan and mountain hares, most eagles and peregrines there do not have to move away in winter. Also, these prey animals live all the year round on hill ground virtually free from contamination. So the eagles and peregrines in the north-east have continued to rear large broods, and their breeding stocks have remained high.

Peregrines nest at greatest density on hills used as grouse moor, but you will see few eagles there because of persecution. The eagles reach greatest abundance in deer forests further west, where most stalkers leave them alone. On average, a pair of eagles has 4500 hectares in upper Deeside, but 7300 hectares on the Argyll mainland where grouse and hares are scarce. The eagles build most of their eyries in crags, but a few may be found in old pine trees.

Gamekeepers persecute hen harriers because they kill grouse and spoil some grouse drives by scaring the birds off. But nevertheless many do nest on mainland grouse moors. Others breed in new forestry plantations until the trees crowd out the moorland vegetation and so

The twite, a member of the linnet family.

reduce the numbers of voles, pipits and grouse that the harriers need for prey. Particularly large numbers spend the summer on the Orkney moors, where they hunt on rough grassland and farmland, taking many Orkney voles and pipits. More harriers and merlins occur in the east Highlands than in the west, nesting mainly below 460 metres where pipits are most abundant. By contrast, ravens breed rarely on eastern moors, though commonly in the west where their main food of dead sheep abounds. Many immigrate to eastern deer forests in autumn, and spend the winter living largely on deer carrion.

Short-eared owls have their home on rough grassland, where their main prey – the short-tailed vole – finds good cover and food. They do best on afforested moorland, where the thicker grass that abounds for a while after planting offers the voles ideal conditions. The owls concentrate where voles are locally abundant, and lay more eggs in years with maximum vole numbers. Kestrels also do well in high vole years, but because their diet is more varied and includes big insects, their numbers fluctuate less from year to year. They nest on crags and hunt over all hill ground except the highest tops.

Buzzards have increased greatly in east Scotland, where they were scarce before the 1950s. They usually nest in woods, but often hunt rabbits on lower moors and grassy valley bottoms. You will see most buzzards in the west, where they feed mainly on rabbits, voles and carrion on lower ground. In recent years goshawks have appeared more often on the hill. They hunt grouse there, and also a variety of prey in woods and farmland next to their nesting trees. Formerly exterminated in Scotland by game preservers, they have come back with the decline in the number of gamekeepers and the increase in woodland. A recent spectacular addition to our birds of prey is the snowy owl. A pair has bred for some years on Fetlar in Shetland, where these normally lemming-eating arctic owls feed mainly on rabbits.

Seagulls abound on some lower moors: many colonies of common gulls nest on heather, and black-headed gulls on bogs and tarns. They often hover to catch moths and crane flies low above the vegetation, and move up to the arctic-alpine ground when insects are temporarily abundant. Rooks and starlings also fly up to the lower hills to feed on insects in June and July, when their food of leatherjackets and other invertebrates on arable farmland becomes scarce. People seldom think of ducks as moorland birds, but mallard and teal occur on most Scottish moors, nesting in thick heather and taking their young to nearby bogs, streams and lochs. Also, many red-throated divers breed on peaty moorland pools in the west half of the Scottish mainland and on the islands.

Exciting days on the hill come when migrants fly through the hill passes in poor weather or over the high tops in good weather. You will often see flocks of greylag geese in October and April. An even finer sight is a herd of whooper swans flying over on a dark November day, giving their wonderful, whooping calls. Swallows and house martins often migrate over the passes in late summer, and in every summer month you may see swifts flying over the hill, here one day, gone the next. In October thousands of redwings and fieldfares land to feed on blaeberries, crowberries, and insects in sheltered spots. You will often hear them calling at night as the flocks fly south. Unusual vagrants come occasionally to the hill, such as the odd robin or bullfinch found dead on the snow in the Cairngorms.

The ptarmigan has a distribution that covers the arctic-alpine zone. North Americans call it the rock ptarmigan, and in fact the birds are most abundant on ground with screes and rocks, and spend much time using big rocks as look-outs. The highest stocks occur over lime-rich rocks, where the food plants have higher nutritive value than over granite. Ptarmigan feed mainly on blaeberry and crowberry shoots, with some heather and various other plants such as least willow. On some hills they are almost as abundant as red grouse on the best-managed grouse moors. They grow a white plumage for the winter. After snowstorms, ptarmigan pack and move to ridges where winds have blown snow off the vegetation, and each bird spends the night in a hollow scratched out of the snow. The ptarmigan is one of the hardiest birds in the world.

Other species of birds are scarcer on the tops than lower down, as one would expect from the sparser vegetation. The meadow pipit is often the commonest of the small birds, but a few wheatears and ring ousels breed up to the summits. Golden plovers and dunlins nest on high peat bogs and also on some grassy ground without peat. You will see the biggest stocks over rich rocks. One of the most fascinating of the rare birds of our high tops is the dotterel. A little jewel of the tundra, this small wader returns to the high plateaux in May, and leaves in August to winter on the deserts of the Middle East. The hen defends the territory and courts the smaller, duller-coloured cock, whereas he incubates the eggs and rears the young. This reversal of roles occasionally allows a hen to produce two clutches, one for him and another for herself to incubate.

The other special rarity of our high tops is the snow bunting. Abundant during summer in the Arctic, in Scotland it occurs in big numbers only in winter, on moors, coasts and hill farms. In summer a few nest on the most arctic-like hills, especially the Cairngorms. The hen nests down a hole in the boulder fields. Even the most favoured hills seldom hold more than a few pairs, so here we have one of Scotland's rarest breeding birds. A special thrill is to listen to the cock's far-carrying, sweet song in a wild corrie.

Other arctic birds occasionally appear. In several summers since 1940 a male snowy owl has been seen on the Cairngorms. Shore lark and Lapland bunting have reared young on upland in Scotland in recent years, and in summer 1977 and 1978 pairs of Lapland buntings

A hen golden eagle refurbishes her nest with a fresh branch of rowan.

35

The largest golden eagle's eyrie in the world is in the Cairngorms. The nest consists of hundreds of branches built into this Caledonian pine tree. The tree is over 200 years old and the oldest branches in the nest have probably been there for 150 years.

appeared in several places. Bird watchers have seen sanderling and long-tailed skua in summer, on ground quite like their usual haunts on arctic tundra. These exciting events emphasize the wildlife value of our high tops.

Recent trends

What major trends affecting the Scottish hill and its wildlife have occurred in recent years? What future changes are likely? And, if these changes are harmful, what can be done about them?

Grouse shooting has increased in the last fifteen years. So has the illegal laying of poisoned meat on grouse moors, and the resulting deaths of many eagles, buzzards, ravens and others. Heather management has improved on some moors, thus increasing the diversity of vegetation and other wildlife. In most places the expansion of hill cattle has probably benefited wildlife, by increasing plant diversity and soil fertility. Due to taxation, many private estates have been sold to corporate owners such as insurance companies and foreign financiers. These new owners are obviously more remote, and this lack of personal interest may harm our wildlife. Major increases have occurred in the numbers and geographical range of hen harriers, goshawks, buzzards, peregrines, foxes and wildcats. This may be partly due to fewer keepers being employed, but it may also be a result of the vast areas of hill that have been changed by afforestation, as predatory animals are harder to find in thick woods than on open moorland. A new shooter has appeared, not the aristocratic Briton but the foreign business man unused to British shooting traditions. Because he dislikes walking far, hundreds of bulldozed tracks have appeared, often badly made – several have scarred some of the finest areas for wildlife and scenery on the Scottish high tops.

General tourists and hill walkers have greatly increased, but their disturbance of game is often exaggerated. Research in the Peak District National Park and at Scottish chair-lifts shows that big increases of tourists have not reduced grouse numbers. Nevertheless, bird watchers and climbers have caused some eagles to desert their nests or fail to hatch their eggs, and more nests of eagle and peregrine have been robbed as a result of the high prices paid by foreign falconers. Tourists' sandwiches have led to an increase in pied wagtails and gulls nesting on the hill, and have drawn flocks of snow buntings in winter to lay-bys and car parks. Attracted to the high tops by scraps of food left by tourists, crows have adopted a new habit of taking ptarmigan eggs. The many feet of tourists have widened popular paths and eroded hillsides on Cairn Gorm, Stac Polly, Ben Nevis, the Lairig Ghru, and many other places. Some ski centres have scarred the hillsides through insufficient care being taken in the early stages of construction, and the resulting soil erosion has had to be repaired by reseeding and fertilizing. The domestic reindeer taken to the Cairngorms were an inappropriate introduction to a National Nature Reserve, particularly as domestic reindeer in Alaska and Sweden were known to have severely damaged the vegetation.

The chief influence on the wildlife of the Scottish hill is still the heavy grazing of sheep and red deer, combined with burning. Deer have increased greatly in recent years. The Red Deer Commission has exhorted owners to shoot more, so as to prevent many dying in hard winters and to avoid damage from starving deer marauding farmland and woodland. In such conditions, regenerating scrub and young trees have even less chance of survival. As sheep are one of the few farm products in which the Common Market is not self-sufficient, our sheep stocks may well rise. This would increase the harmful consequences of continuous and heavy sheep grazing.

Irresponsible burning of hill vegetation has had devastating effects. Due to the higher costs of labour there are fewer people to watch over the burning: many light the heather and then go home, leaving fires to burn all night. Some fires on tinder-dry ground burn off the soil and even destroy the lichen on the rocks. In recent years, fires in Sutherland and elsewhere have laid waste square miles at a time. These practices damage wildlife, and will eventually reduce fertility because of greater soil erosion and a run-down of nutrients washed away by heavy rain.

Unless we fence off certain areas or reduce deer and sheep stocks, some of the finest stretches of centuries-old pine and birch forest in Scotland will become extinct. The same treatment will be needed if we are to have scrub above the tree line. Creation of these habitats in a few

Top: Cowberry in flower at the Bridge of Dye. Also called red whortleberry, it is related to the blaeberry, and has bright red berries high in Vitamin C.
Bottom left: The clustered bellflower, a member of the Campanula family.
Bottom right: Ripening blaeberries. The dried leaves of the blaeberry were used as a substitute for tea.

places of outstanding national value for recreation and science would not be difficult for the Scotland of the 1980s, provided that the political will were there, backed by growing public support.

There has recently been a rash of proposals for developments such as new roads, ski centres, alpine villages and helicopter services on the hill. If implemented, these would spoil the face of many of our finest hills and put their wildlife at great risk. There is an urgent need to designate which areas are of outstanding national value for wildlife, and to refuse new roads or other facilities that would make access easier to such areas. Pressures have become so great that existing organizations and planning arrangements cannot cope with them. Even graver threats to the Scottish hill and to mankind himself have come in the last year, with proposals by the Electricity Boards and the Atomic Energy Authority to explore for uranium mining and for dumping nuclear waste. From Orkney to Harris, the Cairngorms, Scourie, Galloway, Morven – the list of dearly loved names runs on and on. It seems that no part of Scotland is sacrosanct.

There is cause for hope, however. Glen Tanar and Balmoral Estates have fenced red deer out of large areas, and already many young trees have sprung up. Although the main trend in the past was for trees to change to moor, you can see the opposite in the north-east Highlands, such as near Dava, Abernethy, and in Deeside at Dinnet, Glen Gairn and by the Feugh. This happens on ground with few or no red deer, where sheep grazing and burning have declined. In such conditions, once a few scattered trees exist that are tall enough to survive fire and old enough to produce seed, a moderately hot fire can hasten their spread. It does this by destroying ground vegetation and so removing competition from the future tree seedlings.

Another bright spot is the trend towards greater public awareness and appreciation of wildlife. Organizations such as the Scottish Wildlife Trust have grown in strength and influence, and this gives confidence to government bodies such as the Nature Conservancy Council. Better public support is the only basis for the political will needed for safeguarding our most outstanding areas for wildlife.

There is much to regret in man's past and present treatment of the Scottish hill and its wildlife, and indeed also in his treatment of the human communities there and their cultures and distinctive identities. There is also much left of which we may feel proud. Today, man has never had more ruthless centralized power in his grasp, or paradoxically, more awareness of and concern for wildlife and for local human communities. Will we leave the Scottish hill as exciting and rewarding a place for our descendants as we were fortunate to find it? Or will we miss the long-term opportunity that we have, and instead squander our natural resources and heritage for short-term gain, wreck the distinctive human cultures of the hill country, and damage the hill and its wildlife for good?

Chapter 3
Forests and Woodlands

The countryside we now guard so jealously is, in fact, a devastated area, a man-made wilderness.   James Shaw Grant, 1977

These forests could well become in the next century the greatest reservoir of wild plants and animals in the country.
M. E. D. Poore, 1972

The title of this chapter appears to differentiate between forests and woodlands. In fact there is no real distinction: a forest is a large wood. Either may be growing on the site of a 'primary' or 'ancient' wood, or it may have been planted during recent centuries. It is probably true to say that there is no wholly natural woodland, and certainly no natural forest, in Scotland, in the sense of a wood wholly unaffected by the activities of man – by exploitation, burning or grazing. It is probably true also that all forests and woodlands in Scotland, including the twentieth-century forests planted on apparently bare hillsides, occupy the sites of former forests. Some of the so-called new forests of the Borders are growing on the sites of extensive natural forests which have been destroyed in relatively recent times, and whose names are familiar in Scottish history – Ettrick, Jedwood and Galloway Forest, for example.

The past

To understand the present we must know something of the past. The history of Scottish forests is a sad one of steady and relentless destruction by man and his animals, a process which continues today.

It is an immense and well-documented subject which can only be touched upon here. Regrettably there is not space to consider the pre-glacial forests, rich in species now found in America and the Far East, however tempting it might be to claim ancient Scottish nationality for many of the exotic species commonly planted today. Norway spruce and silver fir appear to have come back during inter-glacial periods, but failed to return after the last ice age. Native species are taken to be those which established themselves during and after the final retreat of the glaciers, starting perhaps around 10,000 B.P. It is thought that there was a climatic optimum about the year 7000 B.P., when virtually the whole of the country, including the northern and western isles, was covered with forest, save only on ground too rocky, wet or unstable.

Two fine examples of Scottish trees: (top) Caledonian pines in Glen Lyon, and (bottom) autumn splendour of natural woodland in Glen Banchor.

It is sometimes thought that this, the true ancient Caledonian forest, was one of Scots pine and birch, with broadleaved trees restricted to fertile and sheltered sites mainly in the south and west. This is not so. Probably more ground was occupied by broadleaved trees – oak, birch, elm, ash, alder, hazel, lime, bird cherry, aspen, willows, holly – than by pine. In favoured areas oak would have grown to a large size, in other parts the forest would have been open or scrub-like. Scots pine associated with birch would have been predominant in the north and east on granite soils, but even here broadleaved forest would have occupied the more fertile ground. Above the forest proper would have been a scrub zone of birch, willows and juniper, such as still exists in Scandinavia, but which has almost vanished above the few remains of modified natural woodland found in the Scottish mountains today.

Before man appeared in numbers sufficient to make his presence felt, the forest was subject to natural changes and catastrophes – storms, fires started by lightning, floods and changing climate. But it is man and his animals that have destroyed the Scottish forest, starting with the clearance of trees on light lands, to make room for crops and livestock and for use in domestic life, and continuing as numbers increased and tools became more effective. From Roman times on, there is an increasing abundance of written records, both of the location and extent of the forests and of their continuous destruction. Often an extensive wood disappeared within the lifetime of one individual. Although the forest provided shelter, grazing, fuel, wood for domestic use and later for charcoal, iron smelting, housing and

Typical deer forest in Glen Affric: Caledonian pines and birches grow on the lower ground.

shipbuilding, man looked upon it at best as something to be plundered, and he destroyed it. The sonorous names of forests well documented in history, and now reduced to remnants or vanished without trace, make melancholy reading. Ettrick, Jedwood and Galloway have been mentioned; where now is the great forest of Plater in Angus, where are the forests of Torwood, Buchan, Alyth, Garioch, Cabrach, Dunfermline, Strathnaver? There are records from all over Scotland of trees buried under peat and dug up and used during the centuries, records often complete with detailed measurements, showing that oak, for instance, reached a size hardly found in the country today. Climatic deterioration undoubtedly helped to shrink the forest, but man has been the principal agent.

Voices were raised in every age against the wanton destruction of the forest, and efforts were made both by the royal authority and by local magnates to slow down this destruction and take thought for the future, but to little avail. The first forest laws, the Leges Forestarum, are generally ascribed to the reign of William the Lion in the late twelfth and early thirteenth centuries; they forbade the taking of fire or of domestic animals into the woods, and the cutting of oak trees. These were followed through the centuries by many other laws both national and local. Some planting of trees, rather than of whole woods, is recorded as far back as the fourteenth century, and interestingly enough exotic trees were often used – chestnut, beech and sycamore (the Scots plane). In the seventeenth century there was an increase in planting, often just round great houses, but sometimes on a larger scale, such as the planting of part of Drummond Hill in Perthshire. But the eighteenth century was the great tree-planting time, with many enlightened lairds planting large areas, often with exotics such as the newly arrived European larch and the slightly earlier Norway spruce.

Thomas Pennant remarked of the Blair Atholl district during his tour of Scotland in 1771: 'This country is very mountainous and has no natural woods except of birch, but the vast plantations which begin to cloath the hills will amply supply these deficits.' He was of course referring to the tremendous plantings of larch undertaken by the Dukes of Atholl. At this time, and later, the native Scots pine was planted all over Scotland and on many sites quite unsuited to it – it is commonly found nowadays on sites in the lowlands where it has no business to be.

The eighteenth century saw also the large-scale destruction of the many surviving woods both of oak and pine. The exploitation of the Highland forests was by no means always the work of Lowland or English entrepreneurs, as is sometimes thought; it was the Highland lairds who sold their woods through need or greed, often with no thought of replacing them. For every far-sighted improving laird there were others whose management was purely destructive. Oddly enough, the record of the Commissioners for the Forfeited Estates, that early example of state involvement in forest management, is on the whole a good one. They took considerable trouble to conserve what was left of the Black Wood of Rannoch and others.

At this time more enlightened countries in Europe, such as France and the German states, were conserving and putting under systematic management what remained of their natural forests of oak, beech, spruce and silver fir, to their great and lasting benefit. The destruction of forests in Britain as a whole has few parallels in Europe. Even in a small and land-hungry country such as Denmark the remaining forests were brought under protection by law in 1805. Britain had to wait another century for such legislation.

The increasing imports of timber in the nineteenth century led to a gradual loss of interest in forestry. In Scotland the area occupied by forests and woods probably reached its lowest point towards the end of the century. The figure given for 1872 was 734,490 acres (297,364 hectares). The forest had largely gone. True, it gave way in places to fertile and well-farmed arable land, but it left also the bare hills, the grouse moors, the deer forests, the wastes of Sutherland. The familiar Scottish landscape is the land stripped of its forest and in many cases of its fertility.

The Highland Agricultural Society, as it then was, had since its formation in 1798 made representations to successive governments on many aspects of land-use including forestry. The Scottish Arboricultural Society, now the Royal Scottish Forestry Society, took up the cause soon after its formation in 1854, and along with individual woodland owners it urged governments to do something about forest destruction, to encourage owners to plant and manage, and to play an active part in forestry. Successive governments went through the motions of expressing interest, and innumerable commissions and committees were set up, but no effective action was taken. It took the First World War to bring home to the government the necessity of managing the forest resource. As a direct result of the war the Forestry Commission was set up in 1919, and practical encouragement was given to private owners. The state at last became involved in forestry.

The period between the wars was marked by good progress, but also by the usual concomitants of Scottish forestry – governments losing interest and blowing hot and cold; a consequent loss of interest by many private owners; public indifference or active hostility; criticism of the planting of grazing land; the use of exotics. All of this had been experienced before.

The present

The area of forests and woods in Scotland of half a hectare and over in 1977 was 859,000 hectares. This represents some 11 per cent of the land area, and is not far short of three times the area recorded in 1872, though the two figures may not be strictly comparable because of differences in definition. And there are no grounds for complacency, for the old Caledonian forest probably extended to eight times this size. We should go hungry if we tried to get back to this, but at 11 per cent we are still near the bottom of the European league, ahead only of England (but not of Wales), Ireland, the Netherlands and Iceland, but far behind France, West Germany, Belgium and Italy.

But we must look here at forests from the point of view of wildlife conservation, and not in terms of other objectives of forestry. It may be said that for wildlife any wood, and particularly an intelligently managed wood, is richer as a whole than whatever form of land-use it replaces. In my view all forests and woodland in Scotland are part of the Scottish forest, and distinctions should not be drawn between 'natural' and 'artificial' woods, 'traditional' estate woods and 'commercial' forestry – the latter an emotive and unnecessary term of abuse, because commercial considerations must enter into the management of all woods. Even purely amenity woods, even woods which are nature reserves, cannot be left to themselves, and must involve expenditure on protection and regeneration.

Some naturalists and others regret the large-scale planting of exotic species such as Sitka spruce and lodgepole pine, and consider that Scotland should strive towards recreating its ancient woods of oak and other broadleaved trees and of Scots pine and birch. But in terms of good land-use one cannot go backwards: farmers are not urged to revert to ancient unimproved breeds of livestock or crops, or to ancient field systems and common grazings.

Forests can only exist on a large scale if they have some reasonable economic basis, and neither the state nor private owners can contemplate extensive planting of oak or Scots pine on land which will produce far more timber of other species. Exotics should be used sensitively, however. They have no place in a nature reserve, and it is wrong to use them on a large scale to replace old broadleaved woods in the Highlands and Lowlands alike. This was done between the wars by both the state and private owners, and many ancient broadleaved woods were destroyed in the process.

Many barren hillsides and bogs formerly carried oakwoods, but after clearance changes took place in the soil and oak would not grow if planted there today. There are other trees that will, and the important thing in the first place is to restore the forest, to halt soil degradation and to build up forest conditions once more. It may take some rotations of tree crops or several centuries to do this fully, but the moment of planting is the start of a change, the first step on the long

Rassal ashwood, under the corries of Ben Bhan. Ashwood is comparatively rare in western Scotland and this is the most northerly true ashwood in Britain.

road. And wildlife is aware of the change and moves in to take advantage of it. 'Commercial' planters of spruce do not generally envisage a progression towards the restoration of an oak forest; they do not, however, visualize felling their woods and leaving the ground bare once again. Most of them are consciously working towards turning plantations into forests, continuously managed so that felling and regeneration will take place but only of parts at a time, the forest as a whole remaining. This can be seen on some private estates where for centuries the same areas, more or less, have been under trees.

So let us look upon all the forests and woodlands of Scotland as part of the Scottish forest, however diverse they may be. And of course they are incredibly diverse, from the lush sheltered woods of oak, ash, elm and hazel on base-rich sites to scrub remnants clinging precariously to inaccessible rock ledges in the Highlands, from the splendid pine and birch forests of Rothiemurchus, Mar and Glentanar to the great new spruce forests of the Borders. We shall now look at the main types, not so much ecological types as examples of forests and woods as they exist today – a working classification – bearing in mind that they are not clear cut, but intersect, vary within themselves and are subject to constant change.

Remnants of natural woods

What we call natural woods are those of native species, growing on sites which have continuously supported woodland of such species. In almost all cases they will have been greatly modified by man. Felling will have taken place, perhaps burning, perhaps grazing by sheep and cattle. The balance of grazing by wild animals will have been affected by man's activities. The red and roe deer population may be unnaturally high because of the extermination of predators, and because a reduction in the size of the wood in relation to the surrounding bare (deforested) land may have led to a concentration of numbers for shelter and safety. Grazing either of domestic or wild animals will have profoundly modified the field layer and may have destroyed the shrub layer, of such importance to wildlife. Natural regeneration may be grazed off as it appears, and the whole wood may be ageing and on its way to decay and disappearance. The number of tree species present may have been reduced because of selective felling in the past, or because of deterioration of the site and the failure of trees to regenerate. Some planting of native or non-native species may have been carried out.

Nevertheless, there may be within such woods small areas closely approximating to 'natural' conditions, with regeneration taking place. These are the irreplaceable reservoirs, not only of native tree species in all their genetic variety but of associated shrubs, herbs, mosses, liverworts, lichens and fungi, of the insects and invertebrates dependent upon them, and the birds and animals further along the food chain. A woodland ecosystem as defined by man will embrace everything from soil to tree canopy and all living things that comprise it, but a small colony of some butterfly or plant may thrive and perpetuate itself in its own small ecosystem, which is a fragment of the total ecosystem. A certain fly or beetle may need only one particular fungus to ensure its life-cycle and survival as a species.

These remnants of natural woodland may vary in size from a few square yards in an inaccessible gorge to hundreds of acres of pinewood on Speyside or Deeside or in the Black Wood of Rannoch, or the

A stinkhorn fungus, covered with flies. Attracted by the powerful smell, the insects then carry away the spores.

extensive areas of mixed oak, ash, hazel, birch, elm and alder still surviving in the west Highlands. The bigger the area, the more likely is it to have been modified by man. The Black Wood of Rannoch, a wood of the greatest interest to the forester, entomologist and historian, may seem to present a magnificently 'natural' appearance, with pines of all ages, from great spreading veterans to sparse seedlings in the dense heather, with birch, rowan, juniper and open areas of bog. But its present state is largely due to man. There are records over three centuries of repeated felling and logging, and during the last century the wood was used for some years as a deer enclosure. Before man got to work it would have contained stands of tall stately trees, interspersed with birch and alder and open ground, with dense regeneration in the blanks caused by deaths and natural catastrophes. It would have extended up the hill to the tree limit, perhaps with a zone of birch and juniper above. Managing a forest remnant with the object of bringing it back to a 'natural' condition is an uncertain, prolonged and altogether fascinating business. The deer fence and the rifle have to replace the wolf. And the forest must be allowed to 'walk' across the hill, regeneration often occurring more readily outside the wood than within it.

Fortunately, it now looks as though the best surviving examples of native pinewoods will be conserved and perpetuated by the combined efforts of owners, naturalists, foresters, the Nature Conservancy Council and, through a new system of grants, by the Forestry Commission. Fortunately also, the concept of the managed natural forest, always maintained in a few areas on Deeside and

These skeleton roots preserved in peat are often all that remains of the old Caledonian forest.

Speyside, is gaining increasing acceptance. But apart from areas where conservation is the prime objective, owners of semi-natural pinewoods will be bound to have other considerations in mind. They must expect a return in the form of timber, and although the main component of these woods will continue to be Scots pine, owners have for several centuries planted non-native trees such as spruces and larches.

The large-scale destruction and disappearance of the remaining broadleaved woods, or their conversion to conifers, can be looked upon as a thing of the past. The Highland birchwoods, however, whether true climax birchwood or remnants of mixed broadleaved forest or pine–birch woods, present a special problem. For every healthy birchwood with sufficient regeneration to ensure its survival, there are many more now approaching the end of their lives, with little but old and decaying trees, incapable of reproduction even if ground conditions and grazing pressure allowed regeneration. These birchwoods are often valued as shelter and grazing for sheep, cattle and deer, and owners are reluctant to fence off even parts at a time to ensure their survival. The advent of the power saw has speeded their destruction. Tree felling used to be a slow and laborious business. Now it is too easy to go out and fell a few trees and bring them back to the sawbench behind a tractor. Older readers, and some not so old, will call to mind birchwoods remembered as dense woods when they were young, now reduced to scattered old trees on otherwise bare hillsides.

Undoubtedly the richest woods for wildlife are those broadleaved woods most closely approximating to the natural, with a diversity of tree species and ages, a good shrub and herb layer, decaying and dead trees and fallen wood. The variety of plant life supports a rich insect and invertebrate population, which in turn supports a diverse population of birds and mammals.

'Traditional' estate woods

These range from the parks, policies and broadleaved woods, shelterbelts and game covers of the Lowlands to extensive woods on poorer lands and higher ground, containing not only native pine but spruce, larch and other exotic conifers. All these have a vital part to play, both in conservation (including visual amenity) and the rural economy. They cover the whole range, from remnants of natural woods – or at any rate woods of native species – to what appear to be entirely alien plantations. Yet we must be careful about decrying the aliens. Successive generations have differing views of what is natural or traditional, and therefore praiseworthy, and what is new and therefore undesirable. The 'traditional' Border landscape of great rolling bare hills, with cosy shelterbelts and small woods round steadings, and occasional big houses surrounded by older woods, is wholly artificial. The great rolling hills are the sites of vanished forests removed by man. The shelterbelts are of Scots pine from the Highlands, larch and spruce from the Continent, North America and the Far East. The old policy woods, of great conservation value, may have native oak, ash and elm but they also contain non-Scottish trees such as beech, sycamore, chestnut, silver fir and many others.

However artificial and alien, the shelterbelts, policy woods, estate woods and plantations are of great importance for wildlife. There is an increasing awareness that such woods should be managed as a complete resource, and not exclusively for the production of timber, or for game, or shelter, or amenity. All these functions can be

Top: A modern forest of sitka beside Loch Lubnaig. Bottom: Ploughing for tree planting at Tote, Isle of Skye.

Above: A pair of red squirrels feed in an oak tree.
Left: The pine marten is extremely agile, and can leap from tree to tree.

Top right: A male and female crossbill. The crossed mandibles are used to extract the seeds from pine cones.
Right and far right: Male and female capercailzies, inhabitants of coniferous woodland.

combined, and as far as wildlife is concerned there need be little sacrifice of other objectives.

The 'new' forests

A new forest is an old forest in the making. It is fashionable in some quarters to deprecate the intrusion on the landscape of 'square blocks of regimented pines'. Foresters take a longer view, and so should naturalists. Restoring some of the vanished forest has to start somewhere, and has to be paid for by someone, whether private individuals or the taxpayer. It is reasonable to use those species and methods which will result in establishing a plantation, the young stage of a forest, as speedily and effectively as possible. The new forests do often obtrude on the landscape, but it would be unfair to criticize a new house until the building has been completed, the house occupied and the garden given a chance to grow.

Naturalists are understandably more interested in the effect of forests on wildlife than in their effect on the landscape, but by definition they will prefer the natural to the unnatural. A new forest can look aggressively unnatural, and often unnecessarily so. Outside boundaries may have to be straight because they are ownership boundaries. Trees are planted in rows because it is convenient and economic to do so, but the straight lines become softened in time. Worse are straight rides, often unnecessary, and straight boundaries between species, always so. During the last twenty years much has been learned about combining good landscape with good forestry, and seeing that new plantations fit in with the surrounding land features. Much can be done to avoid monotony by varying the species, by leaving rocks and burn sides unplanted, and by conserving tree growth already present.

Some people, even naturalists, complain that spruce forests are gloomy and lifeless. They are certainly not lifeless, and although they can be monotonous this is a passing phase. Even if a particular forest is to be almost pure spruce for several rotations, it will become much more varied when thinning starts, and when parts of it come to be felled and replanted. This stage provides within the forest a diversity of sites, from open ground with a reinvasion of vegetation, through thicket and pole-sized trees to tall old trees, with a variety of woodland margins. Forest managers are aware of this, and will more and more make specific provision for wildlife conservation in their management plans. And foresters who spend their days in spruce forests have little patience with those who complain that such forests are 'lifeless'. Such people, they say, must go about with their eyes, ears and minds closed. Of course a young spruce forest has not a fraction of the richness of wildlife found in an old oakwood, but we are not comparing like with like. It almost certainly has a great deal more than that of the bare hillside it replaces.

So let us be fair to the 'new' forests, the old forests of the future, the houses in the building, the reservoirs in the filling.

Tiny woods

One isolated tree such as an old oak may support an incredible variety of wildlife – insects and other invertebrates, lichens, fungi, mosses, liverworts, flowering plants, birds and mammals (as well as the occasional royal stowaway) – some living in or on the tree itself, others in or on the ground or the vegetation under it. It has been claimed that

Top: A red deer stag backed by Caledonian pines, the true habitat of this animal.
Bottom: Enterkine Wood, a Scottish Wildlife Trust reserve. Woodlands of mixed age such as this, including dead and dying trees, are particularly rich wildlife habitats.

no less than 500 species of insect are to be found on oaks, some confined to them. Nevertheless, one tree does not make a wood, and a wood to be recognizable as such must contain enough trees for them to exert an influence on one another, on the soil and its flora and fauna, and on the microclimate. A narrow belt of trees on an exposed moorland may never form a real wood. But in a sheltered gorge a few trees growing together may form a small woodland ecosystem.

Scotland is full of tiny woods, some deliberately planted for landscape or game, others there because they contain no trees worth felling or occupy no ground coveted for farming, perhaps the remnants of much larger woods. Sometimes so-called weed species – birch, willow, thorn, rowan, elder, alder, blackthorn, whins and broom – invade woodland sites after felling, and will themselves be succeeded by other species if there are seed-bearers at hand and if the land is not grazed by domestic stock or by rabbits. Grazing by sheep and cattle, if at all regular and prolonged, is fatal to the survival of woodlands. Not only are all seedlings eaten down, but the shrub layer tends to disappear, the herb layer to be replaced by a grass sward, and the ground trampled and compacted.

These tiny woods may conserve some of the richness of flora and fauna which has been lost elsewhere with the disappearance of the forest, and in sparsely wooded country they are of obvious importance to birds and mammals. They are often of no particular concern to their owners, and naturalists could do much by seeking out owners and persuading them to undertake elementary conservation, first and foremost by fencing them off from stock.

Wildlife in forests and woodlands

It can hardly be said too often that forests and woodlands are an immensely rich habitat for wildlife. To some species they are essential, to others beneficial either directly or indirectly. To some others they are of course inimical: light-demanding grasses will not thrive in dark woods, nor will those birds which nest on open moorland. But even to these the forest will from time to time offer refuge. When a stand of trees within a forest is felled, there follows an invasion of herbs and possibly of woody species, and for a time the site takes on the characteristics of bare moorland.

The richness of bird life in old broadleaved woods is well known. The widespread afforestation of moorlands (or rather the restoration of woodland on land long deforested) of recent decades has given naturalists many opportunities of observing and recording changes in bird species and numbers. Changes in species are predictable. Open moorland holds few nesting birds, these may actually increase briefly after enclosure of land for planting and the growth of vegetation, they will then disappear, to be replaced during the first ten years or so by species to whom the denser vegetation, increased food supply, and the presence of small trees for perching and nesting is attractive. The most typical are whinchat and stonechat, in some parts grasshopper warbler, short-eared owl and kestrel – the two latter attracted by greatly increased prey in the form of voles. As the trees grow taller these are followed by chaffinch, wren and robin, and in due course by all the more typical occupants of the conifer forest: goldcrest, coal tit, great tit, crested tit (locally), long-tailed tit, willow warbler, siskin

A fine example of old and young Scots pines in the Black Wood of Rannoch; without fencing there is no opportunity for the natural regeneration of these beautiful trees.

(especially if there is birch and alder), tree creeper, perhaps spotted flycatcher, perhaps bullfinch, song thrush, mistle thrush, greater spotted woodpecker, crossbill, capercailzie, woodcock, tawny owl, kestrel, sparrowhawk and of course starling and woodpigeon. Most of these are found also in mixed and broadleaved woods, but a few – goldcrest, capercailzie, crested tit and crossbill – are confined to the conifer forest. The goldcrest is above all others the bird of the sprucewoods. Mixed and broadleaved woods will usually contain in addition, at least locally, chiffchaff, blackcap, garden warbler, whitethroat and jay. (It might be mentioned in passing that the capercailzie, the splendid cock of the woods, was exterminated in Scotland in about 1771. Swedish birds were introduced at Taymouth in 1837, and there were further introductions during the second half of the nineteenth century. The caper has since reoccupied much of its former ground and is flourishing.)

Among the mammals which have been exterminated in the Scottish forest in historical times are the brown bear, the elk, the reindeer, the boar, the beaver, the wolf and the polecat. Wolves were at all times regarded as a major pest, and were frequently the subject of legislation: forests were destroyed specifically to get rid of them. Polecats survived until perhaps 1920, and as they are still found in good numbers in Wales they may well reappear in Scotland. Wild white cattle used to roam the forest, and were later preserved in parks, but they cannot truly be described as wild animals. They are said to be descended from the pre-glacial aurochs, but so are domestic cattle.

The pine marten, essentially a tree-dwelling animal, was persecuted to near extinction, but managed to survive in remote rocky country in the north-west Highlands. Its fur was at one time a valued article of trade, and it was later trapped by gamekeepers and shepherds, but thanks to the efforts of a few individuals to protect it, and to the spread of forests during the last fifty years, it is slowly extending its range and its future seems reasonably secure.

The greatest of the forest mammals are the deer, the native red and roe and the introduced fallow and sika or Japanese deer. It is sometimes forgotten that the red deer is a forest animal, and that it has lived during the last century or two in treeless deer forests only because the original forest had disappeared, leaving the deer no choice. It was fortunate that deer stalking, as practised in Scotland, became a prized and fashionable sport, otherwise it is likely that red deer would have disappeared with the forest. They showed great adaptability in surviving in the open, though reduced in size and weight and antler formation. But access to forests (and farmland) greatly improves their chances of survival in hard winters. In new planting the forester fences them out, or tries to; they will ruin plantations by browsing and bark stripping, the latter especially of smooth-barked species. In old pine forests they do little harm to the old trees, but may totally prevent regeneration. Although red deer are forest animals, and present a problem to the forester, their range and numbers in Scotland is a wider question. It is generally held, not least by the Red Deer Commission, that their present numbers are much higher than can be supported without serious damage to both farming and forestry.

Roe deer on the other hand are always associated with woods, and though they may be seen on treeless hills, they depend upon the forest for refuge. The disappearance of the forest meant the retreat of the roe, though they managed to survive provided they had access even to quite small woods. Replanting and 'new' planting is quickly followed by invasion of roe deer, and they are probably more plentiful now than for several centuries. Until comparatively recently they were looked upon by many woodland owners as little better than 'vermin', and were indiscriminately shot or even snared. Fortunately a more enlightened attitude is now general, for which credit must go to a few landowners and stalkers, a few individuals within the Forestry Commission who were responsible for a proper policy of conservation and control in state forests, and not least to Continental sportsmen who started coming to Scotland after the last war and who valued roe stalking as one of the finest of sports. Roe can do much damage in woods by browsing and fraying young trees, but most foresters now realize that they are part of the forest scene, and that in the long run they can neither be fenced out nor exterminated.

Fallow deer have been in Britain since Roman times, and may have been brought to Scotland during the Norman period. There is a reference to them in Stirling Park in 1283, and by 1587 they were officially classed as wild animals. Many deliberate introductions must have been made by kings and nobles establishing them in deer parks and later releasing them to the wild. They have a wide distribution, though by no means throughout the whole of Scotland. Their habits are quite different from those of roe, but they are equally dependent upon woods.

Sika or Japanese deer are much later arrivals, having been first introduced to Tulliallan, Fife, in about 1870. Other introductions were made to various parts of the north and west towards the end of the century, and they are now established in the wild in some numbers in

A goldcrest with young.

various parts of the Highlands and elsewhere. Although they commonly feed on open ground, they too are forest animals.

Foxes, hares, rabbits, stoats, weasels and badgers include woodland in their habitat but are not dependent upon it, though badgers prefer to make their sets within woods. The wildcat needs hidden and inaccessible places to lie up in and to breed, and finds these most readily in rocky Highland woods. The bank vole and the long-tailed fieldmouse include woodland along with hedgerows and scrubland in their territories; the short-tailed vole is a grassland animal, but commonly increases in number, sometimes on a large scale, when grassy hill land is enclosed and planted, disappearing again when the trees close canopy.

Squirrels are real woodland animals. The red squirrel inhabits conifers and mixed woods, and when present in large numbers can do serious damage to trees, especially to Scots pine. The present wide distribution of the red squirrel in Scotland owes a good deal to a number of reintroductions when it had become scarce. It was very largely extinct over the whole of Scotland in the early nineteenth century. The North American grey squirrel, introduced into Scotland in about 1890, is at home in broadleaved woods and parkland. It has spread to most parts of south and central Scotland, with outposts further north, and is responsible for much damage to young broadleaved trees, in particular to beech.

Wildlife conservation in woodlands

What can be done to improve the management of forests and woodlands in the interests of wildlife? The key consideration is diversity, whether of tree, shrub and herb species, age or structure. A variety of tree species not only provides a habitat for mammals, birds, insects and other invertebrates dependent upon or associated with those species; through the nature of the canopy and the effect of leaf litter on the soil it determines the composition of the shrub and field layers, the species comprising them and the associated species of other forms of wildlife dependent upon them. Age is important. Large areas of trees of the same age are of less value than if they are uneven aged, or containing a range of areas of different ages. Woodland edges, rides and open spaces are important.

The ideal conservation wood is of some size, not grazed by cattle or sheep, containing predominantly native species of all ages, with a rich shrub and herb layer. Natural regeneration will be taking place, and some trees will be allowed to die of old age, to stand until they fall, and then to be left lying until they disappear. There will be open ground in the form of glades, rides, wet areas, open water and unplanted rocky areas. Such woods exist in Scotland, but it would be a mistake to imagine that they will perpetuate themselves if merely left alone. All conservation requires management, however long-term and unobtrusive. Stock must be kept out, fires must be controlled, as must birds and animals harmful to legitimate activities in the surrounding countryside. Regeneration must be ensured. In many cases the owner must look to the wood for some return in the form of timber.

It is a far cry from this type of wood, usually growing on fertile ground, to the sprucewood newly planted on land lost to forest for centuries. Such a wood is more likely to be of two or three species only, of the same sort of age, which will, when they close canopy, kill off the ground vegetation and prevent the formation of a shrub layer. But it is not difficult to create some diversity even at the time of planting. Burn sides can be left unplanted – if there is already natural birch and alder present so much the better. Small areas of rocky or wet ground can be left unplanted, and some native trees and shrubs can always be included in the planting. The larger the 'new' forest, the easier it will be to create a true forest from a plantation, and to obtain that diversity which is so important.

The newly planted forest is the first stage in the re-creation of the Scottish forest. Forests and wildlife go together: wildlife in all its variety is an integral part of the forest. In managing forests, foresters must accept the responsibility of managing wildlife too.

The work of the forester can be rapidly destroyed by the roe deer. Here a roebuck feeds on the top of a young tree; and opposite a recently planted lodgepole pine in the Naver Forest shows extensive bark stripping as a result of the rubbing of roebuck antlers. The stalking of roedeer is a valuable contribution to the total forest economy.

Chapter 4

The Lowlands

Introduction

For many people, the lowlands of Scotland are where the Highlands leave off. To them the term 'Highlands' conveys an immediate, if somewhat glamorous, image with a distinctive landscape and wildlife, while the somewhat neglected lowlands are relegated to that drive-through-as-quickly-as-possible country (with a quick stop in the capital city) before they reach the 'real' start on the A9 somewhere about Perth. There is even a confusion of terminology: spelt with a capital letter, the Lowlands in many minds cover that geographical portion of Scotland south of the Highland line; the more discriminating refer to the land below 245 metres altitude or thereabouts. For no other reason than a personal familiarity with the southern end of these extensive lowlands, I have decided to compromise on these two approaches for the purposes of this chapter, by confining myself to the land below 245 metres south of the Highland Boundary Fault, regretfully omitting the delightful hill country of the eastern Borders and Galloway. (This definition has the added advantage of avoiding causing offence to those resident north and west of Aberdeen, who, altitude notwithstanding, consider themselves Highlanders.)

A further advantage is that it allows me to indulge in the recollection of my earliest memories of the countryside and its wildlife – the smells, sounds and sights that struck my senses on those first forays into the rural hinterland beyond my native Dundee, as a child on holiday or helping on farms in the Carse of Gowrie. The more dramatic experiences of wildlife in later years cannot overshadow for me the first crystal-clear images: cycling painfully up the Powrie Brae, when the boundaries of the city slowly receded to the south in the frosty haze of a March morning and a new fresh day was revealed, with rooks clamouring in the roadside elms and the brilliant colours of a dew-bright pheasant atop a fence post; or in the dusk of an October evening, while the potato-pickers bent homewards under their bonus of free 'tatties', watching and wondering at a long arrow of pinkfeet honking their way across the Tay against a rose-streaked sky. And in July, at the end of an interminable line of raspberries, idly reaching for a particularly succulent fruit and being startled by a stoat, all gloriously russet and cream, rippling alongside the field wall, its curiosity overcoming its fear to rise upright and stare at the reluctant berry-picker, before vanishing into an impossibly narrow crevice. All of these early encounters had the backdrop of hills and the proximity of

The mink is now widespread in Scotland. A notorious predator, it frequents the banks of rivers and streams, but whether it threatens the existence of the otter is not proven.

the sea, for in the lowlands of Scotland neither are far away.

The hills were always to the north, and the Angus glens beyond that line of small towns at their feet – Kirriemuir, Forfar and Brechin – brought a new dimension which is so characteristic of the lowlands of Scotland: the exciting conjunction of upland and lowland, the inbetween country, with a mature settled landscape along the floor of the glen, and the first hint of wildness and a certain freedom on the darker slopes above. It is this meeting point between highland and lowland Scotland along the great river valleys of the Tay, the Clyde, the Forth, the Tweed, and the tributaries of the Solway which provides much of the richness and diversity of wildlife to be found there, together with a coastline which ranges from the dramatic cliffs of Berwickshire to the expanse of saltmarsh on the inner Solway.

Thus these early recollections, so greenly retained, are not of eagle and crag, of moor and stag, but the glimpses of more mundane pleasures – the lolloping hare against a ploughed field, the rustle of a fieldmouse in fallen beech leaves – disproportionately vivid because of youthful senses. For many of those living in the crowded lowland cities of Scotland (where over 80 per cent of the population is concentrated) such simple sights represented a first contact with nature outside the streets. Despite the car and its newer freedoms, they may still do so.

The physical environment

What are the forces that have shaped this lowland country? First, a climate which is as varied as the distribution of the lowlands themselves, with distinct contrasts between the relatively mild wet west and the drier east with its wider seasonal temperature range. The average annual rainfall is usually below 800 mm in the south-eastern lowlands, rising to 1200 mm in the south-west. Another way of expressing rainfall is to compare the average number of days with more than 0.2 mm of rain, which range from 175 in east Fife to 250 in parts of the south-west – in the latter, much of the rain falls in winter; snowfall may be greater in the west but tends to lie longer when it falls in the east.

The climate has of course changed since the latest glacial period about 11,000–16,000 years ago, when the flora had a strong continental–northern emphasis. In the post-glacial period, as the climate moderated, this was largely replaced by the Atlantic element which characterizes the present. Like the rest of Britain now, and in contrast to much of Europe, the general feature of the lowland climate is its 'oceanicity', i.e. cool summers combined with high atmospheric humidity. This equable climate allows for a wide range of geographical elements in our flora, particularly the Atlantic element. Associated with this is a pronounced east–west gradient with increasing oceanicity in the west, which in the post-glacial period allowed for the development of blanket mires and lake deposits. This relatively wet and mild climate, with a distinctly longer growing season than in the highlands and few frosts before the end of the year, makes food supplies available to wildlife over a critical period. Combined with the shelter and diversity of habitats to be found in the lowlands, this is an important attraction for the large numbers of migrating birds, especially wildfowl, thrushes and finches, which stop here *en route* to southern latitudes from Finland and Scandinavia.

Looking east across the Tay towards the Carse of Gowrie.

The physical features of the lowlands have everywhere been shaped not only by the underlying geological structures but also by glacial action. Unlike the highlands, the lowlands have no pre-paleozoic rocks, the main formations being Upper Paleozoic, including Old Red sandstone, Carboniferous and Permian deposits on the lowest ground, with Old Red sandstone, Silurian sediments and some Devonian igneous rocks in the hills. All of these parent materials provide soils which range from strongly basic (those rich in nutrients) to poor acid soils. Thus the arable farming of the Tweed Valley is based on extensive rich loamy soils, in contrast to the poorly draining shallow soils and peats of the south-west. In the central lowlands, sand and gravel terraces are widespread, particularly along the Clyde Valley. It is this combination of soils and climate which characterizes the distinctive ecological regions of the lowlands and determines their history of land-use and settlement.

The distribution of wildlife habitats

Although up to the Act of Union in 1707 the population was probably not more than 250,000, the lowlands have been more profoundly affected by human activity than any other portion of Scotland. By the middle of the twelfth century, when David, King of southern Scotland, died, a pattern of land holding was established in south Scotland which was not only to distinguish it from the highlands, but also signalled the beginning of a process of settlement and mediaeval husbandry which had important consequences for the future landscape and its wildlife. King David distributed large estates to Anglo-Normans and churchmen, and introduced a form of feudal ownership associated with the new French-speaking aristocracy.

It was James I of Scotland in the mid-fifteenth century who ordained that poaching was to be prohibited, including the fishing of salmon out of season, and that rooks and wolves were to be kept down. 'Civilization' had arrived. The reference to the wolf is of more significance than merely the attempt to exterminate a predator on the increasingly important domestic grazing animals, since it also encouraged the destruction of its woodland habitat which up to Roman times had clothed much of the country with a forest of oak, ash and elm. Many of the early Cistercian monasteries of the Tweed Valley established the first sheep walks along the fringe of the surviving forest, and in turn, these flocks helped to maintain open grazing at the expense of the native woodland. Between 1400 and 1700 there was a vast expansion in sheep rearing in southern Scotland, which together with the use of oak for charcoal in iron smelting, led to a dramatic decrease in woodland cover.

By the early eighteenth century, woodlands had become a rarity. Quite apart from the use of wood for timber and fuel, the run-rig system of agriculture with common unenclosed grazings for cattle and sheep prevented regeneration. The Agricultural Revolution in the latter part of the eighteenth century caused the old pattern of infield and outfield to be abandoned and replaced by the regular design of large square fields with individual farm buildings at their centre. D. Fraser in *The Flower People* records how the noted Angus botanist George Don located a rare hawksbeard on the edge of an Iron Age fort near Forfar towards the end of the eighteenth century. When forty years later another botanist went to the exact spot described by Don, he found that the site had been claimed for a new turnip field. At this time also, hedges and sporting and ornamental woods were extensively laid out by the lairds. Thus today's rural landscape in the lowlands of Scotland, unlike the ancient Anglo-Saxon patterns of much of lowland England, is a completely planned one, dating largely from the Agricultural Revolution.

More than in any other region of Scotland, the wildlife of the lowlands is dominated by intensive agriculture, and it is worth while dwelling a little on its modern farming, and the trends which have brought about today's pattern of land-use. The natural contrasts between east and west emphasized earlier are clearly reflected in differences in agricultural systems, but to avoid repetitive comparisons the central area round Stirling has been selected as an example. Although it has several unusual features, its agriculture is typical of the wider flat valleys known as 'carses' and has elements of both the western grassland farming and the arable lands of the east. It is also interesting in that it demonstrates the relationship between lowland proper – i.e. the mixed arable and livestock farming of the Carse of Stirling – and the upland sheep grazing of the surrounding Ochil and Fintry hills.

In 1973 over 50 per cent of the arable ground in the Stirling area was under grass, and nearly 40 per cent under cereals, mainly barley, with the remainder occupied by root crops for stock feeding. As in the rest of the country, there has been a dramatic switch from oats to

The River Forth loops its way through rich agricultural land. A local saying runs: 'Ae link of the Forth is worth an earldom in the North'.

barley due to the greater yield of the latter, largely as the result of the growing of improved varieties. The increase in yield was brought about in the ten-year period between 1963 and 1973, and is similar if less dramatic for all crops over this period, resulting not only from the growing of more productive varieties, but from a substantial increase in the use of fertilizer and improved weed control. It is this combination of factors, together with economic pressures, which has led to the general intensification of arable agriculture in the lowlands, with important consequences for wildlife there.

This improvement in yields of cereals has resulted also in increases in livestock, as 80 per cent of the crops is used for stock feed; more efficient use of grassland has contributed to support this higher livestock production. A particular feature of the Stirling area is the importance of hay, both for livestock and as a cash crop. Timothy grass is a Carse speciality dependent on heavy fertilizer applications for yields of up to 10 tonnes per hectare. What is significant is that the area on which this crop is grown, the flat impermeable carse lands of the Forth Valley, has been reclaimed by the large-scale removal of enormous quantities of deep peat in the late eighteenth and early nineteenth centuries. The tenants around Doune at that time were encouraged to clear the peat, which was floated down specially dug channels in the bog to the Forth, sometimes with the aid of water wheels to improve the flow. In this manner a vast area of natural bog was excavated, the remnants of which are described on page 70. The agriculture of the Stirling area, with its persistent trends towards more efficient modern farming and consequent intensification of cultivation and alteration of natural habitats, exemplifies the new agricultural revolution which has affected the lowlands as a whole. The scene is set to consider the nature and pattern of wildlife which has resulted from this interaction of man and his environment.

By definition, there are no altitudinal limits to the extent of deciduous woodlands which must have been the natural climax vegetation over virtually all of the lowlands. We have seen how this important wildlife habitat was almost extinguished at an early stage in man's history of settlement and subsequent agriculture, and it is interesting that present-day remnants are mainly confined to the steeper valleys, largely because of their density and inaccessibility to both stock and man with his primitive tools. It is the great river valley systems with their woodlands and wetlands which not only differentiate lowland Scotland into the identifiable wildlife areas of the Tweed, Forth, Tay, Clyde and Solway, but also provide the continuity and contrast between the uplands and the coast, of particular importance to species which move from one to the other. It is these valleys with their more fertile soils, rich feeding and cover which enable much of our upland fauna to survive.

These generalities come into focus when we look at the broad pattern of distribution of wildlife habitat in selected areas. In the 10-kilometre square centred on Melrose, almost all of the land, apart from the Eildon Hills, lies below 245 metres around the River Tweed in one of its renowned sections celebrated by Scott, at its confluence with the Leader Water. Here the agricultural system is broadly divided between arable fields and improved pastures. Apart from the river itself there are very few stretches of open water, 11 of the 15 lochans being under two hectares in extent. This is characteristic of the Border region as a whole, where over 50 per cent of the open waters have a surface area of less than 0.5 hectares. Further, many of these are artificially dammed for mill ponds, farms, industrial and local domestic use. Mires carrying natural peat vegetation within the 10-kilometre square are even scarcer and are confined to very small depressions in this gently rolling country, but to the south, particularly in the very broken country bounded by Selkirk, Galashiels and Melrose, there is a unique concentration of rich mires. In an area covering 10,000 hectares, woodlands occupy only 942 hectares, of which only 122 can be considered semi-natural, mainly restricted to the steeper sections of the River Tweed and its tributaries. Elsewhere there are mixed conifer and deciduous estate woodlands, such as those in the policies of Eildon Hall, but there are at least as much as these two categories combined in small pure conifer plantations and narrow shelter belts, particularly between Earlston and Melrose.

In the west the pattern changes, due to higher rainfall and the predominance of stock-raising under a less intensive system of agriculture. Wildlife habitats tend to be less fragmented, and in Wigtownshire there are extensive low moors behind the coast supporting substantial tracts of blanket bog and raised mires, while larger lochs are more frequent. Natural deciduous woodlands are still extremely scarce, although there are a few remaining valley woods which can be up to 70 hectares in area, and rough unimproved pasture with scrub is common above 90 metres.

To the visitor with an interest in natural history the first impression of the lowlands of Scotland is of a tidy well-farmed scene, not infrequently picturesque – as in the arable lands of East Lothian or the lusher valleys of Galloway – but lacking the more dramatic forms of wildlife. He will have to climb up into the Moffat Hills, the Cheviot on the south-eastern border, or through the great forestry plantations to the heights of the Merrick above Glen Trool before he will encounter anything remotely approaching wilderness in the popular imagination. In the broad valleys and foothills the naturalist must be selective, and seek out those relatively wild places which have been ignored by agriculturalists and foresters, or which, due to the efforts of old estates, have been preserved down the ages specially for amenity and sport. What he will find is a surprising diversity of flora and fauna within a small compass, as well as a number of natural spectacles such as the gannetry on Ailsa Craig, or Loch Lomond and its nationally renowned oakwoods.

Sea buckthorn, an invader of sand dunes that is difficult to control.

Flora

For a considerable time after the destruction of the forest cover in the lowlands, even into the period when arable agriculture became more developed locally, much of the vegetation would have been a form of rough pasture, probably extensively grazed by domestic stock. This lowland grassland is now considerably modified by intensive grazing, drainage and application of fertilizers, characteristic of a pre-dominantly settled agricultural countryside. Much of this grassland occurs in the west, where under heavy rainfall the soil is neutral to acidic. Examples of grasslands on more calcareous soils are to be found on the shelly sand dunes such as those of Aberlady Bay in East Lothian and on the Ayrshire coast between Dunure and Maidens. Often this is associated with scrub such as sea buckthorn and hawthorn. Where drainage is impeded marsh communities may develop, characterized by sedges and the showy marsh marigold. Taken together, these different grassland types in south Scotland provide an impressive list of plant species: in the neutral grassland category alone, south Scotland supports some 147 grasses and flowering plants, including a dozen of Continental distribution.

Many of these species are to be found along our hedgerows and roadside verges. Unlike the adjacent fields, these areas are not usually grazed or cultivated, and therefore contain remnants of the tall herb and grassland plant communities which flourished before industrialization and modern agriculture. The commonest species are the grasses themselves, particularly cocksfoot and Yorkshire fog, often with herbs such as white clover and creeping thistle. Several of the so-called weed species are extremely valuable for insects and the birds which feed on them. A recent survey in Strathclyde has estimated the area of roadside verges at not less than 2400 hectares, which is approximately half the total area of deciduous woodland in that region. The same survey showed that an average 30-metre section provided 30 different plant species, and sometimes over 45 species.

Because of the importance of this habitat, the Scottish Wildlife Trust has pioneered the designation of a range of roadside stretches as reserves, for specific management by local highway authorities. A sample list of species in these reserves contains:

Agrimony	*Agrimonia agrimonoides*
Spiked sedge	*Carex contigua*
Blue sow thistle	*Cicerbita macrophylla*
Hemlock	*Conium maculatum*
Maiden pink	*Dianthus deltoides*
Giant horsetail	*Equisetum telmateia*
Northern bedstraw	*Galium boreale*
Hedge bedstraw	*G. mollugo*
Meadow cranesbill	*Geranium pratense*
Common rock rose	*Helianthemum chamaecistus*
Field scabious	*Knautia arvensis*
Creeping Jenny	*Lysimachia nummularia*
White butterbur	*Petasites albus*
Hoary plantain	*Plantago media*
Bistort	*Polygonum bistorta*
Field rose	*Rosa arvensis*
Monk's rhubarb	*Rumex alpinus*
Danewort	*Sambucus ebulus*
Orpine	*Sedum telephium*
Hoary ragwort	*Senecio erucifolius*
Pepper saxifrage	*Silaum silaus*
Goat's beard	*Tragopogon pratensis*
Guelder rose	*Viburnum opulus*

Control of management, such as cutting, burning, and spraying, is important to maintain the diversity of flora, particularly flowering herbs. With the expansion of the motorway programme in Scotland, there would seem to be considerable opportunities for developing the potential of this marginal habitat, which is after all the most obvious to today's car-borne visitor.

The wetlands of lowland Scotland are particularly noted for a number of rare species. Loch Lomond at the mouth of the River

Endrick is one of the few localities for waterwort and the Scottish water dock, and holy grass is found in a number of mires in the Borders and Galloway. Here, recent survey work on the marshes of the River Dee has revealed a number of plants with interesting distributions, such as the most northerly location of sawwort which is common in England and Wales. The herb baldmoney, usually found on scrubland, is here on the southerly limits of its range, while whorled caraway has a strongly western distribution. More surprisingly, those prominent landmarks of Edinburgh, Arthur's Seat and Castle Rock, provide one of the few locations in south Scotland for the red catchfly. The pale mauve flowers of mountain milk-vetch normally found on upland rocks, has its only location in southern Scotland at the exposed Mull of Galloway, where the rare yellow vetch also occurs, as it does on other parts of this south-west coast. An interesting possible association between a localized plant and fauna is demonstrated by the case of the yellow marsh cress, one species of which (*Rorippa islandica*) is known in only seven localities in Britain, one on the Solway coast, in an area frequented during winter by geese. This is a feature of all localities of the species, and there is some evidence that these populations of *Rorippa* may have resulted from transport on the feet of geese, notably Greenland whitefront from as far away as Iceland or Greenland, where the plant is abundant in the same wet muddy habitat.

A female otter with a four month old cub. Cubs are born mostly in the spring and although suckled for six months they are also soon taught to eat fish.

Fauna

Mammals

There are some twenty-two native mammal species in lowland Scotland – none of them particularly rare, although the natterer's bat, for instance, does not occur north of the central belt – and eight introduced or 'feral' species. Some of the native species such as wildcat have in recent years shown exciting signs of a more regular return to the south (the last wildcat recorded in the Borders was in 1849).

The roe deer is a rapidly expanding species common throughout the lowlands, notably in the Border area, where extensive young conifer plantations have recently been established adjacent to good arable farmland, a combination providing excellent cover and easily available feeding. In these favourable conditions there will be an annual recruitment to the population, and these animals will be forced to seek new territories – thus maintaining rapid expansion until territory in suitable unoccupied habitat ceases to be available. The roe is a very adaptable animal although it prefers woodland with frequent glades and rides; in dense young conifer crops it will cause devastating damage by bark stripping, fraying, and browsing of young plants.

The pine marten, extinct generally in south Scotland since 1900, is now occasionally recorded, notably in south Ayrshire. One less desirable expansion has been that of the grey squirrel, plentiful since its introduction a century ago in the central belt, but now spreading into the Borders and as far north as Deeside. Elsewhere there is at least circumstantial evidence that this inhabitant of deciduous woods, as well as urban parks and gardens is occupying the mainly coniferous habitat of the red squirrel, whose range has been contracting since the 1940s. A more doubtful effect is that of the introduced mink on the otter. The mink, escapees from farms, have increased their range following the expansion of the mink farm industry in the 1950s, mainly in lowland Scotland. In 1965 no less than 324 mink were trapped by the Department of Agriculture, by which time there was no doubt about the species' capacity to adapt to the wild in Scotland and breed successfully, with populations thriving on most of the main rivers.

The otter itself is a species of considerable topical interest, having recently been included in the Conservation of Wild Creatures and Wild Plants Act in an attempt to arrest its apparent decline in England and Wales. This delightful but rarely seen nocturnal creature is extremely sensitive to disturbance, and not surprisingly is much more common in the highlands than in lowland Scotland where suitable breeding conditions in dense riverside and loch vegetation is restricted. A current national survey, in its provisional results for a quite populous part of the lowlands, indicates that outside cities there are no large areas with a complete absence of otters, as indicated by the characteristic 'spraints', or droppings. Local hunt records suggest relatively stable numbers of this species even in well-farmed countryside, which one hopes is indicative for the Scottish lowlands as a whole. However, a major contributory factor to the decline of the otter elsewhere (in Norfolk, for example) may be the disturbance created by recreational boating and fishing, and as the demand for this use of leisure time grows, so could the risks facing the otter, particularly on our more accessible lochs and rivers.

Most terrestrial mammals in Scotland favour woodland as a

Top: Common otters at play. Bottom: The natterjack toad puffs itself out to an enormous size when croaking.

Above : The Tweed valley at Sir Walter Scott's view of the Eildons.
Right : An aerial view of St Abb's Head, a Scottish Wildlife Trust reserve particularly noted for guillemots and razorbills.

Left : The pine marten — a member of the weasel family — has dense fur, and hair on the soles of its feet to increase its grip.

habitat, particularly where there is a range of cover types and vegetation such as is associated with ungrazed mixed deciduous woodland, with berry and nut-bearing trees and shrubs. Some species of bats are almost entirely dependent on mature deciduous woodland for suitable roosting sites. On the other hand species such as water shrew, water vole and otter clearly depend on productive unpolluted water courses. All mammals require relative freedom from regular disturbance. This diversity of habitat and protection from disturbance is probably found most frequently on the older estate, which combines agriculture with forestry and sporting use – particularly if the latter is under enlightened management allowing for both the natural development and the deliberate creation of wildlife habitats, together with a tolerant attitude towards the so-called 'pest' species. At least one estate in the Loch Lomond area which possesses these characteristics is known to support 21 out of the 22 known native mammal species in south Scotland. It is difficult to over-estimate the importance of game preservation in the last 150 years as a factor controlling wildlife populations in southern Scotland, where the early decline in such carnivorous species as the pine marten and wildcat has only been reversed with a gradual decrease in activity by gamekeepers since the end of the First World War.

Roadside verges are colourful reserves for many plants.

Estate management calls for many skills: the rearing of lambs, chickens and pheasants requires that the levels of some predators are kept down. Dougie Simpson of Fintry is a retired fox trapper who still goes out on shoots.

The trapdoor spider emerges from its nest.

Invertebrates

Most of the insect species recorded to date are of local rather than of national importance, although at least 20 sites are especially noted for their insect fauna, a high proportion of these being old woodland. A good example is the ancient open park woodland of Dalkeith, outside Edinburgh, noted for its rare wood-boring and fungus beetles which are dependent on mature and dying timber, particularly oak. Likewise the mixed deciduous woodland clothing the steep slopes of Abbey Craig below the famous Wallace monument at Stirling supports a large number of beetles (including a recent new record for Scotland) dependent on this rich habitat, while similar woodlands in the sheltered Avon Gorge section of the Clyde Valley are known as localities for beetles at the northern limit of their range in Britain.

Aquatic beetles are a special feature of several of the mosses of the Borders, which include a unique assemblage of no less than six very rare species in one locality alone. Several of these species have Arctic affinities, and represent glacial relics closely associated with shallow mossy pools of these boreal fens, restricted to the Borders. One of the most interesting aspects of the invertebrate fauna of lowland Scotland is the northerly distribution of southern species such as the 24-spot ladybird on the Solway coast and on the mild Clyde coast; the trapdoor spider inhabits the most favoured south-facing Solway Bay at Auchencairn, which is also notable for its rich lepidoptera. The mild Solway coast supports at least 20 species of butterfly, which include not only the more widespread such as the green-veined white and common blue, but also such distinctly southern species as the dingy skipper and the wall brown.

Amphibians and reptiles

The amphibians and reptiles of lowland Scotland have likewise received little attention, although all the common British species are represented. Widespread species include the common frog, common lizard and, in suitable dry moorland, the adder, while the common toad and slow worm are more localized. The restricted distribution of several species of amphibians is almost certainly due to a paucity of suitable wetland sites, many of which in the lowlands have been drained, filled in or polluted, especially by farm waste.

An interesting local study of this situation was carried out in the Lothians by the Scottish Wildlife Trust over the period 1972–6. A detailed survey was made of some 440 pond sites, and these were assessed primarily on the range of amphibians present, particularly breeding species. Sites with more than two species of breeding amphibian were unusual, as were those containing the now scarce great crested newt, which appears to be absent from Midlothian, despite its occurrence in at least three ponds in 1963. Many of the pond sites are old quarry workings which are now likely to be filled in, particularly in the vicinity of towns. Elsewhere drainage and water abstraction is taking its toll: in the predominantly agricultural East Lothian, for instance, nearly 50 of the 150 sites were found to be dry.

Birds

Generally, lowland agricultural land supports a restricted range of the commoner species, but frequently these occur in large numbers, such as the vast mixed flocks of lapwings, oystercatchers and starlings which can be seen feeding on leatherjackets on stubble fields in winter and early spring, together with the ubiquitous woodpigeon and large mixed parties of finches.

The ornithological interest of farmland depends to a large extent on the availability of marginal habitats – including small woodlands and hedgerows, ponds, and proximity to rough grazings and moorland – and on the intensity of agricultural management, especially in arable districts. Marked changes in land-use can have a significant effect on bird populations, particularly with the trend towards simplification to provide maximum production of crops. On the other hand, even within the lowlands there has been considerable new woodland planting, mainly of fast-growing conifers. By diversifying the available range of habitat, such plantations can initially support high densities of breeding birds, usually associated with the presence of dense ungrazed ground vegetation.

Approximately a dozen of the breeding bird species of lowland Scotland are predominantly northern in their distribution in Britain, while about four are mainly southern; these include the gannet, eider and redwing, the latter rare in southern Scotland. Of the predominantly southern species, the great crested grebe is widespread over a range of moderately rich lochs, but other wetland species of southern distribution, such as kingfisher, willow tit and marsh tit are often very localized in southern Scotland. Since there seems to be no obvious climatic barrier to their spread, it must be assumed that they are restricted by the scarcity of damp woodland and riverside habitat. The green woodpecker on the other hand has been steadily extending its range northwards; a breeding record in Aberdeenshire in 1975 marked the then most northerly extension of its breeding range in Great Britain.

The sparrowhawk has been the subject of intensive and highly significant research, particularly in Dumfriesshire, carried out by Dr Ian Newton and others. Nesting sparrowhawks are highly territorial, preferring to breed mainly on sites in coniferous woodland where there are open flyways such as rides, and accessible to feeding areas outside the woodland in farmland and other habitats. Cock sparrowhawks feed mainly on small birds such as finches and tits, but the larger female can take such sizeable species as woodpigeon, which consume large quantities of agricultural seed. Following the introduction of DDT as an agricultural pesticide in 1947, sparrowhawks have laid thin-shelled eggs, many of which are doomed to accidental breakage or hatching failure. Subsequent use of the even more toxic compounds such as aldrin and dieldrin as seed dressing caused widespread death among the species, virtually wiping it out in lowland arable areas, while other organo-chlorine compounds used in industry and infiltrating the environment contribute further to embryo deaths. Despite restrictions on the use of several of these chemicals after 1962 and 1976, pesticides (especially DDT) are still widely used in lowland Scotland. There is very considerable evidence of the relationship between breeding failure of the sparrowhawk and the continued application of chemicals in agricultural areas; even extremely low levels of these can cause a progressive and serious decline of populations far from areas of usage, because of the tendency of such pesticides to disperse throughout the environment.

Habitats and conservation

The conservation of wildlife is much less a matter of direct protection of the species concerned than the management of the habitat they occupy. The range of interesting examples of research and management of wildlife in the lowlands cannot be covered in this chapter, and a sample has been chosen to characterize important areas of coast, woodland, wetland and agricultural land, including some of the conservation problems associated with our nature reserves.

Coast

In southern Scotland the coastal zone ranges from the Mull of Galloway, with its botanically interesting cliffs rising 100 metres above the Irish Sea, to the low dunes of St Cyrus on the east coast between Stonehaven and Montrose. Elsewhere, as in the Clyde Estuary and the Inner Solway, there are extensive sand and mudflats, while much of the remainder is a low rocky coast interspersed with higher cliff sections and dune systems, often developed as golf links to landward, as in East Lothian and Ayrshire.

The most obviously interesting fauna of the coast are the great flocks of birds: the massed colonies of seabirds which breed on the higher cliffs of the mainland and islands (notably the gannetries of Ailsa Craig and the Bass Rock) and the razorbills and guillemots of St Abb's Head which fill the air with their almost melancholy sighing in late spring. Southern Scotland has the unique distinction of providing both the oldest recorded (1516) gannetry in the world at the Bass Rock – from which the species takes its scientific name *Sula bassana* – and the youngest on the small group of islands in Luce Bay known as the Scar Rocks, where the first breeding record of this species was in 1939. The estuaries of the Tay, Forth, Clyde and Solway are renowned for their variety and abundance of coastal bird species. Off the north-east coast of Fife, for instance, the population of breeding eider reaches a peak of 3000 pairs and is therefore of international importance. Of no less significance are the dense winter concentrations of diving duck, especially scaup and pochard which frequent the rich waters off Leith in the Forth.

To the casual observer, the uniform low salt marshes with their off-shore mudflats stretching apparently endlessly in such estuaries as the Solway appear uninteresting to say the least. The flats themselves have a limited variety of fauna, but what they lack in this they make up for in the sheer abundance of algae and invertebrates, providing rich feeding in winter for many thousands of wildfowl and waders. It is the physical and chemical composition of the substrate which determines the abundance of such animals as the mud snail or the small amphipod crustacean *Corophium volutator*, and the feeding patterns of estuarine birds is closely related to the distribution of such species: shelduck feed on the former and redshank on the latter. The Solway is primarily renowned for its goose populations, notably greylag, pinkfoot and its own wintering barnacle flock, but its numbers of waders – knot and blacktailed godwit – put the estuary into the top league in Britain for such species.

The Caerlaverock marshes in the Solway, among the largest in Britain, are unusual in their formation on a high tilted shore, which is subject to quite spectacular erosion and deposition from the action of the rivers Lochar and Nith on either side of the 'merse' as it is known here, resulting in a decrease over the last hundred years of over 500 hectares. Sea meadow grass is the pioneer sand colonizer, building up very low mounds which are later invaded by such species as thrift and sea aster. This relatively narrow zone is succeeded by a mainly grassy sward, predominantly composed of red fescue, with varying proportions of sea milkwort, sea arrowgrass and, particularly towards the eastern end, sedges. One such species is chestnut sedge, which at Caerlaverock represents one of the most extensive populations of the species in Britain, while sea lavender is a particular feature of the Solway marshes. Pride of place, however, must go to the winter barnacle goose from Spitzbergen which, following the establishment of a National Nature Reserve in 1959 at Caerlaverock, has risen from a population at that time of under 1000 to a peak of 6800 in 1978 under a closely controlled wildfowling scheme.

Much less well known as a feature of the Inner Solway coast is the breeding population of the natterjack toad, of special interest because of its extremely localized occurrence on the coast and heathlands of Britain. An interesting preliminary study has recently been made by R. Bridson on the factors affecting breeding success of the natterjack at a site on the Inner Solway; this showed that cattle trampling in breeding ponds at a critical period has a devastating effect on tadpoles, by a combination of direct hoof impact, churning of the pond bottom, pollution by defecation, etc., to the point where all the tadpoles are destroyed. Evaporation of shallow ponds may also be significant and there is a particularly interesting link between excessive enrichment of farm ponds as a result of heavy fertilizer application, and lack of development of tadpoles from spawn.

The history of Tentsmuir National Nature Reserve on the north Fife coast is interesting, since much of the dune area has developed as a result of massive accretion of sand within this century, the first foredune having formed after 1905 on the original spit. At the present time new mobile dunes are constantly forming, and the reserve appears to be extending seawards about 30 metres every ten years. Although there is considerable variation in the vegetation from one part of the dune system to another over the four main dune ridges and intervening depressions ('slacks'), there is a typical recurrent series of plant communities from the coast inland. Another difference is that the slacks tend to be drier than for instance on west-coast dune systems, and are frequently invaded by a scrub woodland of alder, willow, birch and sea buckthorn.

The latter species poses a particular management problem, in common with several dune areas elsewhere. This woody plant, which can grow to a height of 4.5 metres and produces a crop of brilliant orange berries in late autumn, has been introduced so extensively as a sand stabilizer that it has become firmly established on many dune systems, and at Tentsmuir was planted by the Forestry Commission for this purpose in 1925. Although it has the merit of providing food and cover for birds, it is a highly aggressive colonizer, forming dense and sometimes impenetrable stands as in the southern part of this reserve. Like many other exotic invasive species, it is extremely difficult to eradicate once well established and is propagated by both suckers and seeds, frequently dispersed by birds. A control policy has been devised for nature reserves on a national scale, and at Tentsmuir attempts are being made to eradicate the buckthorn by cutting and uprooting seedlings in the northern compartments, while other parts of the reserve are surveyed regularly to monitor the spread of the species.

Woodland

Entirely natural oak-dominated deciduous woodland – that is woodlands known not to have been managed or planted and which have been self-perpetuating since Roman times – are extremely scarce in the lowlands. Most existing oak woodland is of relatively recent origin, planted for amenity or sport in the neighbourhood of large houses or, as around Loch Lomond, for wood distillates. In the Borders hardwood areas are estimated to have declined by 50 per cent in the years between 1947 and 1965, and in that region there are now no native deciduous woodlands over 20 hectares. At the same time, modern coniferous plantations have undergone a dramatic expansion throughout southern Scotland, much of this on the poorer upland grazings. Indeed it may be said that the single biggest change in land-use in southern Scotland since the war has been the quite remarkable expansion of commercial forestry over what was previously open moor and sheep walk, with very considerable changes in wildlife populations as a result.

The native deciduous woodlands which remain in the lowlands are broadly of two types, distinguished by soil type. Thus on the deeper base-rich soils, often associated with the steeper valleys, a mixed deciduous type occurs; this is characterized by sessile oak, with ash, elm and occasional hazel, such as is found in the Clyde Valley and the woods of east Loch Lomondside. The second type occurs on more acid soils under high rainfall conditions in the west, and tends to be dominated by sessile oak, often with quite high proportions of birch and sometimes alder on wetter peaty ground. Good examples are to be

A buzzard lands at its prey – in this case a dead rabbit.

found in the Cree Valley south of Glen Trool in Galloway, and outstandingly on the Loch Lomond islands – Inchcailloch in particular is one of the best examples of this native forest type in Britain. Many of these woodlands have in the past been grazed or managed for coppice so that they are now in a moribund condition, with a poor understorey and lack of tree regeneration, except where actively managed as nature reserves. It is a cause for some concern that the total area of native deciduous woodland of any significance in lowland Scotland, excluding fragments of 20 hectares or less, is unlikely to be in excess of 1500 hectares, a sadly depleted relict of the natural climax vegetation of the region.

There are some 236 species of vascular plants (excluding trees and tall shrubs) associated with native woodland, but a much smaller number – about 70–80 – are more or less exclusive to woodland because of their shade and soil requirements. Many of these oceanic species occur in the woodlands of lowland Scotland, notably the ferns and mosses characteristic of the western oakwoods; hard fern is particularly common, together with common polypody and oak fern. The much more variable mixed deciduous woodlands can support more than 20 different tree and shrub species, including ash (which is often plentiful) and bird cherry, and a very large number of herbaceous species such as dog's mercury, herb robert and primrose.

The Loch Lomond woods were intensively used from the second half of the seventeenth century for the production of oak bark in the tanning of leather, which subsequently involved a system of rotational coppice cutting and the removal of 'barren timber' such as ash, elm and alder. At the same time sheep numbers rose rapidly, and the intensive woodland management, which involved planting and subsequent heavy domestic grazing, considerably altered the structure of the forest and its species. Loch Lomond coppice, being based on what remained of the natural forest, differs from English coppice which was largely planted and therefore relatively uniform.

The island of Inchcailloch within the National Nature Reserve has been protected from sheep grazing for some time, and supports a summer bird population of 34 species, all typical birds of continuous broadleaved woodland which has a few small clearings. There are two notable absences from Inchcailloch, that of the green woodpecker and pied flycatcher, the latter especially associated with the very open grazed woodlands elsewhere on Loch Lomondside. Indeed a number of other species such as wood warbler, tree pipit and redstart appear to favour woodland where the shrub layer is absent, often due to grazing. Garden warbler, blackcap and dunnock are often to be found on Loch Lomondside in woods where there is a well-developed shrub layer, and on Inchcailloch the exceptional density of wrens has been linked to previous coppice management there. Thus the bird species present, their diversity and abundance, may be very closely related to the history of woodland management going back for a considerable time.

A completely different woodland type is found on another of the islands of the loch. Inchlonaig is one of the very few yew woodlands in Scotland, with massive ancient scattered trees, some exceeding 300 centimetres in girth, which by legend were planted by Robert the Bruce for supplying his bowmen. In 1663 it was converted into a deer park and is famed for its herd of fallow deer. An even earlier reference to this species on Loch Lomondside, in about 1540, is given by G. K. Whitehead, who quotes an instruction sent to a keeper to the Duke of

Montrose 'to kill two fat bucks as His Majesty and his Gentlemen will be visiting the island [Inchmurrin] and they are sure to have sharp stomachs'. A recent survey has shown that on Loch Lomondside generally fallow deer numbers have declined over the past 120 years to about one quarter of their previously known level (at the beginning of the nineteenth century Inchmurrin supported about 240 fallow deer), although they have spread from their original deer parks and now range over a much wider area than formerly, moving readily from the islands to the mainland.

Wetlands

There are several excellent reasons for selecting Loch Leven, near Kinross, as an example of a lowland loch for the purposes of this chapter. Apart from being the largest natural nutrient-rich lake in Britain, holding the biggest population of breeding ducks of any site in the country and renowned as a brown trout fishery, it has been subject to intensive scientific research. These investigations into food chains linking trout, perch and tufted duck have also brought to light the considerable changes which have taken place in the ecology of the loch, mainly as the result of man's activities. Indeed it was the appearance on the loch of extensive algal 'blooms' thought to be caused by artificial enrichment from surrounding nutrient sources which in 1964 stimulated some very detailed cooperative research involving several universities and other research institutes and the then Nature Conservancy. This research made a unique contribution to the International Biological Programme, culminating in the publication of a special volume of the Royal Society of Edinburgh in 1974, and Loch Leven became one of the best known lakes in Britain in terms of its fundamental ecology.

With its high natural nutrient status and history of modification due to the influence of surrounding land-uses, Loch Leven represents a microcosm of the situation of many lowland waters throughout the country. All the streams into the loch drain from arable farmland and carry large quantities of nitrates and phosphates, one-third of the latter derived from sewage and industrial discharge at Kinross. The loch therefore exemplifies the changes due to the inflow of large amounts of agricultural fertilizers and industrial wastes, a process of enrichment ('eutrophication') which favours the production of intense blooms or suspensions of blue-green algae in the upper levels of the water, producing an unattractive pea-soup effect. One important result of these algal blooms is to reduce the light penetration necessary for the growth of such submerged aquatic plants as *Potomageton* and *Myriophyllum* species, which have virtually disappeared over the last fifty years. The lack of protection by shore vegetation has probably contributed to the present accelerating erosion of exposed sections.

In the lowlands, raised mires occur on flood plains of the older river systems – especially on alluvial deposits of estuaries, although they are very localized in their distribution. Two excellent but contrasting examples are found at Kirkconnel Flow, a National Reserve adjacent to the River Nith in Dumfriesshire, and at Flanders Moss in the Upper Forth Valley, part of which is a Scottish Wildlife Trust reserve. The latter is the largest raised mire in Britain, the series of bogs extending 11 kilometres in length, with the largest, East Flanders Moss, occupying 15 square kilometres, although extensive afforestation has drastically reduced the area of natural bog. As with

Top: Oakwoods on Inchcailloch Island, in Loch Lomond National Nature Reserve.
Bottom: A stoat with its kill.

many other mosses, there has been considerable modification by drainage, and in parts by burning, and both sites have been subject to traditional peat cutting on their perimeter. In the south-west part of Flanders Moss, the vegetation is dominated by *Sphagnum* which forms a more or less continuous carpet, often associated with ling, cross-leaved heath and cotton grass. Two species of localized distribution, bog rosemary and cranberry, are locally plentiful in common with many of the raised bogs in southern Scotland, with the former species at the northern limits of its range in Britain. A species of particular note on Flanders Moss is *Ledum groenlandicum* which occurs in small quantities in the centre of the bog – a rare northern acid mire plant which here almost certainly persists as an escape from cultivation.

Kirkconnel Flow shares many characteristics with Flanders Moss, including a history of disturbance, with considerable cutting away of peat at the edges leaving only the central dome of the original raised bog, a fraction of the area of Flanders Moss. It is probably the removal of peat for fuel and associated drainage in the past which has been responsible for the lowering of the water table: by 1850, some seven miles of ditches had been dug into and around the boundary of the present reserve. This has contributed to the most striking feature of the site, which is the extensive colonization by Scots pine from original plantings last century, ranging from large mature timber on the periphery to thickly grown small to medium-sized pines elsewhere, often over a heather dominated vegetation more akin to moorland than bog, with dense carpets of lichens.

Agricultural land and estates

Earlier in this chapter emphasis was placed on man's historical influence on his environment in the lowlands. The Hirsel, at the extreme south edge of the Berwickshire Merse, is a good example of the old estate. It has been in the ownership of the Earls of Home since 1621, although from 1166 it formed part of the foundation charter of the Cistercian Priory of Coldstream and now comprises 1200 hectares, of which 240 hectares are woodland. As in so much of lowland Scotland, extensive grazing and cultivation had almost destroyed native deciduous woodland in the district round the Hirsel by the eighteenth century. Since then estate policies have been developed to produce fine mixed conifer and deciduous stands, and some of the land of low arable quality has been planted to give justly famed stands of oak and beech, despite the tendency elsewhere to convert these older mixed-policy woodlands to exotic plantations.

In the two 10-kilometre squares adjacent to the Hirsel there are only 28 hectares of native deciduous woodland, while exotic plantations (with some indigenous species) cover 617 hectares. The Hirsel makes the single largest contribution to the total woodland, apart from extensive parkland. In addition, the Hirsel Lake, created in 1787, provides (with one exception) the largest open water within a 20-mile radius. The lake is a winter duck roost, with up to 2000 mallard and high populations of shoveler, goldeneye and tufted duck, while the Leet Water is a tributary of the nationally important River Tweed system. Not surprisingly, with its southerly situation, diversity of habitat and sympathetic estate management, the area is a haven for bird life, with almost 100 breeding species among over 160 seen on the estate; these include the great spotted woodpecker, sedge warbler, dipper, stonechat, redshank and barn owl, reflecting the range of

Top: Peat cutting. Peat is still widely used as fuel in many parts of Scotland. Bottom: The Montrose basin, a Scottish Wildlife Trust reserve. The picture shows an ox bow at the head of the basin.

available breeding conditions, including the particular open woodland requirements of such species as the pied flycatcher which nests regularly.

Conclusion

This chapter started with early recollections of adolescent hunting grounds, and with true territorial instinct I shall return there for the final words, looking out on a blustery March morning from the window of a cottage in Glenisla, in Angus. At first sight there is nothing particularly special about this location: a typical winding glen road to one side below plantations of pine and spruce, the low heathery mass of Craiglea Hill intervening between the River Isla to the west and the cottage surrounded securely on three sides by a remnant of woodland – some fine planted larch, and a much-grazed slope of birch on an outcrop of block scree. To the south, the flatter lands of the valley bottom sometimes merge into rougher peaty moorland above – at this time of year with that look of particular spring wetness with flooded patches near the river, which comes from a late thaw – and the air has the brightness of expectancy of late flurries of snow. From the fields below the cottage comes the almost constant intense bleating of first lambs, whose mothers have been brought down from higher pastures to enjoy the relative comforts of the glen's 'maternity wing'.

Two miles to the south, the Isla thunders over the waterfall of

Inchcailloch Island, Loch Lomond National Nature Reserve. Inchcailloch is one of a chain of islands in the loch which lie along the line of the Highland boundary fault. The fault itself can be seen on this island.

Reekie Linn, a more than usually spectacular demonstration of the effects of faulting on the highland boundary line. Lying almost exactly on the 245-metre altitude level which we have used arbitrarily to separate highlands and lowlands, everything towards the south and Strathmore is softer, more settled and typically lowland, while to the north a short walk above the cottage gives a panorama of the upper glen, even here beginning to take on the more sombre hues and rougher contours of the highlands. We are at the meeting point of lowlands and uplands, inhabiting a sort of transition zone between the two. For here there is a complex inter-digitation along the glen and its tributaries of the typically lowland with the characteristically highland habitats. It has always seemed to me that this is a particularly rich and interesting ecological zone, combining the attributes of the two faces of rural Scotland and offering a choice of wildlife not available elsewhere. George Don, almost exactly two hundred years ago, first recorded along the streamsides of this glen many mountain plants unknown at that time in Britain, which had become established by seed washed down from the high cliffs of Caenlochan, linking mountain and valley.

What makes this ordinary patch of glen remarkable is entirely personal: what one knows is wholly the result of one's own discovery, usually quite casually in the business of routine outdoor tasks or unplanned walks. Because of this there is the special delight of surprise, and if one will admit it, the gratification of staking a claim to that particular experience. Perhaps this is the secret of the distinctive pleasure provided by lowland wildlife. In a countryside which has long been tamed, and where our senses are more often than not programmed to urban stimuli, nature comes upon us unexpectedly in the odd corners of experience, and in this way is intensely personal.

Chapter 5
Lochs and Rivers

Scotland is a land of many waters. One has only to look at a map to see the abundance of lochs and rivers, and it has been estimated that there are over 9000 bodies of freshwater of more than 0.3 hectares in area in Scotland. The Isle of Lewis from the air appears to be more water than land, and you wonder if you can walk more than a few yards without getting your feet wet. The rivers are fast and torrential, rising in the mountainous areas of the country and flowing swiftly to the sea. In 1799 Robert Heron, writer and traveller, in his book *Scotland Delineated* had this to say of the lakes:

> The *lakes* of this country are numerous, and some of them very extensive. Any attempt to describe, or even to enumerate these, in this place, would greatly exceed our limits. But such is their picturesque beauty, and such the fine scenery, that neither the happiest strokes of the pencil, nor the warmest glow of poetic enthusiasm are adequate to convey an idea of the charming prospects they afford.

On the rivers he expounded further:

> The *rivers* in Scotland are in general rapid and remarkably transparent. In so narrow a country, however, we cannot expect to find rivers equal to the Rhine or the Danube. But, when their rapidity, and the shortness of their courses, are kept in view, we must allow that the Scottish streams are by no means inconsiderable. Half the water they discharge, would, in a level country, make very broad and deep rivers.
>
> Though there are many large and rapid streams in the northern and middle divisions, yet the Spey may be reckoned the most northerly great river. It descends from the centre of Inverness-shire with all the fury of a mountain torrent when swelled by rains or melted snow, running along impetuous and irresistible. The Don and Dee, which pass through Aberdeenshire, are large rivers; and the Tay discharges into the sea at Perth, the greatest body of water perhaps of any river in Britain. In the southern part, the Tweed, the Forth and Clyde are noble rivers; the pride of the natives and the admiration of strangers. After this we may notice the Esk, the Annan, the Nith and the southern Dee, which, with several other fine streams, fall into the Solway Firth . . .

A fish pass on the Loups of Burn, River North Esk, Angus.

This is a most accurate and concise summary which still applies to our lochs and rivers today, except that, due to pollution, some of our rivers are not always so transparent, and, as we shall see, water abstraction has in some cases lessened their flow.

The lochs

Lakes in Scotland go by the name of lochs, though they may be called lochans if they are very small. Only one Scottish lake is referred to as such and that is the Lake of Menteith; at one time it was called Loch Inchmahome but the name was changed by the owners who had strong English connections.

We are fortunate in having a great deal of information on the physical and geological features of our Scottish lochs, largely as a result of an exhaustive bathymetrical survey carried out between 1897 and 1909 by Sir John Murray and Laurence Pullar, during which time 562 lochs were surveyed. The results and bathymetric maps run to six volumes; published in 1908, they are a most valuable source of information and are now hard to come by.

From this survey we know that the largest lochs in Scotland, according to their length, area, and maximum and average depths, are as follows:

Length (kilometres)		*Area* (square kilometres)	
Loch Awe	40.98	Loch Lomond	71.09
Loch Ness	38.98	Loch Ness	56.41
Loch Lomond	36.42	Loch Awe	38.46
Depth (maximum in metres)		*Depth* (average in metres)	
Morar	372.5	Ness	158.6
Ness	276.2	Morar	104.0
Lomond	228.2	Lochy	83.8

Although Loch Awe has since been impounded by the North of Scotland Hydro-Electric Board's Awe Barrage, this has made no difference to the total area of the loch, as the barrage has in fact only raised the water in a short stretch of the river channel to the same level as the loch without altering its level, which is regulated within its natural range. Loch Morar and Loch Lochy have also been harnessed by the Hydro-Electric Board, but their levels have not been altered.

Scottish lochs are all in a region which has in recent geological times been covered by an ice sheet, and although most have been formed by glacial activity, others have been created in different ways. Some have resulted from water lying in hollows in, or surrounded by, peat, or from the action of the wind which intercepts the drainage of sand dunes – the latter has created such waters as Loch of Strathbeg near Fraserburgh and numerous lochs on the west side of South Uist. Others have been formed either by river action and the formation of 'oxbow' lakes, or by wave action on the seashore, where sheets of water have been enclosed by gravel bars. Chemical action, too, has produced lakes, and Loch Borralaidh and Loch Croispol on the limestone plateau near Durness in north-west Sutherland have been formed by corrosive action on the limestone.

Those lochs created by glacial activity resulted either from the irregular distribution of glacial drift or from occupation of rock basins gouged out by the action of glaciers. The former include those lying either in boulder clay or 'kettle-holes' and those resting on morainic deposits. Good examples of kettle-hole lochs, formed by the accumulation of fluvio-glacial sand and gravel formed around masses of ice during the glacier's retreat, are to be found in eastern Scotland and include Loch Rescobie in Angus, Loch Lindores in Fife and Loch Leven in Kinross. The glacial lakes occupying rock basins on plateaux, in valleys and corries tend to be long and deep – a fact revealed clearly by the briefest look at a map of Scotland. The smaller circular lochans lying in the hills often mark the site of a glacier's origin, where the snow and ice accumulated. Two of our largest lakes are the result of major faults in the earth's surface. They are Loch Ness, in the Great Glen, and Loch Morar. Both show the general characteristics of tectonic lakes, as they are called, being long, narrow, steep-sided and deep.

The productivity of our lochs is largely dependent on their shape, their nutrient content and the nature of their bed deposits. If we take a brief look at the classification of lochs we will see how easy it is to put them into either a rich or poor category, and so give us an understanding of why certain forms of plant and animal life are present in some and not in others. Lochs with a low nutrient content are called 'oligotrophic' (mineral poor); those with a high nutrient content, 'eutrophic' (mineral rich). Oligotrophic lochs are usually deep, have a small shallow or littoral zone, where most of the productivity of a loch occurs, and lie on infertile rock such as gneiss,

Loch Ness, the second deepest loch in Scotland and almost 39 kilometres long. It occupies part of a major fault in the earth's surface and shows the characteristic long, narrow steep-sided shape associated with tectonic lakes.

schist and granite. They are poor in dissolved nutrients such as phosphorus, nitrogen and calcium. Their waters are acid and have pH values ranging from 5.5 to 6.9 (pH 7.0 is neutral). Most of the lochs in the Scottish Highlands and mountain areas of the Borders and the south-west are oligotrophic. Eutrophic lochs lie on mineral-rich rock such as limestone and Old Red sandstone in the lowland areas and are relatively shallow with a large area of shore rich in plants and animals. Loch Forfar in Angus, Loch Leven in Kinross and Duddingston Loch in Midlothian are all good examples of eutrophic lochs.

There are many lochans in the mountainous moorland and boggy areas of Scotland which do not quite come into either of these two categories, and these are referred to as 'dystrophic' lochs. They are shallow and rich in organic matter consisting of undecomposed peat and other humic material. Their waters are acid and often stained brown, with pH values often around 4.5. Because of their acid nature and a deficiency in calcium there is little decomposition. This results in a large accumulation of organic matter but a scarcity of nutrients in solution. The peat-stained water of these and many Highland lochs limits to a few metres the depth to which sunlight can penetrate and therefore also limits plant growth. This almost universal mantle of peat in the Highlands, which extends to an altitude of 600 metres wherever the land is not too steep, therefore has far-reaching biological consequences for these lochs and their flora and fauna. Although most of the poor lochs occur in the Highlands of Scotland and the richer ones in the Lowlands there are some exceptions where outcrops of basic rock raise the pH of the water. In north-west Scotland there are a number of limestone lochs which are very rich: Loch Croispol near Durness, for example, has a pH of 8.8.

The study of a geological map will give an idea of the nutrient content of the lochs in a particular area, but this is also affected by the nature of their deposits. A loch with deposits of an inorganic nature or with a rocky or bouldery bed is less likely to provide a good substrate for aquatic plants or food for invertebrate animals than one which consists of organic matter (the remains of plants and animals living in the water) and material brought down by inflowing streams. There are exceptions to this, however, and the shell sands of marine origin of the west coast and island machairs are important sources of calcium which strongly influence the nutrient content of lochs lying over Lewisian gneiss – Upper Loch Kildonan on the Isle of South Uist is such a water, with a pH of 9.0. The amount of nutrients present may also be influenced by inflowing streams draining different rock strata. This is shown very clearly from the studies on Loch Lomond made by Dr Harry Slack of Glasgow University, where the chemical analysis of seven principal inflowing streams yielded the following values of calcium, arranged in order of place of inflow from north to south:

River Falloch	2.2 p.p.m. $CaCo_3$
Inveruglas Water	5.8
Douglas Water	3.5
Luss Water	7.7
Finlas Water	5.4
River Fruin	10.3
River Endrick	15.8

Top left : The great crested grebe on its nest in the reeds. The breeding success of these birds is dependent upon an adequate supply of fish for their young.

Bottom left : The red-throated diver, despite its beautiful plumage, is an ungainly bird on dry land.

Right : This stonefly (or gadger) has just emerged from its nymphal skin, which lies beside it at the streamside with liverwort and moss.

Below : Damselflies mating.

Below right : The golden-ringed dragonfly at rest, with wings closed.

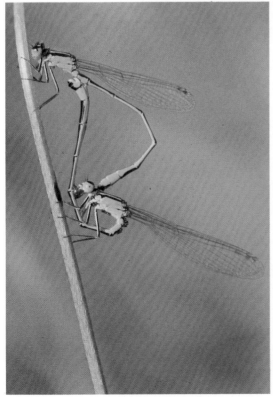

Lochs therefore, although they may be affected by inflowing rivers and streams, tend to be closed systems, and their productivity is generally influenced by their immediate surroundings. Rivers, on the other hand, are open-ended systems, changing considerably from source to mouth: their physical, chemical and biological characteristics are influenced by changing geology, inflowing tributaries, land-type and man.

The rivers

In northern Scotland the rivers rise in areas of high rainfall and flow over acid rock. Rivers flowing east are much longer than those draining to the west, and in their lower sections may have long, flat reaches running through base-rich land. Because the land rises steeply from the west coast to a summit ridge not far inland the west coast rivers are generally short, steep and rocky. In the south, with a more central mountainous area, the rivers flowing west are much longer than the west coast rivers further north, although only one of the six largest rivers in Scotland flows west and that is the 170-kilometre long River Clyde; the others – the Tay (188 km), the Spey (177 km), the Tweed (154 km), the Aberdeenshire Dee (145 km) and the Forth (106 km) – all flow east.

Rivers can be divided into zones based upon the dominant fish species normally present. The headstream or highland brook is small and shallow, with an irregular course; it is often torrential with no pools, and has a low water temperature. The only forms of plant life are mosses and liverworts. There are no fish in this zone.

The troutbeck is larger and more constant than the highland brook; its current is usually more rapid and so the water, being also deeper, is capable of carrying objects in suspension. A typical troutbeck has a steep gradient, and its sides are strewn with rough boulders and coarse pebbles. Areas of fast water alternate with irregular pools. The resident fish present in this zone include the brown trout, which is a strong swimmer, and the stone loach which shelters among the stones. The troutbeck is also visited at spawning time by adult salmon, whose young also temporarily occupy this zone.

In the minnow reach or grayling zone the current is not so fast and, although the river still flows swiftly, the conditions are not torrential. There is therefore less erosion and some silt may be deposited in the quieter, smooth-flowing areas. In the areas with a moderate current threadlike algae may grow on the stones during the summer, and where silt is deposited other plants can gain a foothold and further silt accumulates among their roots. The areas of fast-flowing water now alternate more regularly with long pools. The fish which are characteristic of this stretch are the minnow and, in some areas, the grayling. The fish of the troutbeck are also present, and so too is the eel.

The last zone is known as the lowland course or coarse fish reach. Here the river is deep and slow-moving. The sluggish flow in this zone results in the deposition of silt, forming a muddy bottom on which many water plants can grow. Although some of the fish characteristic of the upper reaches of the river may be present in this reach, conditions are not normally suitable for the successful completion of their life-cycle. Conditions here are more suitable for other species of

Inhabitants of the riverside: (top) a water vole peers from a hole in the bank, and (bottom) wild irises bloom.

fish such as the cyprinids, the roach and the chub.

In a large river such as the Tweed, which exhibits all four of these zones, changes in nutrient level may be seen from source to mouth as the river flows over different rocks and receives tributaries of varying richness. In its upper and middle reaches, the river is distinctly oligotrophic and flows over Silurian deposits poor in nutrients. There is a slight change near St Boswells when Old Red sandstone replaces the Silurian rocks. Then a marked change takes place at Kelso as the geology alters to calciferous sandstone and then carboniferous limestone and the nutrient-rich River Teviot joins the Tweed, all helping to make it noticeably eutrophic. Not only do the pH and alkalinity values increase progressively downstream but so also do the figures for nitrate and total phosphorus. The nitrate values fluctuate considerably, but generally the higher values, attributable to a great extent to sewage effluent, are more common in the lower reaches. In addition moderate amounts of nitrogenous, phosphatic and potash fertilizers, as well as lime, reach the Tweed and its tributaries from surrounding farms and forestry plantations.

In a river such as this, with a wide range of fish species, it is possible to see quite clearly how the steepness of the river influences the distribution of the fish. A survey carried out on the fish fauna of the Tweed and its tributaries by myself and two students showed a distinct relationship between the gradient of a tributary and the number of fish species present, and it was possible to formulate a rule, as follows:

Gradient (per cent)	Number of fish species
6.0	1
3.0–6.0	2–3
1.4–2.9	3–6
1.3	4–11

Lochscape of North Uist: from Beinn Mhor towards Lochmaddy.

High water levels can noticeably influence the distribution of plants and animals, and exceptionally large floods are not infrequent in Scottish rivers. They can be an awe-inspiring sight besides which many man-made phenomena pale into insignificance. South-east Scotland is famous for abnormally high rainfall which periodically occurs in August and produces exceptionally high flows known as Border Floods. The largest of these floods in recent years was on 12 August 1948 when, at Kelso, the combined waters of the Tweed and Teviot rose 5.48 metres above normal. Probably the most famous Border Flood occurred on 1 August 1294, when the Teviot and Tweed overflowed their banks and the bridge at Berwick was washed away. In other parts of Scotland floods are equally large, and marks recording flood levels have been cut into the upstream side of the right bank buttress of the old Tay road bridge in Perth which indicate the extent of flooding over the years. A most vivid account of the damage inflicted by the Moray floods in north-east Scotland in August 1829 is given by Sir Thomas Dick Lauder in a book of that title published in 1830.

Plant life

In rivers the type of plants present depends upon the rate of water flow and the presence of silt, the chemical content of the water and the amount of sunlight. Plants with strong stems and deep roots can stand up to the strain of a fast-flowing current, and types such as the water milfoil and river crowfoot can withstand very high water velocity. In slower moving water, where silt is present, other plants become established and gradually spread, and a distinct plant community is formed, generally consisting of a number of species of pondweed and water crowfoot.

A most comprehensive survey of the vegetation of the River Tweed and its tributaries was made by Dr Nigel Holmes in the early 1970s – without doubt the largest survey of its kind on any river in Scotland. In this, 180 different macrophytic growths were recorded, including 31 algae, 5 lichens, 83 water mosses, 59 flowering plants and two macroscopic microbial communities. The results show the nature of plant zonation very well: it was found that there is a striking dominance of water mosses in stretches with greatest current velocity, and that submerged flowering plants prevail in the slowest reaches.

River crowfoot: the divided leaf is an adaptation to flowing water.

A study of aquatic plant communities in Scottish lochs reveals an amazing variety of associations, and nowhere is this more apparent than in the shallow lochs of the Highlands. These larger aquatic plants have very distinct zones, with a succession that leads from open water to reed swamps and marshland. The zones, moving from open water to the shore, consist of (a) submerged plants, rooted and floating, such as the water milfoil and certain species of pondweed (eg. *Potamogeton crispus*); (b) rooted floating plants like the water crowfoots, the amphibious bistort, the water lilies and some pondweeds (eg. *P. natans*); (c) emergent and erect plants, known as reed-swamp plants – the bulrush, occurring in the deeper water, and then the common reed, which is the main swamp-forming species, the reedmace and the bur-reed; and (d) emergent and erect plants, such as the sedges, rushes, bogbean, brooklime, meadowsweet and yellow iris.

The invertebrates

The most conspicuous forms of invertebrate life in and around lochs and rivers are the insects which spend their larval life underwater as nymphs and their adult stage as winged forms above water. The best known are the damselflies and dragonflies which flash and sparkle like jewels as they dart to and fro across the water in search of smaller flies upon which to feed. Many of our small hill lochans graced by these insects are given the air of an ornamental pond. On a hot July day, with just a little breeze to keep at bay the biting midge, it is a delight to sit and gaze at the carpet of white and yellow water lilies and the bog lobelia with its light violet-coloured flowers standing delicately in the shallow water, and follow the flight of the electric blue and red bodies of the damselflies skimming over the water surface. Every now and then the larger tiger-striped dragonfly will make its appearance and snap its jaws audibly as it devours another fly.

Other conspicuous insects, particularly to trout anglers, are the sedgeflies, mayflies, stoneflies and non-biting midges. The stoneflies are generally absent from still waters due to their preference for the fast-running, cool, well-oxygenated waters of the upper two river zones. All the above insects have certain times for emerging from their nymphal or pupal skins as they make their way to the surface water film. Their emergence depends on the season of the year and the time of day as well as on climatic conditions and water temperature. On the upper Tweed for two or three weeks in April the march brown mayfly will emerge each day over a period of one or two hours around midday, while the iron blue mayfly emerges throughout most of the summer and early autumn, but usually when the weather is cold and blustery and frequently after rain showers. The tiny white brookwing mayfly often emerges on a June evening, and frequently in such numbers that, while fishing the Tweed at such times, my clothes have been white with the masses of resting flies.

Stoneflies live longer in the adult stage than mayflies, and on emerging tend to hide under stones and in trees – they can usually be found by turning over stones by the waterside. A particularly interesting member of this group is the large carnivorous stonefly, or the 'gadger', as it is called on Clyde-side. It makes its appearance in late May, and if you turn over large stones by the side of upper Tweed or upper Clyde at this time you will see these long and narrow dusky brown flies, their wings folded down along their backs, scuttling away for shelter. You will often find the empty nymphal skin or 'shuck' stuck to the underside of the stones.

Many of the studies made on invertebrate animals in Scotland have been with regard to their being a source of food for fish. In recent years there has been some concern among Tweed anglers over the apparent scarcity of certain forms of aquatic fly life, particularly the march brown. Several reasons for this scarcity have been suggested, such as the Border Flood in 1948, silt from land drainage, fertilizers, insecticides, pollution from sewage and detergents and water abstraction. A survey along the length of the Tweed of the mayflies, stoneflies, sedgeflies and non-biting midges was therefore carried out by myself and a student in 1973. The distribution of many of the insects recorded can be explained in terms of the natural physical, chemical and biological changes in the habitat as progress is made down the

A mayfly emerges from its pupa.

river from the torrential, stony and unstable conditions in the uplands to the more smooth flowing stretches and stable conditions with more abundant plant growth in the lowland reaches. For example, the stoneflies were most abundant in the upper part of the river down as far as Walkerburn, but downstream of that point the only group of stoneflies present in any numbers was the genus *Leuctra* or 'needleflies'. The greatest number of sedgeflies tended to increase downstream of Stobo, where the river tends to grade into the minnow reach where conditions are more stable. There were some anomalies, however, and the march brown was practically non-existent downstream of Walkerburn, which might have been due to a deterioration in the environment. Since then the march brown has gradually returned and in 1978 was quite prolific.

This shows the importance of such surveys, from which future trends can be predicted and the physical and chemical factors that limit the distribution of the species found. Much more work needs to be done in this field and information on the distribution of certain groups is needed. This does not imply that such requirements give *carte blanche* to every naturalist to sally forth and collect specimens for the sake of collecting, but wise collection and careful recording is recognized as necessary. The dragonflies tend to be a neglected group, as do the swan and duck mussels. There have been only three records of the swan mussel in Scotland since 1950. One of these records is from the Castle Loch near Lochmaben in Dumfriesshire, which has the eutrophic conditions they require. The duck mussel has an unusual distribution in that it frequents lochs, sluggish streams and canals in the lowlands and central belt, and elsewhere in Scotland has only been recorded from north-east Caithness. The pearl mussel is also interesting in its distribution, as it occurs in many calcium-deficient rivers in the north-west such as the Kerry, the Little Gruinard and the Polly, and it obviously has the ability to extract for its shell the necessary calcium when this is present only in very low concentrations.

Only a few forms of invertebrate life have been mentioned so far, but those that have are very important as, with the exception of the chironomids and mussels, they are all lovers of clean, cool, well-oxygenated water and are the first to disappear when these conditions change. Their absence is thus one of the first signs of polluted waters, so they serve a useful purpose in enabling biologists to assess the purity of our waters, as well as providing a rich larder for our fish.

The fish

The fast-flowing gravelly and rocky rivers and cold oligotrophic lochs are the ideal home of our two dominant fish species, the salmon and brown trout. They provide the clean, cool water and high dissolved oxygen concentrations which these fish require for the well-being of themselves, their eggs and their young.

Early travellers in Scotland were amazed at the abundance of salmon in our rivers, and the Norsemen gave their name for salmon, *lax*, to our rivers Laxford, Laxay and Laxdale. Even in these modern days of commerce the salmon is fortunately still prolific, and the average annual net and rod catches of salmon for the period 1966–75 is 475,188 fish. It is quicker to list the Scottish rivers which contain no salmon, for there are at least 200 salmon rivers in Scotland, and this does not include the small streams in which the fish only run in late autumn to deposit their eggs under several inches of gravel. One of our largest rivers, the Clyde, alas has no more salmon returning from the sea to its waters, and only the salmon emblazoned on Glasgow's coat-of-arms provide evidence that they at one time frequented this river now so grossly polluted in its lower reaches. The largest salmon rivers are the Tay, Tweed and Spey, but probably the most prolific salmon fishery for its size is the little Grimersta River system in west Lewis, which consists of a small river and a chain of lochs including Loch Langavat, the largest freshwater loch in the Outer Hebrides. The smallest salmon lake in the world is Loch Laxdale, which lies in west Harris and is little more than a peaty lochan.

The brown trout has two forms, a migratory and a non-migratory form, known respectively as the sea trout and brown trout. The sea trout frequents most of the salmon rivers and lochs on the mainland and is dominant in such lochs as Stack in Sutherland, and Maree and na Sheallag in Wester Ross, which are celebrated for the standard of their sea trout fishing. The main home of the sea trout, however, is in the lochs of the Outer Hebrides – particularly Harris and North and South Uist – and the Shetlands. Unlike the salmon, the sea trout does not travel vast distances in the sea and may return to the river to spawn several times during its life. Some large West Coast sea trout, weighing over 5 kilos, will have spawned eight or nine times.

The brown trout is ubiquitous, and there can be few lochs or lochans either on the mainland or on the islands without a population of these fish. Many of the small lochs in the Highlands contain large numbers of slow-growing trout. This slow rate of growth is caused not so much by the acid nature of the water or the low average water temperature as by the density of fish following good spawning conditions in the inflowing and outflowing streams, which results in a high recruitment. In a study in 1961 Niall Campbell showed that the growth of trout in some Scottish lochs with little or no spawning facilities was much better, regardless of the pH and alkalinity, than in lochs where spawning facilities were good. Certainly the richer lochs are able to support more trout of a large size than the more acid ones, and the eutrophic Loch Leven supports the largest naturally maintained trout fishery in Scotland. The greater part of the recruitment to this 8120-hectare loch comes from the large spawning areas in the South Queich stream, enriched with nutrients from surrounding farmland and sewage and industrial effluent from neighbouring townships. Campbell also found that the longest-lived trout occurred (a) in large soft-water lochs where a proportion of the trout matured at a relatively old age and the population density was low, and (b) in lochs with no spawning facilities where introduced trout matured but were not able to spawn.

The growth of brown trout in Scottish rivers has not been studied nearly so extensively. The rivers where some work has been done in this field include the River Bran in Ross-shire, where I examined the scales from 518 trout, and the River Tweed and tributaries which was studied by myself and three students and from which 1421 sets of trout scales were collected. The results indicate that the growth rate is slightly slower than that of the trout sampled by Campbell. The observed differences in the growth of trout in the various waters of the Tweed Basin can be related to the chemical characteristics of the water: the richer conditions which prevail in the lower reaches of the

A catch of large grayling from the Eden Water. This is one of our most beautiful freshwater fish; the dark zigzag stripes mark the limits of the rows of scales. The grayling prefers swift running water with a stony or rocky bottom. It was probably introduced into Scottish rivers.

main river and in the lower tributaries produce faster-growing trout. But higher average water temperatures might also contribute to the differences in growth rate, as may differences in population density, for recent work on the Tweed indicates that the density of trout is higher in the less rich streams.

A salmonid fish which is much more common in our lochs than is generally realized is the charr, which dwells mainly in the cold oligotrophic lochs north of the Highland Boundary Fault. It is a pretty fish, particularly at spawning time when its belly and flanks are bright red, contrasting sharply with its black back and the white stripes on its fins. It tends to feed mainly on zooplankton, particularly water fleas and midge larvae. The charr has always been associated with the large brown trout known as the 'ferox' trout. These fish, which are very heavy, are thickly marked with large black spots merging on their backs and extending to cover almost the entire flank of the fish, over a background of deep gold. Niall Campbell surveyed charr and ferox trout lochs in Scotland and found that of 88 lochs containing charr, 57 of them also contained ferox trout and 37 of those containing ferox were over 200 hectares in area.

A most interesting study of charr was made in 1976 by Ronald Campbell, who compared the diet of two Hebridean loch populations of charr, one that does not share its habitat with the brown trout (allopatric) and one that does (sympatric). The allopatric charr population in Loch Meallt on the Isle of Skye is probably unique in Great Britain; unfortunately it is threatened both by local anglers who wish to introduce trout, and by the fact that the loch lies on a deposit of diatomaceous silica which can be used industrially.

Another interesting and less common genus of the salmon family is *Coregonus*, a white fish resembling the herring. Two species occur in Scotland – the powan which dwells in Loch Lomond and Loch Eck, and the vendace which only occurs in the Mill Loch near Lochmaben and is now almost extinct.

Two introduced species of salmonid whose distribution throughout Scotland is increasing as a result of being brought into many lochs by angling clubs are the rainbow trout and North American brook trout. While no one objects to these introductions, there should be some control over the elimination of native species in order to make way for them. Many lochs, particularly in central Scotland, are being cleared of pike, perch and roach in order to introduce rainbow trout, and even our native brown trout is being excluded from some waters due to it being more fastidious than these domestic, easily caught 'broiler-type' fish. We could if we are not careful find ourselves with lochs full of this one domesticated fish species, having completely lost our gene pool. Some rivers in North America are now almost entirely reliant on domestic stock fish as a result of this short-sighted policy.

There is one wild species of salmonid which was introduced into at least one river in Scotland in the last century – the grayling, which was introduced into the Clyde. It also occurs in the Tweed and its tributaries, the Nith, Earn, Isla, Tay and Tummel, but no further north; whether or not it was introduced to these rivers at one time is not known for certain.

There are a number of other fish species which occur in Scotland, and all are worthy of some protection. The pike and perch are widespread and occur as far north as Ross-shire in some of the slightly more productive oligotrophic waters referred to as mesotrophic lochs.

Top: Whooper swans on Loch Lomond, with Ben Lomond in the background. Bottom: Water crowfoot (foreground) and water lilies on Loch Lomond National Nature Reserve.

The river with the most interesting fish fauna is the Tweed, which has at least 16 species of fish including the gudgeon and the dace. The latter species may well have been introduced within the last two decades by anglers, as has the minnow to many waters north of the Highland Boundary Fault. The Annan, too, has an interesting fish fauna and is one of the few rivers in Scotland to have the chub.

Another species which has a very limited distribution in Scotland and is really at the limit of its range is the carp, and it is hoped that it will be protected in the few lochs in which it occurs. One of these waters is Danskine Loch near Gifford; this is a Nature Conservancy Council SSSI for marsh and scrub habitat, but the presence of the carp makes it of added value.

A fish which is likely to receive more attention in Scotland, particularly in the realm of fish farming, is the eel. Huge numbers of young eels or elvers, which have drifted across the north-east Atlantic from the Sargasso Sea with the Gulf Stream, ascend in May many Scottish rivers on the west coast such as the Shiel, the Ailort, the Morar and the Nell. When at its height this elver migration gives the appearance of a solid black mass of tiny bootlace-like fish swarming over every obstacle in their path. Countless numbers of them will die soon after reaching the river, as the oligotrophic nature of these west coast rivers cannot support such large numbers of fish, and in this respect it is interesting to speculate on the contribution of nutrients from their decaying bodies for the maintenance of the river's productivity. The survivors take up residence in the deep waters of lochs such as Morar and Shiel, where they remain for twelve to fifteen years before returning to the sea as silver eels with the first of the autumn floods. One commercial organization is now catching these elvers and transporting them to a farm where they are reared on an artificial diet, their growth rate hastened by the warm water produced by the firm's industrial process.

Without doubt the loch which is most similar to the coarse-fish lakes in England is Castle Loch at Lochmaben, and it is the only Scottish loch in which the common bream is found.

One fish which has been found to be more widely spread than was at one time realized is the tench, and it occurs in many semi-ornamental lochs in central Perthshire (it was probably introduced to these waters some time in the distant past as an ornamental fish). It is to be hoped that this species is not eliminated in order to make way for the 'fish of the moment' – the farm-reared rainbow trout. Already the Scottish Wildlife Trust have resisted approaches from an angling club to remove tench from Hen Poo Loch in their Duns Castle Reserve with a view to stocking with rainbow trout.

The birds

Many birds may be seen by the water's edge as well as on the water, and a checklist of these would be of formidable length. However, there are certain birds which are truly characteristic of Scottish inland waters and for this reason deserve particular mention. Two birds found almost exclusively on remote Highland lochs are the black-throated and red-throated divers. These divers, the 'loons' of North America, are beautiful birds. They make their presence known in the spring through their eerie banshee-wailing cry, which echoes through

Top: Two sea trout jump the falls.
Bottom: The fine markings of the brown trout, widespread in lochs and rivers throughout Scotland.

a silence broken only by the gentle lapping of the waves on the gravel-studded shores. In the summer a visit to the lochs haunted by these divers will be rewarded by a sight of the birds floating far out on the loch, seemingly unconcerned, although the female will have carefully covered her eggs with vegetation before slipping into the water.

The future status of the great crested grebe is of much concern, and although a survey of this bird in 1965, carried out by Ian Prestt and myself, found that there had been a steady increase in numbers from 1949, there is no room for complacency as this bird is certainly open to danger from oil pollution while frequenting coastal waters during the winter. Their breeding success is also dependent on a supply of fish to rear their young, and an absence of fish from their breeding ground would result in no young being fledged. Such a situation occurred on Duddingston Loch in Midlothian some years ago when there was a total kill of fish as a result of the waters becoming deoxygenated. That season, and the following, no grebes nesting on the loch were able to rear their young for the lack of fish. The situation was rectified by the introduction by the Scottish Wildlife Trust of roach and tench, two fish that can tolerate the expected low dissolved oxygen conditions of this water.

One group of ducks which require special mention are the sawbills or fish-eating ducks, the goosander and red-breasted merganser. Goosanders need particular consideration as they are the quarry of many people with interests in fisheries. As they receive no protection in Scotland under the Protection of Birds Act 1954, they are shot by gillies and bailiffs who feel that their removal must result in an increase in the stocks of salmon. There is no evidence that desultory control measures do have the desired effects, and as these handsome birds are not over-numerous they should be left unharmed. This also applies to the red-breasted merganser, a smaller but equally handsome relative which haunts the lower reaches of river systems and the sea lochs of the West Coast, and feeds as much on the fish of rocky shores as it does on freshwater species.

One duck which is a recent addition to our resident population is the goldeneye, which has been found nesting in northern Scotland in nest boxes erected on trees by the Royal Society for the Protection of Birds. It rarely feeds on fish but tends to confine its diet to invertebrates such as sedgefly and midge larvae.

The mammals

There are only four truly aquatic mammals frequenting Scottish freshwater: the water vole, the water shrew, the otter and the mink – the latter an introduced species originating in North America. Alas, although the beaver was at one time found in the Highlands it became extinct in Scotland sometime between the fifteenth and sixteenth centuries.

The water vole is found throughout Scotland where the conditions of lush vegetation favour its requirements, and for that reason is more abundant on lowland rivers than on northern waters. A dark and slightly smaller form does occur in the north and is considered to be a subspecies (reta). The little black and white water shrew is not often seen but is, for all that, fairly common. It is generally feverishly active collecting stores of water beetles and sticklebacks, but it is not always sufficiently active to avoid its predators the pike, goosander and mink.

The otter is to be found throughout most of Scotland and is particularly numerous on the West Coast. As the angler spends more time by the river than most folk it is he who sees the most otters. I frequently had the pleasure of watching them in a small West Coast river, and on one occasion found them fishing in the same pool as myself. It was such a fascinating sight that I did not begrudge them their salmon. Most anglers have the same attitude, and I know a number of salmon proprietors who are quite unconcerned at finding a dead salmon on the river bank with only one bite of flesh removed.

There is much concern over the spread of the mink because of its prey. John Cuthbert has studied the food of feral mink in Scotland and from an analysis of 722 mink scats from three Scottish rivers found that fish (mainly trout, salmon and eels) formed the most important food (67 per cent), with mammals such as water voles and short-tailed voles (16 per cent), waterside birds, mostly ducks and moorhens (7 per cent), amphibia (1.5 per cent) and invertebrates (8.8 per cent) of secondary importance. By sharing the same habitat and food supply as the otter, mink may be considered to be a potential competitor, and it is thought that the otter avoids areas frequented by mink.

The influence of man

Perhaps surprisingly in such a wild country as Scotland, man has, through his varied activities, had a very marked impact on many of our lochs and rivers. The rivers were the first to be affected in the last

A black-throated diver brooding on its nest; before returning to the water it will completely cover its eggs. These birds of remote Highland lochs make their presence known in the spring by their wailing cries.

century by pollution from the increasing discharge of poisonous and oxygen-demanding effluents resulting from the rapid expansion of industry and rise in population. Fortunately, as a result of the untiring work of the River Purification Boards and Salmon District Fishery Boards and the advent of more effective legislation, pollution is slowly becoming less of a problem.

There are still many rivers in Scotland, however, which we can hardly be proud to hand on to our children in their present state. The Clyde is grossly polluted in its lower reaches, and the Carron flowing into the Forth estuary is practically devoid of life; some of the tributaries of the Almond in West Lothian, affected by pulp, sewage and open-cast coal mining, have lost their oxygen-loving invertebrates which have been replaced by organisms such as *Tubifex* worms, chironomids and leeches, more characteristic of organically polluted conditions. In Fife open-cast coal mining has made the waters of the Lochty, with a pH of 3.0, too acid for any form of life, and the rivers Ore and Leven are still polluted. Further north the River Don is only just beginning to recover from years of serious pollution from paper mills. On the credit side we have in recent years seen the recovery of the North Esk River running through Penicuik and Dalkeith as a result of the closure of the paper mills, and the Tyne in East Lothian is now free of a carpet of sewage fungus which at one time extended downstream from the old sewage works at Haddington; the oxygen-loving trout are once more returning to their old haunts. The Spey no longer suffers from the effects of 'pot ale' from the distilleries since the distillers found that the oxygen-demanding effluent could be made into animal feed.

Lochs have not been unaffected, and some lochs now rich in nutrients have undergone eutrophication from receipt of additional nutrients from sewage effluents and fertilizers. This may occur naturally, as in Duddingston Loch where increased nutrients resulting from the droppings of the large wildfowl population, plus the accumulation of organic detritus from decaying reed beds and a lack of rapid turnover of the loch water, led to eutrophication. The same effect may be achieved by the input of nutrients from man's activities, and Loch Leven reached this state as a result of run-off of nitrogen into the feeder streams from a number of intensive poultry units, and increase of phosphates from the discharge of sewage from the townships of Kinross and Milnathort and effluent from a woollen mill.

Changes in land-use also affect rivers, and nowhere has this been more apparent than in afforestation. Ploughing and draining leads to more rapid run-off in streams and rivers, which in turn brings about movement of gravel and silt. The planting of conifers has seriously affected the productivity of our streams, leading to a paucity of invertebrate and fish fauna in sections of stream flowing through mature forest with a dense tree canopy.

In recent years the river environment has suffered indirectly from the development of new industries. The North Sea oil and gas development and pipeline construction down the length of Scotland resulted in the beds of many east coast rivers being temporarily disrupted, with high levels of suspended solids leading to the choking of salmon spawning and nursery areas. Gravel has also been needed for various construction works, and the River Nairn was badly affected by the removal of gravel for the oilrig platform yards at Ardersier. The upper reaches of the Clyde, too, have been seriously affected by gravel workings extending over a number of years.

With an increase in industry and population there is an ever-growing demand for water and, according to the government publication *A Measure of Plenty* (1973), the total water consumption by the year 2001 is likely to double from its 1971 figure of 2130 megalitres per day (Ml/d) to one of 4414 Ml/d. This is perhaps not a lot of water when one considers the extent of our water resources. Over Scotland as a whole the average rainfall is around 1400 mm a year. Making allowances for evaporation and other losses, it is calculated that the total quantity of water which runs off the surface of the mainland and down our streams and rivers to the sea is some 73,000,000 Ml/d a year, or an average of 200,000 Ml/d. That being so, with our population of 5.1 million the total quantity available is equivalent to about 400,000 litres per head. The average consumption from public supplies in 1973 was about 400 litres per head for all purposes, domestic and trade, or about 1 per cent of the available supply.

However, because the rainfall varies over the year it is necessary to be able to store water; this requires either the formation of reservoirs through constructing dams across river courses and laying pipelines to put the water into supply, or the construction of river intakes. The development of Scotland's water resources for public supplies up to 1971 has resulted in a total of 380 reservoirs and lochs being developed and 259 river intakes being built.

The effects of water abstraction on the river and loch environment and its flora and fauna are numerous. The most serious effects on the river are caused by changes in the rate of flow, which can result in a reduced dilution of any polluting effluents entering the river downstream and may affect the upstream movement of migrating fish. Reservoirs tend to be unproductive bodies of water, due to the water fluctuating, sometimes rapidly, over a wide range of levels. This results in an unstable rocky shore constantly exposed to rain, frost and wave action – a hostile environment for many forms of invertebrate. A comparison of the littoral fauna of two reservoirs (Talla and Fruid) and a natural loch (St Mary's) in the Tweed Basin shows this clearly: not only were fewer organisms present in the samples from the two reservoirs but there was less variety in the types of animals found. This difference in numbers and species is largely due to the increased range of water levels experienced in the reservoirs, but it is also probably affected by the different substrata, as much of the land surrounding the reservoirs consists of man-made rock embankments and slumped hillsides, with a general lack of vegetation.

Writhing elvers of the European eel. The elvers enter Scottish rivers in large numbers in May, having been carried in the ocean from their spawning grounds in the Sargasso Sea. They remain for up to fifteen years in lochs and rivers, before returning to the sea for their long migration back to the spawning grounds.

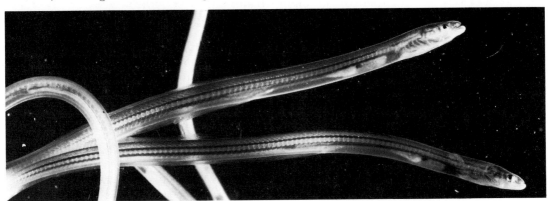

Our water resources have been developed not only for domestic and industrial use but also for generating electricity. Hydro-electric development schemes in Scotland increased after the Second World War with the passing of the Hydro-Electric Development (Scotland) Act in 1943. Since that time as many as 25 schemes have been developed by the North of Scotland Hydro-Electric Board and South of Scotland Electricity Board. Some of these have been very extensive schemes involving the formation of reservoirs, the raising of the water levels of existing lochs and the diversion of rivers and streams by pipeline and aqueducts. Fortunately both boards have put a great deal of care into looking after the welfare of the migratory fish in the affected rivers. By the construction of fish passes and fish screens, the opening-up of previously inaccessible spawning grounds, the erection of fish hatcheries and the provision of compensation flows and freshets, the stocks of salmon and sea trout have been maintained in these waters.

Furthermore some of the reservoirs – and this applies to water supply reservoirs as well – have created excellent wildfowl habitats. In a survey of wildfowl on hydro-electric reservoirs in the Highlands, Duncan MacIver and I found that the reservoirs most suitable for wildlife are the ones with gently sloping sides and those that do not experience rapid fluctuations in water levels. The result of such rapid fluctuation has been seen all too clearly on Loch More, the header reservoir of the Loch Ness pump storage scheme, where the breeding success of the resident Slavonian grebes has been significantly affected.

Below left: The Clunie dam on the River Tummel in Perthshire. The salmon move round the dam by means of the terraced fish pass on the left of the picture.

Below and right: Stripping (hand-spawning) salmon. The eggs are extruded from a ripe female by gentle pressure; a large cock fish is brought from the net, then the 90,000 eggs which have been fertilized go to the hatchery for rearing.

Conservation

It is vital that, through a knowledge of the ecology of fresh water, we should be aware of the ways in which man's developments can be detrimental to our inland waters. In this way we can take action to protect the waters and their flora and fauna; we can insist on wise management and on adequate provisions to ensure the survival of the habitat being incorporated into any development scheme. Reserves and sites of scientific interest must be created to this end, and the work of the Nature Conservancy Council, the Scottish Wildlife Trust and the Royal Society for the Protection of Birds has led to the protection of a number of interesting freshwater habitats. A further advance was made in 1976 when the River Tweed was designated by the Nature Conservancy Council as a Site of Special Scientific Interest, the first time an entire Scottish river system had received such a designation.

If such reserves are to be of real value they must not remain static areas but be actively managed and maintained. Changes in neighbouring land-use, for example, could well affect the area it was planned to protect. For this reason security of land tenure is important, as is the social conscience of neighbouring landowners and other water users.

But in the end it is up to us: our own vigilance will be of most value in safeguarding our heritage of lochs and rivers, unsurpassable anywhere in the world for their variety and beauty.

Chapter 6
Estuaries and their Bird Life

Characteristics of Scottish estuaries

Physical characteristics

Estuaries may be defined not only as places where rivers enter the sea, but more precisely as the region of varying salinity between the mouth, where the water is fully saline, and the river proper where it is fully fresh. Physical conditions within estuaries are often very complicated, depending on the rate of flow of the stream, on the rock formations underlying the stream bed, and on whether the estuary is fed by one river or by several. In addition, the shapes of estuaries constantly change through natural processes; the forces of tide and wind are rarely constant, so that sand or gravel bars are continually created and destroyed, and sediments redistributed.

Estuaries are among the few natural habitats remaining in Britain. Except where there are towns, they are more subject to natural influences and less to human disturbance than most other areas. It is reasonable to suppose that their natural history has remained largely unchanged for hundreds of years and that they are good places to study natural processes.

At the head of an estuary, the nature of the inter-tidal banks tends to be that of the lower reaches of the river. Around the mouth, shores are exposed to the waves and are usually clean sand, shingle or rocks, like the open coast on each side. In sheltered places further up the estuary, the settled sediments become finer, and there are usually large banks of soft, glutinous mud. In some estuaries most of the sediments are brought down by the rivers, forming extensive deltas. In other cases the sediments are apparently derived largely from the sea. Streams running through miles of rich arable countryside usually have big deposits of silt near their mouths, while the estuaries of streams passing through little farmland usually have little mud. This is clearly seen in Scotland, where eastern rivers have muddy estuaries while many in the west do not.

The outstanding feature of the animals and plants living in muddy estuaries is their high productivity, due to the constant supply of nutrients. Estuaries and tidal marshes are among the most fertile natural areas in the world: up to seven times as productive as a typical wheat field and twenty times more so than the open sea.

Although the fresh waters of a river are always moving seawards, the flow in the estuary is influenced by the tides. Sometimes the force of fresh water running directly into the sea is sufficient to prevent the sea

Top: Caerloverock marshes, one of the largest salt marsh areas in Britain, used for breeding and nesting by many waders.
Bottom: Looking across the Firth of Forth from Fife to the Lothian coast (note the Bass Rock on the far right). The Forth is a particularly valuable estuary for wildfowl.

Left : The distinctive eider drake (top) ; it is the only waterfowl that is white on top and black below. The female eider (bottom) is very drab, and well camouflaged on her nest.

Right : Whooper swans in flight across the moors. Below : Research scientist Dr Sandy Anderson at work on the Ythan estuary.

entering, with little mixture of waters. But in the typical estuary the force of the river is insufficient to prevent the entry of the sea when the tide is rising. This damming of river waters sometimes means that the effect of the tides is felt far up-stream. Conversely the effect of fresh water may be felt far out to sea, and in the bigger Scottish firths it may be difficult to decide where the estuary ends and the sea proper begins.

Marine animals capable of surviving in brackish waters can penetrate for considerable distances up the bottom of an estuary with a vertical salinity gradient, provided that the salinity at the bottom is maintained at neap tides. This is important for the wading birds which eat mainly marine invertebrate animals (others eat mainly freshwater ones), and the distribution of birds in an estuary is obviously greatly influenced by the distribution of their prey. In many estuaries a circulation is set up in which the movement of fresh water seawards at the surface is to some extent balanced by a movement of salt water upstream along the bottom.

Estuaries provide different habitats at different stages of tide, from shallow water to dry mud. In smaller estuaries, diving ducks may be seen only when the tide is in; on the other hand, wading birds will be found on the mud flats exposed when the tide is out. To be really suitable for birds the estuary must also have safe roosting places nearby, where the birds can rest until the tide changes. Other birds use the estuaries only as roosts and obtain their food elsewhere. This is true of some geese, for example, which feed inland, or of terns which feed further out to sea.

Although most estuarine birds depend on invertebrates, others eat fish. Kingfishers winter on estuaries as far north as Aberdeenshire, and ospreys on migration are seen on estuaries throughout Scotland. Mergansers and cormorants regularly follow the tide up smaller estuaries, chasing mainly various mysids, shrimps, flounders, gobies, butterfish and coalfish. Goldeneye and long-tailed ducks often occur in estuaries where they take small fish, as well as similar foods to wading birds. Herons stalk flounders and eels in the channels left at low tide, and terns can often be seen diving after sand-eels and fish fry.

Mud in estuaries is richer in nutrients than sand and carries more numerous and diverse invertebrate animals. Tiny snails (*Hydrobia*) and shrimp-like creatures (*Corophium*) which form the main food of many ducks and small wading birds are commoner on soft muds, while the abundant lug-worms, which are an important food of larger, long-billed waders, are most numerous in muds and sand. The depth and extent of the mud and the degree to which it intermixes with sand and gravel mainly determine the invertebrate populations, and these in turn influence the use of the estuary by birds.

The kingfisher

Estuaries are of little intrinsic interest to people who are not naturalists, and who see little point in walking or wading through the soft mud and often dangerous creeks. Over the centuries areas of rich mud and associated marshland have been reclaimed for agriculture (for example, parts of the Wash) with unknown but presumably large effects on their birds. Modern threats to estuaries include reclamation for water storage or for docks, and there has been much interest recently in the Wash, Dee, Ribble and Severn estuaries. One of the main problems facing ecologists working on estuaries is predicting the effects on the wildlife of changes in their use and shape. To make such predictions we need to know about the behaviour and food of the birds involved, and especially whether estuaries already hold as many birds

A greylag goose and her goslings. Although wintering on fields near the coast, this bird breeds on moorland and in thickets.

as they can. Other risks to birds are pollution of the estuaries from industrial and oil installations, or their use as dumping areas for waste and human effluent. No one who has walked the Scottish coastline can have failed to notice the pipelines carrying sewage into the sea from mansions, hamlets, townships or cities, and the debris littering the shores of the Firth of Forth is a sign of how little man has cared for his natural environment. Fortunately there is increasing awareness of pollution, and the new sewage disposal unit at Edinburgh will do much to clean the Forth, though paradoxically this may lead to a big reduction of a large concentration of the sea-ducks which congregate and feed on the sewage. Nonetheless estuaries remain at risk from industrial and recreational development, and the effort of the Scottish Wildlife Trust in preserving the rich mud basin at Montrose is greatly to be commended.

Most of Scotland's richer estuaries are on the east coast. This is partly because the rocks north and west of the Highland Fault are mostly acidic, giving rise to poor soils and relatively low-quality farmland, and poor silt in the rivers. So the mud in estuaries in the north and west tends to contain fewer invertebrate animals than in the east. In addition, the rivers rising in the west tend to be short and, because of the high rainfall, subject to frequent big spates which carry sediments out to sea. Western estuaries are usually small and sandy, but where rich feeding places do occur, as on the Clyde and Solway, birds are found in large numbers.

Bird numbers

A heron at rest in a rowan tree. The powerful dagger-like beak and long legs are adaptations to its wading and fishing life.

Counts of ducks and geese have been made in Britain and north-west Europe for many years by the Wildfowl Trust and the International Wildfowl Research Bureau respectively, and the populations of these areas are known with some accuracy. More recently, the British Trust for Ornithology, together with the Wildfowl Trust and the Royal Society for the Protection of Birds, organized counts of waders and ducks on British estuaries, and the Irish Wildbird Conservancy on Irish estuaries. The surveys provide a basis for the scientific evaluation of different estuaries, and enable each one to be rated in relation to the others in Britain and elsewhere in north-west Europe.

An estuary is regarded as nationally important if it supports regularly one per cent or more of the estimated British population of any one species. The scientific value of the Firth of Forth has long been recognized, and its main value is in its diving and other ducks. Scaup have reached 22,000 birds, pochard 8000, goldeneye 6000, shelduck 2800, long-tailed duck 300, common scoter 1240 (with many more in spring) and velvet scoter 550. There are also very large numbers of eider, which have increased spectacularly both in number and range in Britain during this century. The Firth of Forth is the only estuary in Britain and Ireland which holds an internationally important concentration of goldeneye: nearly half of all goldeneye wintering on the east coast of Scotland are on the Forth. In addition, twelve species of waders occur in numbers of international importance. The Forth is particularly important also for great-crested grebes, for it is here that most of the Scottish breeding population is found. Up to 768 great-crested grebes have been counted (and there are probably many more at times) and up to 45 wintering red-necked grebes. Among other birds, over 1400 cormorants occur; for this species, the Forth is one of the two most important wintering areas in Scotland, with numbers much the same as on the Solway (up to 1340).

Three other Scottish estuaries support wildfowl populations of international importance. These are Loch Gruinart and Loch Indaal on Islay with an average of 18,000 birds, mainly barnacle geese; Outer Tay with an average of 17,200, mainly eider; and the Moray Firth. A survey of the Moray Firth between Burghead and Inverness in 1973/74 showed a peak of 22,600 sea-ducks in January (14,600 scoter and 7000 longtails), compared with about 38,000 in the Firth of Forth. In 1971/72, the Dornoch Firth held 650 longtails and a mixed flock of about 2000 scoters. The latter is probably a regular feature. Over 1000 longtails were observed on several occasions in Burghead Bay in 1970/71 and 1971/72, and up to 2400 in Scapa Flow in the mid 1970s. The main counted winter sites for eiders are further south, mainly in the mouth of the Firth of Tay (up to about 20,000), the Forth (2900), Inner Clyde (1350), and Rattray Head (1200), but also in Outer Dornoch Firth (1000). Mergansers peaked in the Moray Firth (600) and the Forth (500); and in 1973 there were about 400 goosanders on the Beauly Firth. 'Several hundred' goosanders were reported in 1976 wintering on the Tay estuary between the road and railway bridges.

Many of these flocks have been counted only a few times in the last decade, but where counts have been frequent, numbers vary from month to month through the winter and from one year to the next. For example, in 1971/72 more than twice as many shelducks were counted as in 1970/71, when the total north-west European population was estimated at 105,000. About half of these normally come to Britain, but in 1971/72 perhaps 70 per cent did so. The main Scottish wintering sites are near Grangemouth in the Firth of Forth (2000 in 1971/72 compared with 1600 in 1970/71, north shore of Solway (1450) and Eden (1200). In January 1973 the regional total was even higher at 125,000; the total for the Forth was 2900, but this was a maximum, reducing to peaks of 1500 and 2200 in 1974 and 1975. In 1974/75 more shelducks were recorded on the Inner Solway (2400) than on the Forth. The Inner Solway, the Forth and the Eden are sites of international importance, with 1250 or more shelducks recorded in at least three of five seasons in which counts were made.

Turning now to dabbling ducks, the most important (though not necessarily the most numerous) species in Scottish estuaries are wigeon and pintail. Concentrations of over 4000 wigeon were recorded in at least one year of the five at Dornoch (average 6200), Cromarty Firth (6000-plus regularly) and Inner Solway (4300), and 500-plus pintail at Inner Solway (average 1300). There are no other internationally important concentrations of dabbling ducks in Scottish estuaries. Estuaries are particularly important for inland ducks when fresh waters freeze. Maximum numbers on estuaries were generally recorded between December and February, whereas at many inland sites maxima most often occurred in November. The upper Forth near Kennet Pans is a good hard-weather refuge, but numbers varied between seasons – teal, for instance, decreased in the upper Forth from about 5000 in 1962 to less than 300 in 1967–8. Tufted duck sometimes accumulate to around 700 in the same area when inland waters freeze; in the very severe weather of early 1963 they reached 2300. Compared with the mild winter of early 1964 when this 15-km stretch held about 1400 dabbling ducks (580 pintail), in January 1963 there were over 6000 dabbling ducks and 3500 diving ducks.

There are six Scottish estuaries with more than 10,000 waders:

the Solway, Firth of Forth, Inner Clyde, Cromarty Firth, Moray Firth and Montrose Basin. Again the Solway and Forth emerge at the top, but the two northern firths are also important. On the Solway, the area from Gretna to Kirkcudbright Bay supported a quarter of the Scottish wader population in winter 1972/73. The Forth and Solway are surpassed elsewhere in Britain only by Morecambe Bay (260,000), Ribble (219,000) and Dee (105,000) in north-west England, and by the Wash (168,000). Numbers at Lindisfarne, an extremely rich area, are much the same as the Forth. The next best Scottish estuary for waders was the Ythan (9000); five other estuaries had 5000–7000 birds, nine had 3000–4000, and five had 1000–2000. All were in the east or in south-west Scotland. In most cases, numbers were much the same in different years, but at the Moray Firth they were considerably lower in 1974/75 (16,000) than in 1973/74 (28,000).

The surveys provide useful information on individual species, including the months in which each reached peak numbers each year. Knot were much the most numerous in January, reaching 65,000 in 1972, 25,000 in 1973, and 49,000 in 1974, followed by oystercatcher and dunlin at around 40,000, redshank 20,000–25,000, and curlew, bar-tailed godwit and golden plover around 10,000. Curlews were most numerous in autumn, and so were oystercatchers in 1971 and redshanks in 1973. Otherwise peak numbers were reached in middle or late winter, up to March. The annual variation in numbers was quite considerable – partly due to differences in observer effort – but in 1970/71 there was an enormous influx of knot and dunlin at mid-winter. Totals for grey plover varied from less than 100 in 1970/71 to 633 in 1974, and then fell to 300–400 in 1974/75.

Pollution

The sandwich tern is endangered through its eggs being stolen. Its nests are also vulnerable to natural disasters, such as being swamped by blown sand or exceptionally high tides.

There is much concern at the potential harm to large concentrations of sea-ducks from oil spillages or other pollutants. Concentrations of scaup and goldeneye are nearly always found in areas where unnatural feeding (e.g. on grains or other sewage) results from man's presence, and other sea-ducks occur in large, shallow sandy bays, usually at the mouths of estuaries where industry has easy access to the sea.

Ninety-five per cent of the scaup counted were on the Forth, making this species extremely vulnerable to any oil disaster there, which could devastate the entire Icelandic breeding stock. Eiders, with a very large concentration at the mouth of the Tay, are also liable to suffer seriously from oil pollution. Large numbers of sawbills, sufficient for an oil incident to affect the population as a whole, occur in the Beauly Firth (both red-breasted mergansers and goosanders) and the upper Forth (mergansers only). Great-crested grebes are at risk in the middle Forth, off Edinburgh. Shelduck are particularly concentrated in the upper Forth, at Grangemouth, and in the Solway and Cromarty Firths. Big concentrations of ducks are also threatened by developments in the Moray Firth and in the Scapa Flow.

Not all waste dumped in estuaries is harmful, and some is even beneficial to birds. Mute and whooper swans, for example, feed on distillers waste in the Cromarty Firth. Eiders too seem to benefit from sewage: at Seafield, in the Firth of Forth, these ducks are mainly winter visitors between October and May and have increased locally from 270 birds in 1959 to about 2000 recently. In the Seafield area industrial and domestic sewage effluents, including grain from maltings, form a slick which can be seen for several miles out to sea. Fifty eiders feeding in this area were collected for stomach analysis between November 1969 and March 1970. Molluscs – mainly the blue mussel – were found to be the main food, occurring in 94 per cent of the stomachs and making up the bulk of the contents. Thirty stomachs contained mussels alone. The second most important food was crab, and barley husks were found in only 6 per cent of the stomachs. This was the only plant material consumed and originated from the sewage. It appears that the eiders were not benefiting directly from the sewage, but from an increase in the mussels that grew on the strength of it. (Little wonder that these mussels are unfit for human consumption.)

Harmful pollutants may be classified in four main groups: oil; toxic chemicals, including numerous synthetic chemicals derived from petroleum such as chlorinated hydrocarbon and alkyl mercury compounds, and heavy metals and their organic derivatives; a variety of manufactured objects (e.g. rubber bands); and micro-organisms (e.g. botulism) and parasites. All of these may occur as pollutants in estuaries, but the most serious are oil and toxic chemicals. Birds may be poisoned by oil and they are also vulnerable to the effects of thin oil floating on the sea, through its physical action on their plumage. As the residue becomes thicker, they may be able to clean themselves without poisoning, but they often damage their feathers in the process. The recovery rate of oiled dead birds (which were put back into the sea and subsequently looked for) has varied from 5 to 56 per cent, and thus the

Cleaning up an oiled guillemot. The recovery rate of such birds returned to the sea varies from 5 to 56 per cent.

numbers of bodies found can only indicate minimum numbers of birds dying from this cause.

Very large numbers of birds are at risk from oil pollution in other parts of the world, so that active conservation in British waters to compensate for these enormous losses is of great importance internationally. Oiling incidents in British estuaries are increasing and are potentially very harmful. About 150 birds were killed in Poole Harbour in 1961, and 900 great black-backed gulls and other birds in the Medway estuary in 1967. At Loch Indaal, Islay, in 1969 one of the largest flocks of eiders wintering on the west of Scotland was contaminated. Over 300 eiders were killed, although fortunately the important flock of barnacle geese escaped.

Fortunately too, most of the huge eider flock wintering in the Tay escaped in an incident in 1968, when at least 88 tonnes of oil escaped through a crack in the hull of the *Tank Duchess* into the Tay estuary near Dundee. Local biologists recommended that the oil should be removed from the surface of the water by surface dredging, and any that came ashore by shovelling. But no early remedial action was taken, with the result that beaches were fouled and oil remained in the estuary for two weeks. Over the next three months 182,000 litres of detergent were used to wash the beaches, and a great deal of the resultant detergent/oil/water emulsion ran into the sea. As many as 1368 birds, most of them eiders, were known to have been oiled, and the total killed may have been higher. In this one incident 7 per cent or more of the British eider population perished; many could have been saved if the *Tank Duchess* had discharged her oil as soon as the crack in her hull was reported, and if the oil had been cleared from the water immediately instead of being allowed to float about for two weeks.

In the Moray and Cromarty Firths thirteen cases of oil pollution were recorded up to April 1974. Fortunately there have not been many since. In early 1978, an escape of oil in the Forth affected a high proportion of the Scottish population of great-crested grebes and many wintering ducks as well. About 241 grebes and about 900 other birds of several species were oiled; 200 of these grebes, 276 ducks and 43 other birds were found dead. The amount of oil spilled was tiny (less than a thousand litres), but it affected a lot of birds.

Oil pollution exerts its worst effects on swimming species in cold water where the oil remains liquid and retains its toxic components longer. Birds are particularly vulnerable in cold conditions if the insulating capacity of their plumage is destroyed. It is clear that big flocks of ducks wintering in Scottish estuaries present a major conservation responsibility. To deal with the problem naturalists need to know details of the distribution of bird flocks and their movements with time of day, weather and state of tide, as well as arrival and departure dates. The aim should be to keep the oil away from the birds or at worst scare them out of its path as it arrives. Oil presents particular problems in an estuary, as it may be swept back and forth by the tide for days, polluting inter-tidal feeding grounds as well as endangering swimming birds. A further difficulty is that the distribution of seabirds in estuaries may be different from that of the more obvious sea-ducks. In the Forth the latter are mostly seen along the south shore, whereas auks concentrate in the middle of the firth, with adults and young birds sometimes in different places.

The dangers of oil pollution are obvious and have worried naturalists for decades, but toxic chemical pollution has only recently started to cause concern and its effects may be insidious. While it is comparatively simple to test for and identify the better known chlorinated hydrocarbons, other toxic substances may be reaching the environment unnoticed and producing unknown symptoms in the wildlife affected. The best known chlorinated hydrocarbons are DDT and its derivative DDE, which have notable effects on raptors feeding on seabirds, particularly on peregrine falcons in which the effects have been well documented. In Holland chlorinated cyclodienes decimated the population of sandwich terns, and another cyclodiene, Dieldrin, is suspected of causing the death of birds on the Clyde.

Heavy metals, notably mercury, have been found in relatively high concentrations in eiders nesting at Aberlady Bay on the Firth of Forth, in a red-throated diver and in a merganser from Aberdeenshire, and also in waders from the Wash. But not much is known about this – neither where the heavy metals originate, nor natural concentrations in the birds, nor their ability to deal with it.

Nature conservation on estuaries

Nature reserves on Scottish estuaries are managed by the Nature Conservancy Council, the Royal Society for the Protection of Birds, the Scottish Wildlife Trust and East Lothian District Council. The NCC has several long-established national nature reserves on estuaries, for example on the Solway (Caerlaverock), River North Esk (St Cyrus), River Tay (Tentsmuir), the Ythan (Sands of Forvie), two parts of the Cromarty Firth and Loch Fleet. These places are of interest mainly on account of wintering geese, concentrations of nesting ducks and terns, and migrant ducks and waders. The RSPB owns or manages several islands with tern colonies, notably Inchmickery in the Forth, and some terneries or potential terneries on the Moray Firth. The Scottish Wildlife Trust has recently protected the Montrose Basin, once an important goose wintering ground, and the East Lothian District Council manage a local nature reserve at Aberlady Bay and a country park at Tyninghame Bay.

All these organizations have sought and in most cases achieved excellent relations with the Wildfowlers' Association of Great Britain and Ireland, as well as with local wildfowlers whose own interests are often fostered by co-operation with nature conservationists. These good relations are very important in the establishing of new protected areas, and the conservation and sporting organizations have the management of estuarine birds very high in their priorities.

The co-operation of oil-related industries is crucial for the conservation of birds on estuaries. Besides the hazards of pollution and the vital importance of preventing spillage, the development of new installations may involve real threats to the feeding grounds of waders and wildfowl. These industries favour flat land with access to deep water, and many schemes – for example in the Forth and Cromarty Firths – involve substantial reclamation of the important inter-tidal area. This can have two major effects. The first, most obviously, is in reducing the area of available bird habitat, and the second is in interfering with normal patterns of sedimentation. Where this is combined with the filling-in of ponds and lagoons to landwards (for the dumping of fly-ash from power stations, for instance) another alternative feeding ground and high tide roost is removed. Such reclamation is a major threat in Nigg Bay in the Cromarty Firth and a proposed fate for Skinflats in the upper Forth.

None of the conservation organizations is taking active statutory or other steps to manage any of the big flocks of sea-ducks or other birds feeding at the junction of sea and fresh water in estuaries, which are extremely vulnerable to a variety of forms of pollution. This is presumably because of the difficulties in taking positive action and the complexity of other organizations involved. Nonetheless declaration of statutory responsibility for sea-ducks at sea by the NCC would seem to be long overdue. At the very least, this would involve a regular scientifically organized programme of both guarding against and monitoring oil incidents, and a defined programme for co-operative action to protect wildlife from spillages. The latter is perhaps the more important practical point. It is difficult to protect birds once a major pollution incident has occurred, but knowledge of their biology and behaviour should be fully utilized in the clearing up procedures.

The history of recent cases, not least the oil discharge in the Forth in February 1978, shows a lack of co-ordination in supplying relevant information. In March 1972 W. R. P. Bourne noted that if urgent action had been taken in the Cromarty Firth it would have been extremely easy to scare roosting geese away from the path of approaching oil, and criticisms in the case of the *Tank Duchess* have been noted above. Statutory powers with regard to offshore spills are held by the Department of Trade, and by local authorities when oil reaches the shore. Prosecuting for pollution from land-based installations is the province of the River Purification Board, and of the Board of Trade when the source is shipping. The NCC and the voluntary bodies seek, through local planning and through liaison with the Scottish Development Department and many other agencies, to highlight the importance and sensitivity of areas important for wildlife. They back their case with factual evidence from local and national monitoring and survey work, often financed by NCC funds. Unfortunately there seems to be little evidence of shared responsibility, and organizations which are empowered to take action seem unwilling if 'only birds' are involved. Whether designating the water areas of big estuaries as national nature reserves or sites of scientific importance would be of much value *per se* may be doubtful, but improved communication and liaison over action seems an obvious priority.

Conservation of smaller estuaries is also important, particularly since these may provide alternative feeding areas for ducks and waders dispersing when further developments reduce the food supply in the big estuaries. This of course assumes that the little estuaries are not full already. If they are – which would be the biologist's view – conservation measures may need to be directed at improving food supplies in 'safe' places. Conservationists are well aware of the risks, and both the NCC and RSPB are financing and carrying out surveys on bird numbers and distribution in these important places.

Ways in which birds use estuaries

Geese and swans

In Scotland, most east coast estuaries provide secluded roosts for pink-footed geese which feed inland, sometimes many miles away, and usually fly at dusk to the estuary to drink, wash, preen and sleep. Unlike greylag geese, which will sometimes roost in hundreds or even thousands on quite small lochs (but which also use estuaries), pinkfeet need greater seclusion for their roosting places and are very wary of disturbance. The Montrose Basin and the estuary at Tyninghame were favourite roosting sites for pink-footed geese feeding inland in Strathmore and East Lothian, but increasing pressure from wild-fowlers has resulted in a falling off in the use of these mud flats as roosts. It will be interesting to see whether these geese adopt the new sanctuary at Montrose as they did at Aberlady Bay, and whether Montrose will resume its importance as a roost for pinkfeet. Brent geese formerly fed on eel grass in many Scottish estuaries, particularly in the Moray and Cromarty Firths but also at Aberlady Bay; with the disappearance of the eel grass these geese have gone too, and it is now rare to see more than stragglers. Bean geese, once very numerous in Scotland, have also almost disappeared, though a few occur most years with the other geese at the Ythan estuary and elsewhere in Scotland, notably in the south-west.

The Solway and the Firth of Forth are visited by large flocks of geese, the Solway particularly being a wildfowler's paradise. The Solway's chief claim to fame lies in its barnacle geese, which in winter are centred on the National Nature Reserve at Caerlaverock or across the water on the English marshes at Rockcliffe. Barnacle geese are protected in Britain except in the western islands, where they may cause considerable damage to spring grass and where concentrations of birds may need to be dispersed. Unlike brent geese, barnacle geese graze mainly on pastures adjacent to the estuaries, and in some places they may compete strongly with human interests. In October 1970 their diet at Caerlaverock was found to consist of 44 per cent seed, mainly of mud rush, but also 14 per cent clover, mainly stolons, and 42 per cent grass and other material. In 1977 an experiment showed that young barnacle geese preferred ryegrass and red fescue to bent and meadow grass. They also preferred fertilized to unfertilized ryegrass.

The Wildfowl Trust has recently established a highly successful refuge for barnacle geese at Caerlaverock, which provides excellent viewing facilities for concentrations of the geese. One of the initial problems was to attract the birds to fields within the refuge rather than equally suitable fields outside. In Holland it was found that groups of model geese set out at night in fields frequented by barnacle geese acted as a nucleus around which geese landed as they arrived from the roost each morning, and thus can influence where they feed.

The pink-footed goose is also particularly numerous in the Solway, reaching 20,000 or more birds for short periods in most winters. This is the main stronghold of this species in west Scotland. Big numbers of pinkfeet on estuaries occur only where there are large areas of rich farmland inland, hence the importance of eastern estuaries and the Solway. This is less important for barnacle geese, which feed on poor-quality pasture.

Near some estuaries, notably the Solway, Tay and rivers in the north-east, greylags and pinkfeet sometimes occur in mixed flocks. Unlike pinkfeet, greylags tend to feed near their roosts, and if feeding conditions change, they will change their roosts. The two species usually keep separate. Greylags are much less restricted to the vicinity of large lakes and estuaries. While they tend to feed in much the same way as the pinkfeet, they have a more diverse diet so that they can persist in inland wintering places in weather that would cause pinkfeet to shift. It has been suggested that the main differences in the food of the two species is associated with the greylag's larger bill; root crops were found to comprise 23–34 per cent of the greylag's diet, compared with 11–18 per cent in the pinkfoot.

In 1973 a study was made of geese in an area in south-east Scotland which included 59–73 per cent of the total immigrant greylag population and 64–93 per cent of the pinkfeet. The features which made a site safe for roosting included intrinsic ones such as situation, area and openness, and extrinsic ones such as the degree of disturbance. Nine large mud or sand flats, in or near estuaries, were available in the area. The smallest mudflat used by geese for roosting covered about 3 km², but the area of a site was less important than the distance it spread from the shore. Greylags roosted within 1 km from shore, but pinkfeet up to 3 km.

Total numbers of greylags and pinkfeet wintering in Britain are much the same, fluctuating at around 70,000 birds of each species (up to 89,000 pinkfeet), and both have increased from about 26,000–30,000 in 1960 to their present levels. This increase is presumably associated with a succession of good breeding seasons, but security on roosting grounds is another important factor. Numbers of grey geese are now at levels where there are increasing clashes with farming interests. The main management problem is how to break up large concentrations of feeding geese, or to provide more reserves for such concentrations.

Mute swans are often seen on estuaries, and sometimes occur in very big herds. They eat a great variety of macrophytic plants and algae and also graze on nearby pastures. Most stocks of mute swans in Britain depend upon or are greatly influenced by man, and only a few stocks can be regarded as entirely natural. One of these is in the Outer Hebrides, in the islands of North and South Uist and Benbecula. Here breeding birds are confined to fresh water, but non-breeders occur in flocks on some of the larger inland lochs and also on some sheltered inlets of the sea. Although these are not estuaries they are saline, and the principles governing swan numbers here may be found to apply elsewhere. Interestingly, the total numbers of these wholly wild birds, both breeders and non-breeders, fluctuate within extremely narrow limits from year to year and from season to season. Presumably there is a detailed adjustment to food supply, whether this consists of fresh water macrophytes or marine *Enteromorpha* or *Zostera* or whatever, and probably a similar mechanism applies in the east coast estuaries where other flocks of non-breeding swans occur.

Mute swans occur in numbers on several east coast estuaries, notably in the Moray and Cromarty Firths, Ythan, Dee, Tay and Firth of Forth, while in the west flocks occur on the Clyde. Like many other waterfowl, mute swans migrate to large lochs or estuaries to moult. In most of these places their numbers are sometimes affected by human food refuse, and the processes involved in the regulation of their numbers, if they occur, may be difficult to detect and assess.

The two other palaearctic species of swans, whooper and Bewick's, are typically freshwater species, and the main staging posts for whoopers in Scotland are at Loch Leven (around 200), and Loch of Strathbeg (up to 820). Both species fly to the security of estuaries for roosts – in East Lothian (Aberlady Bay) and Aberdeenshire (Ythan), for example – when disturbed by farming operations.

Terns

Sand spits at the mouth of estuaries provide good nesting sites for common and arctic terns. Little terns are scarce and decreasing, although they are still widespread on pebbly beaches. They are usually found in scattered pairs, though occasionally in big colonies in some years, as at a few places on the north-east coast. Sandwich terns occur in a few localities, most of which are now protected as these birds are particularly vulnerable to disturbances. Their nests are prone to robbery, for their eggs can fetch big prices, and they are occasionally vandalized too – as in one notorious case at Aberlady Bay when scores of eggs were stolen only to be left in litter bins in nearby Prestonpans. Nests on sand spits are vulnerable to combinations of summer gales and high tides which lead to flooding. Blown sand can also cover nests: one remedy is to surround the nesting area with a 10-mm mesh netting fence rising about 15 cm above the level of the sand. Debris soon collects in this, providing a screen against blowing sand. Some of the problems faced by terns are natural, and may influence numbers adversely only when added to the growing human influences. Sandy beaches are favourite places for recreation, and bathers can unwittingly cause desertions. Removal of gravel is another risk. In Scotland, tern colonies on sand spits at the entrance to the Moray Firth may need special protection from oil industry developments.

Nesting terns are in special need of protection against these various threats, and the East Lothian District Council deserves mention for its protection of the ternery at the mouth of Aberlady Bay. This is very near a big city, with obvious risks from disturbances, but also with a high educational value which might be put to good use by constructing hides from which the birds could be watched undisturbed. Terns, however, are notoriously difficult to protect because not only are they vulnerable to many disturbances, they are also fickle in their attendance at many sites. A colony may be apparently fully occupied, when suddenly the majority of birds leave it for no obvious reason. This may happen as late as the middle of May. The NCC protect a colony of little terns nesting on shingle beaches at the estuary of the River North Esk on the national nature reserve at St Cyrus in Kincardineshire. Between 1971 and 1976 the number of pairs fluctuated between about 10 and over 100, and in 1974 this colony was the largest in Britain. In other years the birds seem to move up and down the coast, probably at least as far as the Ythan estuary and Buddon (where a tern ringed at St Cyrus has been recovered). Numbers of arctic and common terns change equally unpredictably.

Recent studies of ducks and waders

Shelduck

In western Europe the shelduck is the estuarine duck *par excellence*, and is well known as such to all Scottish birdwatchers. Shelduck feed very largely on the tiny marine snail *Hydrobia ulvae*, and need a quiet, secure place with plenty of easily accessible food when in late summer they become flightless during moult. European shelducks mostly gather together to moult in big flocks in the Waddensee, but smaller numbers also moult in the Bristol Channel and the Firth of Forth.

After moulting they move to other areas, Britain being the main wintering area for shelduck in north-west Europe. Important wintering areas in Scotland include the Solway and Clyde estuaries, the upper Firth of Forth near Grangemouth and the River Eden near St Andrews. The birds seem to shift northwards gradually, but show marked differences in dates of return. At Aberlady maximum numbers are reached early in January, whereas at the River Ythan near Aberdeen the highest numbers are not usually found until April. These big differences are surprising. Winter conditions are considerably more severe in Aberdeenshire than on the Forth or in Fife, but what is probably more significant is that the Ythan is narrower than the southern estuary and has more wildfowling. Shelduck also return later to the enclosed estuary at Tyninghame, East Lothian, which is heavily shot over, and this estuary is at the same latitude as Aberlady and, if anything, more sheltered. There is also a suggestion that some shelducks return to the Moray Firth earlier than to the Ythan.

Shelduck distribution in the Firth of Forth has not changed much over the past forty years. Spring populations of more than 100 birds occur at Grangemouth, Aberlady, Kennet Pans and Tyninghame Bay, but only about 80 of the birds at Aberlady breed. Smaller breeding stocks occur in the Almond estuary and near Tullibody island, with scattered pairs elsewhere. The total spring population of the Firth of Forth is about 700–1000 birds. At most places there was no major change in spring numbers between about 1960 and 1971, but they increased at Aberlady Bay. Breeding success is variable, with isolated pairs or small populations tending to breed more successfully than bigger populations.

At Aberlady Bay, the numbers of resident breeders and non-breeders were stable from 1967 to 1978. Too few young were produced at Aberlady to maintain these numbers of resident adults – only between 9 and 34 were reared in most years (although in 1969 there were 122) – and this poor breeding was attributed to effects of high density. The adult population level was thought to be maintained by young birds coming in from elsewhere, although it was possibly the

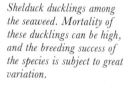

Shelduck ducklings among the seaweed. Mortality of these ducklings can be high, and the breeding success of the species is subject to great variation.

result of a hierarchy in the winter flock. Birds high in this hierarchy would feed in good areas and later establish territories; those low in it would fail to get territories, would not breed and would perhaps go elsewhere. Such a hierarchy was shown to exist in the winter flock in the Ythan. Here, breeding success was also low, with 24 per cent of clutches and 76 per cent of ducklings lost. Furthermore, 87 per cent of fledglings failed to return after their first-year dispersal. This very low recruitment was not enough to replace the annual losses of adults, and the mean population in May dropped from 210 in 1962–4 to 160 in 1968–9. Breeding output tended to be better in years with a lower spring population.

Eiders

Eiders are widely distributed around Scottish coasts where there are blue mussels, their principal food. They are usually associated with rocky shores, and are seldom seen more than a few hundred metres from salt water, except occasionally when nesting. They do however occur locally in big numbers at some estuaries in north-east and east Scotland, particularly from Aberdeenshire to East Lothian, where they nest in heather, on golf courses and even in woods and in the middle of open fields. Elsewhere they nest on islands where there are no foxes. This uncharacteristic behaviour in east Scotland may be associated with the former scarcity or absence of foxes in these places, and it will be interesting to see whether their habits change as a result of the recent invasion of foxes into the coastal strip of eastern Scotland.

The huge flock of up to 20,000 eiders wintering over big mussel beds near the mouth of the Tay estuary contains birds from as far away as Aberdeenshire, 110 kilometres north-east. Smaller flocks have been seen in many other places, including the west coast (500 at Loch Indaal and at Loch Carron, for example) and the northern isles, and the NCC and RSPB are investigating the extent to which they are at risk from pollution.

A lot of work has been done on eiders at the big colony on the Sands of Forvie National Nature Reserve on the estuary of the River Ythan in Aberdeenshire. This population seems to consist of two parts, possibly distinct genetically. One of these sub-populations winters near the breeding area and the other moves southwards to winter off the coast of Angus and Fife. The number of eiders wintering on the Ythan estuary increased from about 400 in 1956–9 to about 900 in 1961–70. In summer, peak numbers were about 3000 in 1961–3, increasing to 4700 in 1965–7. Then many eiders were killed by oil, reducing numbers to the previous level, but by 1970 the summer peak was again about 4600. Numbers now seem to be stationary at this level. This increase at Forvie paralleled similar increases throughout the birds' British range, and elsewhere in Europe.

At Forvie there were about 1600 nests in 1961 and over 2000 in 1970 (and about 1900 pairs in 1976), but in 1964 there were only 800. The mean clutch size over the ten years was about 4, but significantly fewer eggs were laid in 1964 and 1969. The difference was associated with cold weather at laying time, but it may have been due to individuals laying fewer eggs in 1964 and 1969 than in other years, or to only late nesters – which are known to lay fewer eggs – nesting in those years. The proportion of eggs hatching varied from about 42 per cent in 1969 to 74 per cent in 1965. Most losses resulted from the robbery of eggs by gulls and crows, especially from late clutches.

Following hatching, duckling mortality was very high, and at least 55 per cent died in the first week of life. Mortality varied from year to year, and while 98 per cent or more died in four years, about half survived in 1963. In 1972–4 less than 10 per cent of ducklings survived.

It is these differences between years in numbers of eiders nesting, clutch-size and hatching success, as well as the variable but usually extremely high duckling mortality, that are the main interests of this study. Very high mortality of ducklings was also discovered in a Dutch study, and findings are similar in studies of other ducks (for example shelducks, sea-ducks and freshwater ducks at Loch Leven) as well as eiders. It is also interesting that the Ythan and Dutch eider populations increased despite very high duckling mortality and pollution incidents, and would presumably increase faster if the mortality were reduced. The late laying, small clutches and reduced numbers of nesters at the Ythan in some years were attributed to cold weather, but the reason for the exceptionally good breeding in 1963 was not known.

Most broods of eiders combine into crèches, with one or a number of adults accompanying them. Both the numbers of ducklings in crèches and the numbers of attendant adults were found to vary. The ratio of duckling to adult changed in different weeks from 1:1 to 5:1, and the mean number of adult females per crèche (over four years) from 4 to 18, with extremes of 1 and 87. The crèche system was manned by a constant turnover of breeding females who stayed with their young for a few days and then abandoned them and left the crèche as other females took over. The adult and duckling eiders fed on different foods. Whereas the adults fed mainly on mussels, the ducklings ate *Corophium*, *Hydrobia* and periwinkles. These two food supplies occurred in different parts of the estuary, so the adults had to leave their young in order to feed. At the end of incubation, during which they did not feed, adult females needed to spend as much time as possible on their own feeding areas in order to regain condition. So the crèche system seems to have evolved as a compromise in which a succession of adults look after the ducklings in their feeding area while all the other adults feed elsewhere. When eiders do not form crèches but mother and young stay together in family parties until fledging, it is in places where both are able to obtain food together.

In a study in 1972–4 it was found that 80 per cent of the mortality of ducklings was due to predation by large gulls, and this predation was four times as high in bad weather as in good. The disease coccidiosis killed other ducklings. Thus predation of nests and ducklings is important in the breeding biology and behaviour of eiders. Inaccessible coasts or islands with no foxes and few gulls, and with food available in the same place for both adults and ducklings, would seem to be the best place for them to nest and rear their ducklings.

Oystercatchers

Whether estuaries have rocky, sandy or muddy shores, the groups of birds that most characterizes them is the waders. Some species breed locally in Scotland and are to be found on our estuaries all the year round, others are mainly winter visitors, and some are passage migrants. Some feed on invertebrates in mud, others in sand; some feed on inland fields, visiting estuaries to drink or roost.

In recent years controversy has surrounded one species of wader in particular, the oystercatcher. This bird is typically associated with large sandy estuaries where it can find a wide variety of inter-tidal invertebrates including annelid worms, but mainly bivalves such as the edible mussel *Mytilus edulis*, the cockle *Cerastoderma edule*, and *Macoma balthica*. Oystercatchers attack mussels in two characteristic ways. They may open them *in situ* by stabbing through the open shells, or carry them to a suitably firm patch of ground to use as an anvil, leaving behind small piles of empty mussel shells.

Although oystercatchers clearly eat a variety of foods, much interest has centred on their predation of cockles. They stalk cockles as the tide is receding, when the cockles are filtering the water through an extended feeding tube. The birds insert their bill into the partly open shell and snip the muscles so that the cockle is helpless. In this way they can obtain quite large cockles. When the tide is out, the birds pick the cockles from the sand and carry them to a hard surface where they hammer the shells open just as they do on occasion with mussels. Whether or not oystercatchers seriously compete with fishermen for cockles and how much they are to blame for declines in some cockle fisheries has led to conflict between ornithologists and fishermen and to an official government investigation.

Redshanks

The food of redshanks has been studied on the Ythan estuary, at the Wash and in other places in south England, from direct observations, from gut samples, and from analyses of pellets found on roosts. The diet was found to be varied. In summer and autumn, pellets at the Wash contained crabs, shrimps, small cockles, *Macoma balthica*, and *Hydrobia*; but *Hydrobia* predominated from October to April, with crabs, ragworms and *Macoma* appearing in May. Amphipods (*Corophium* and *Orchestia* spp.) were numerous only in June. On the Ythan, redshank ate mostly *Corophium* at all times of the year, depending on the temperature of the mud. When this was above 6°C, *Corophium* formed the bulk of the food taken, but when the temperature was lower, it was mostly *Macoma* or ragworms. These changes in diet appeared to be related to changes in the behaviour of the prey which affected their availability. In addition, in winter the birds obtained less than half their food from the estuary in daylight and had to get the rest at night or inland. All this suggests that redshank on the Ythan had difficulty in getting enough to eat in winter because of the short days,

Redshank roosting. These birds feed at low tide on small shrimps, worms and Hydrobia; when the tide comes in they are forced off their feeding areas and roost to await the ebb.

cold weather and poor availability of food.

At the Ythan, higher densities of redshank occurred where there were higher densities of *Corophium*, but in south-east England *Nereis* probably contributed more than *Corophium* to the birds' diet. In a comparison of different estuaries, numbers of redshanks were found to correlate significantly with the density of *Nereis*.

Although redshank preferred places where there was an abundance of *Corophium* on the Ythan, and elsewhere of *Nereis*, the resulting tendency to congregate in the best sites was counteracted by a tendency for new arrivals to avoid places with a high density of birds. How the birds adjusted their numbers so that most occurred in the places where food was most abundant is not yet fully understood.

Conclusions

The Firth of Forth is very important for the conservation of Scottish wildlife. It has an extremely high rating in the 'index of importance' in the 'Birds of Estuaries Enquiry'. But , so far, the Nature Conservancy Council has no statutory responsibility for the conservation of wildlife in or on the sea, and it is hard to define where the estuary of the Forth ends and where the sea begins. This means that although the advice of the NCC may be sought and readily given in potential catastrophes from oil or other pollutants, the very large flocks of sea-ducks found here (unique in Britain) are not the responsibility of a national organization, and their safety is not watched constantly as it should be. A strong case can be made for declaring the whole Firth of Forth from, say, Alloa to Gullane Bay a national nature reserve. In the event of incidents from pollution the NCC may then be able to strengthen the hand of the River Purification Boards and the Department of Trade in organizing effective prosecutions and consequent heavy fines. The attitude that 'only birds' are involved must be changed. Organizations empowered to take action should have a statutory responsibility to do whatever is necessary to protect the birds.

Since the big concentrations of sea-ducks depend largely on human effluent, it is important to monitor what happens to these ducks when sewage input declines. The building of the sewage disposal unit at Edinburgh may lead to the dispersal of the big flock of scaup and goldeneye, or perhaps to a reduction in the overall British populations. In the case of dispersal, it is important to know where they go, and to see if they need protection. While estuaries are among the very few habitats that are still more or less natural, they are very vulnerable to pollution and other human development.

Estuaries are threatened too by development of many kinds, including that of recreation. Many of these developments may greatly benefit our community, and conservationists need to consider particularly carefully the grounds on which scientific interests can objectively seek priority. In many cases all too little is known about the behaviour and food requirements of birds which may be threatened. Ecologists may be asked to say which are key species on national and international criteria, and to predict the effects of change. Our understanding of the interacting factors influencing bird distribution patterns is advancing but there is still a long way to go before such predictions can be made with confidence. Spending of public money on research on the ecology of estuarine wildlife can be well justified.

Greylag goslings in their downy nest in the heather.

Top left : Barnacle geese feeding ; note the white bird. Bottom left : Pink-footed geese coming in to Loch Leven National Nature Reserve, with another white intruder — this time a snow goose.

Right : A pair of oystercatchers. The long bill is used for opening cockles and mussels. Below : A young male bar-tailed godwit. The joints that are clearly seen are the bird's ankles, the legs being elongated as an adaptation to wading.

Chapter 7
The Bird Islands

In the turbulence the light aircraft swung alarmingly, lost height, bumped and thumped. The pilot had warned us that it would be so before we took off from Plockton for a photographic fly-around over the rock stacks of St Kilda. Banked over at a steep angle I had a distorted view of black rock teeth thrusting through the swirling cloud – the Cuillins of Skye. Rain battered the perspex. I wished I was on the ground. Then cheer, and a surge of happiness. Below were glimpses of silver sea, and on the horizon was St Kilda, lumpy and grey-blue in a clear sky. Luck indeed, and I wondered what I would see, for it was exactly twenty years earlier, in 1957, that I had last seen it. On that occasion we had landed with materials for the servicemen who were building a beach-head for a rocket base.

I had not long to wait before we were banking over Village Bay, flying slowly over the white squares of the garrison building and to the dome of a hilltop radar station. It had not lost its attraction. Seen from the air I had a new appreciation of the layout of the old village, its rigs of cultivation sloping in narrow strips to the yellow sands of the bay.

Even so I felt a certain nostalgia for the St Kilda I had known the first time I landed on the island in 1955, when it was very much as the villagers had known it. There was an aura of true remoteness then. Even to get to it meant hiring a fishing boat and sailing from Tarbert Harris with tents and enough food for three weeks. After ten hours' sailing we felt we had truly arrived on the edge of the world, with 555 hectares of land and 14 km of ferocious cliffs to explore.

In comparison with that pioneer visit, the second visit was made tawdry by the work camp and explosions and the noise of stone-crushers shattering the peace. But in companionship it was rich, for I had the late Kenneth Williamson and Dr W. J. Eggeling of the Nature Conservancy for company and we had exciting times, setting mist nets and entangling spring migrants en route for the Arctic: Icelandic wheatears, meadow pipits, white wagtails, whimbrels and many other.

The month was May and there was a fair amount of bird movement going on. What we didn't know was whether or not we were too early to find petrels on the breeding cliffs. There was only one way to find out – to sit out through the darkness on Carn Mor. We took sleeping bags and found an old stone cleitt for shelter. By 2 am there was nothing doing, and Joe Eggeling had just turned in for a snooze while I sat outside, when something brushed my cheek and I heard a slight thump on Joe's sleeping bag. In the torch beam the slaty-grey little bird with fork tail and white rump sat quietly while I nudged the

Stac Lee, white with gannets, is one of the most dramatic of the St Kildan stacks.

sleeper and let him pick up the first Leach's petrel he had ever seen.

What an inspiring amount of natural history work has been done since then on St Kilda, by professionals and amateurs, thanks to the ease of transport between the mainland and the rocket tracking base. And what a setting for study it is. On the boulderfields of Carn Mor, Manx shearwaters scream round your head in the darkness before thumping down in the stones, and you have to be quick with your torch if you hope to catch them before they wriggle underground into their burrows. The petrels come later, the first indication of them being the little laughing call which tells you they are Leach's. You strain your eyes trying to see them, and glimpse the bat-like shape as they nearly touch your face. Then there are nights out on Conachair on the biggest face on St Kilda, lodged steeply above overhangs dropping into invisibility where the waves boom. From there you might experience an unforgettable sight, as the red ball of the sun climbs out of the ocean and pauses between mighty Boreray and the two attendant stacks which form the noblest gannetry in the world – and the biggest. I had memories too of puffins going round and round in the air like swarming bees, all going the one way to avoid traffic problems, then settling so close that every boulder was abloom with red legs and red beaks of the white-breasted birds. Fulmars had powder-puff chicks in every niche.

I had hoped we would fly through Soay Sound to look at other favourite cliffs and corners I had explored, but the pilot deemed the buffeting of the wind in that narrow place too dangerous. But he was

willing to take a whirl round Boreray and the stacks for an eye-to-eye view of the gannets, and that was something I had not bargained for. We zoomed in, with me jammed in the tail of the plane, camera at the ready. Then it all happened. A pointed top like the Matterhorn in winter rushed towards us, but the snow was gannets and as we leaned over to come round the face I saw an array of birds that must have been 10,000 strong, each a white dot on the ledges of Stac Lee.

The mind could not register so much in a short time: we rounded Stac Lee and before us was Stac an Armin with gannets pouring off it like spindrift, then we swept up along the green crown of Boreray to look down its 300-metre pinnacles. Each of these fearsome stacks was ringed with boiling sea where the waves burst white. In that short spin I had seen a greater concentration of gannets than anywhere else in the world. The *Atlas of Breeding Birds* gives 59,000 pairs for 1974, out of a world population of perhaps 213,800 pairs.

There are accounts of the St Kildan islanders climbing these stacks to take a crop of birds for food, poised up there at night to seize the adults while they slept. In spring after a long stormy winter the fresh gannets would have been welcome, and as many as 1100 in one night are said to have been taken. But the main harvest was in autumn, when the crop was young fat birds known as gugas, of which perhaps 3000 might be thrown down to the waiting boats heaving below. Both these figures are for the period between 1847 and 1895: as far as we know the raids stopped of their own accord about 1910.

Just what it was like to climb Stac Lee, fiercest of the stacks, I

The National Nature Reserve of St Kilda contains more breeding gannets than anywhere else in the world.

learned from Dick Balharry, who with Dr J. Morton Boyd forced a way to the top in May 1968 – the first ascent since St Kildan times. On their way to the stack strings of gannets and fulmars followed the boat, but so deep was the swell that in the depths of the trough the stacks were invisible. Then they were under it, the point of the 160-metre pinnacle, dark against grey sky, aswirl with the white wings of gannets; there was not a scrap of vegetation, only rock and water and countless thousands of birds. 'It was supposed to be a reconnaissance, but I was so busy looking for a route that I had no feeling of fear, only a terrific sense of excitement in the boom of the sea as it crashed against the brown rocks, shooting straight up the face, to be sucked back into the ocean.' To land they simply waited for their boat to rise on the highest swell, stepped smartly out grabbing what hand and footholds they could, and after 6 metres of near vertical climbing paused for breath.

They had brought modern climbing gear with them, hammer, pitons, rope-slings, rope, and they needed it 30 metres higher up when they were faced with a blank smooth wall where the weathered rock had sheared away. 'It looked impossible, and the thing I had to master was the noise and the verticality. The birds were screaming like an excited crowd at a football match. Straight below was the sea, and the next bit was actually overhanging. I drove in a piton for security and committed myself.' They were now on '. . . a great bevelled roof of gannets and walking up ledges of slimy guano. You sank in at every step. Now and then gannets would reach out and grip your arm with their beaks, gannets, gannets and more gannets. Even the stones were covered in grey whitewash, so dry and encrusted that you broke through rather than sank in. When the gannets rose they created a dust storm, as happens when a helicopter takes off from dusty ground.'

On top there was room for only one gannet's nest; below it was a wee bothy, beautifully dry inside and capable of holding two men, but now taken over by two fulmars. Describing the whole experience Morton Boyd said: 'The gannets were an excuse. The primary object was to reach the top. And we'd made it. I felt this was my *ultima Thule*.' The real mission was to take close-up photographs of the gannet ledges as a check on the accuracy of aerial photographs, to provide data for judging the population level of the birds in the future.

All the evidence is that the gannet is doing well. Numbers have risen dramatically since about 1939, yet this species was in decline in the nineteenth century when throughout its range it was being exploited for food. In ten years the St Kilda colony rose from 44,000 to 52,000 pairs, and four years later, in 1974, was shown at 59,000 pairs. The story is paralleled in other gannetries, though not all.

All this makes the case of the disappearing puffin a strange one, for when the St Kildans were in residence it was the most common bird on the island and the one they relied on most heavily for food and feathers. Their burrows were everywhere and they were easily snared. There were millions of birds. But when Jim Flegg made his full survey on St Kilda in 1971 he estimated a maximum of only 250,000 burrows in use. Concern has been expressed over a general decline in puffin numbers in the west coast of Scotland, but for unexplained reasons numbers seem to be stabilizing, while on the eastern side the puffin population is rising.

There is an interesting link between the puffin and the St Kilda wren. Kenneth Williamson estimated that this largest wren in the world numbered 230 pairs on St Kilda, and he associated this with puffins being a source of food. Puffins are careless; they drop some of the little fish that they eat, which decompose and attract insects. Future figures for the St Kilda wren should be worth watching in the light of this knowledge. The St Kilda wren is distinguished from Fair Isle, Shetland and Hebridean wrens by its greyer plumage and stouter bill.

Northwards from St Kilda towards the Shetlands lie three other notable Atlantic islands, each a stronghold of Leach's petrels: first the group of the Seven Hunters – the Flannans – then the gannetry of Sula Sgeir, shortly beyond which is fabled North Rona. Ornithologists who have had the good luck to land on the Flannans say that they belong to the petrels, particularly Eilein Mor. Sula Sgeir is the rock still raided by the Lewismen for a crop of 3000 fat gugas each autumn. Even so, the gannet colony continues to expand, and it stood at 9000 pairs in 1974 compared to James Fisher's figure of 3970 pairs in 1943. Wisely the Nature Conservancy has allowed the raids to continue, since the gannetry can stand the loss and the men of Ness enjoy the challenge of a long sail and a difficult landing for a fortnight of dangerous work.

Next comes North Rona, the loneliest of all the islands that carries a human population and one which casts its spell on all who go there. No one was more affected than the late Sir Frank Fraser Darling, who described to me how much he cherished the memory of it: 'I felt completely fulfilled on Rona. The immensity of the ocean was so absorbing in itself. The seabird cliffs in spring and summer, one of the most thrilling things a man can have to watch. I remember how on August 10, they were gone, and at the end of the month the seals were

Puffins are found on many of the islands described in this chapter, from the Inner Hebrides to the Shetlands. They live in burrows and are quite confiding, allowing you to get near so long as you move slowly.

hauling out and building up in thousands.' Fraser Darling worked on this most northern fragment of the Outer Hebrides right through to winter, sometimes crawling on hands and knees to fetch water for cooking. He experienced every kind of weather tantrum that nature can lay on, until three days before Christmas '. . . the sun was behind the far clear line of the Sutherland hills and the whole of our snowy world was pink. The atmosphere was clear and still, and even as I watched I spied a dot thirty miles away between Cape Wrath and the Butt of Lewis. A ship, undoubtedly, the first we had seen for a month, and it must be a cruiser coming for us.'

Ron is the Gaelic name for seal, but the island might have taken its name from St Ronan who is reputed to have built a tiny cell there in the eighth century. All we know for certain about the original inhabitants comes from Martin Martin, who wrote down what the Parish Minister of Barvas in Lewis told him of a visit to its five families in the seventeenth century. They died when a plague of rats came ashore from a wreck and ate their corn. It must have been winter, or otherwise they could surely have survived on seabirds. Perhaps there were no seals breeding on the island because of the human population.

It fell to Dr J. Morton Boyd to carry the torch lit by Sir Frank Fraser Darling. Morton Boyd, when a university student, had become fascinated by islands, and Fraser Darling had suggested to him a study of Hebridean machairs, financed by a three-year grant from the Nature Conservancy. The work resulted in his appointment as the first Regional Officer for Western Scotland in the Nature Conservancy, as which he led expeditions to North Rona. It is due to the continuity of the work done by Morton Boyd and his staff that we can appreciate the part played by these remote rocks in the ornithology of Scotland.

The autumn expeditions to North Rona, although primarily concerned with the breeding biology of the Atlantic seal, opened a new window on bird migration. Fair Isle, situated midway between the Orkneys and the Shetlands, has been famous since last century as a migration station where birds of Icelandic, Greenlandic and Scandinavian origin cast up every autumn. Then, with the building of the rocket base on St Kilda and the presence of a resident naturalist warden, it was found that St Kilda too had its share of exciting bird movements. The North Rona seal expeditions provided a co-ordinated picture of what was happening on all three islands at the same time. During the period of 1–20 October 1961, for example, the following were recorded: birds of 38 species on St Kilda, 50 species on North Rona (in half the period), and 109 species on Fair Isle. One year later migrant birds of 70 species were recorded on North Rona, and it has been observed that the passage of geese and swans is more noticeable from Rona than from St Kilda or Fair Isle, because it lies on a direct line from Iceland to Scotland. Rona is also within night-flight bird range from Norway. Analysis of the migrants recorded shows a mixture of Iceland and Greenland birds, and those which have drifted off-course from Scandinavia.

In view of the fact that all small and remote islands seem fated to become uninhabited, it is all the more remarkable that Foula, the St Kilda of the Shetlands, should still carry a viable population, though it seems inevitable that its end cannot be far away. An old lady I talked to on the island reminisced about the livelier times at the beginning of the century when over two hundred people lived on Foula, and any croft going empty was eagerly snapped up. 'There was always dancing and singing, but who stays here now but the old, who have to depend on the few young ones to keep the island going?'

The name Foula comes from the Norse, meaning 'bird island'. When I went there in 1959 we sailed from Walls to Valia Sound which indents the westerly arm of the Shetland mainland, a journey of just over three hours on the prevailing wind. As we drew near, the faint outline hardened, thrusting high out of the ocean like a fluted iceberg, and the sea-way filled with birds. Elegant arctic skuas made agile passes at arctic terns, bonxies big and brown as buzzards swung round the boats, auks by the dozen scuttered out of our path.

It was after midnight when we carried our gear north of the harbour and camped on a headland; we awoke to the wailing of skuas and the tittering of whimbrel. Sticking my head out of the tent to see what was going on, I had a northern welcome from a shower of twites descending round me with wheezy greetings. Our position was midway down the 5 km length of Foula, and behind us lay the greatest breadth of the island stretching over 4 km of hills to its west coast, where rising clouds revealed ridge crests green against blue sky, an invitation to explore. But before we had gone very far we were trying to improvise weapons to ward off the attacks of skuas nesting everywhere on the hill, mostly bonxies (great skuas).

Incredible as it may seem, the estimated population of these once rare great skuas was at the time 3000 pairs, plus or minus 300, not counting another 2000 non-breeders. It was gratifying to see them in such numbers, when at the beginning of the century the total breeding

The bonxie in typical aggressive pose. Watch out for your head if ever you are among them, for they will dive-bomb with equal aggression.

population in Britain could be found in only two places – here on Foula, where there were approximately 100 pairs, and on Hermaness, Unst, where about nine pairs were protected by a paid watcher. Now they are widespread in the Shetlands and Orkneys, and have reached St Kilda, Lewis, the Island of Handa and Caithness. Yet although they far outnumbered the two hundred and fifty pairs of arctic skuas, it was the latter which were most dynamic in attack, coming from behind without warning, whereas the bonxies tended to give you warning grunts before swooping at your head. Chicks were everywhere, and it was a relief to find that if you picked up a chick and held it in your hands the skuas invariably left you alone.

Our route lay over the Skordar ridge and down to the bowling-green turf of the North Ness, in a cacophony of terns, oystercatchers, ringed plovers, gulls, skuas and other sounds. Shags stood poised on rock stacks, wings out. Fulmars had nests on the earth floors and chimney stacks of ruined crofts. Kittiwakes flew in from the sea to bathe in a freshwater lochan. Down on the storm beach black guillemots landed from the sea with silver fish, dodging hurriedly underground before they could be caught by marauding gulls and skuas. All was life, movement – and robbery.

Now we took the edge of the cliff, climbing with it from sea-level to 380 metres, to stand on the edge of the most frightening vertical plunge I have seen in Britain or Ireland. Small wonder that it is impossible to count the seabird colonies of Foula from the land when the rock scenery is on this scale. Figures from the *Scottish Bird Report* for

1975 gave breeding guillemots at 30,000 birds, puffins 25,000 pairs, razorbills 6000 pairs, arctic terns 6000 pairs. The mind boggles when you add to these the thousands of kittiwakes and fulmars, and the storm of petrels which come in to their burrows on the Noup when darkness falls.

It is hard even to guess at all that is to be seen on Foula, for the island is composed of so many little worlds. One of the most exciting regions is the Wick of Mucklebrek and the Sneck of the Smallie, where the precipitous coast is gashed with a deep rock chimney 60

The Sneck of the Smallie, Foula – a cavern of nesting birds.

metres high, forming a veritable grotto full of shags and puffins. It is an eerie scramble before you step into daylight and then follow an old bird-fowlers' path traversing the face of the Ufshins to Wester Haevdi, nearest point to the Faroes, Iceland and the 'Wast Ice', which is what the Shetland fishermen call the Greenland Sea. It was surprising up there to come across a party of crossbills seed-picking on the ground.

The ornithologist and bird photographer Chris Mylne, who lived on Foula for two years prior to 1956, made the good point that, because of the size and roughness of Foula, accurate census records are very much related to the number of observers. Even so it is possible to obtain a migration trend which shows that smaller numbers of north-eastern migrants appear on Foula than on Fair Isle. (There are occasions, however, when the same species of birds appear on both islands on the same day, as one September in 1955 when mist and drizzly conditions produced an avalanche of redstarts, tree pipits, whinchats, willow warblers and pied flycatchers.) The marked spread of skuas from high ground to the former croft lands on Foula equates with the decline in cultivation as the population dwindled. Pastures coarsened, favouring the skuas and causing the corncrakes to disappear.

The surge of the bonxies has doubtless diminished the arctic skua population on the island, but even the vast increase of the former is nothing compared to the success story of the fulmar which began in Britain on Foula. The historical discovery of a dozen nests on the Kame was made in 1878, the first outside St Kilda. It was the beginning of a growth which spread round almost the entire coast of Britain and Ireland, and in the Operation Seafarer census of 1970 an estimated 305,600 sites were occupied, of which nearly 90 per cent were in Shetland, Orkney, the Outer Hebrides and north-west Scotland.

Professor George Dunnet, of Aberdeen University, who has studied the fulmar in detail, attributes its spread and remarkable increase in population to the long life-span of the adults and the high survival rate of young and adolescent birds during the first eight years of their lives. But why should a species whose nesting area was the Arctic and St Kilda suddenly explode in all directions round our coasts? The late James Fisher suggested that the expansion was mainly due to the ready supply of food made available by the trawling and whaling industry. Others have suggested genetic mutation, or a gradual warming up of the North Atlantic. Having travelled aboard trawlers to the Faroes and seen the hordes of fulmars – and gannets too – following the fleets for discarded fish guts, I incline to the first view.

Birds and Mammals of Shetland lists nine major habitats, each suitable for different species: moor and hill; cultivated arable land; marshy bottoms; plantations and gardens; sandy flats; sea lochs and sheltered voes; lochs in agricultural land and lochs in moorland; and of course sea cliffs. For a good cross-section of such habitats we go to the island of Fetlar, which it is said was among the first to be colonized by the Vikings because it was so fair.

For all we could see of it when we landed in the mist with our tent, we could have been camping in our back garden – but for the grunts and wails of invisible skuas and the 'cak-ak-ak-ak' of red-throated divers. Indeed it was still misty when we set off to find the snowy owls of Vord Hill, and the first delightful surprise was to meet George and Irene Waterston on an official RSPB visit, and to help bird photographer Eric Hosking to get photographs of the first nest of this species in Britain. The grey world was opening up as we talked. Colour flooded into the land and seascape in pink cliffs, green headlands and gently undulating fields. A herd of Shetland ponies grazed in front of us, and behind them across the water was the last fragment of Britain – Unst – pale blue and inviting. Sounds filled the air, songs of skylarks and pipits and wheatears; golden plover skirled and whimbrels whinnied.

The theatrical clearing had an effect on the owl too, for it rose from the stone under the distant skyline where it was perched and came beating round like a white buzzard to alight on a nearby fencepost. So my first good view was face-to-face through the glass. The feathery 'nose' and round head gave it a strangely animal look, and the eyes were pale silver, slit with black. I was fascinated too by the gold feathers of the legs, extending down over the claws – winter warmers indeed. Swivelling its head like a gun turrent to scan the ground all round, it took off, flew back to its old perch and demonstrated its hunting skill to us.

We didn't see the actual strike but we were sure that the owl's method was stealth. The ground fell away in undulations below the stone where it was perched, and our feeling was that the bird waited until the rabbit was below its own horizon before taking off. This seemed the only explanation for its skimming flight so close to the ground that it was virtually skiing the last part. It disappeared from our view to reappear with its prey, than landed on the ground and stood over the prey for five minutes, perhaps squeezing it to death, before flying with it to the nest.

Later on RSPB watcher Bobbie Tulloch arrived on his boat from

An historic occasion, the discovery of the first nest of snowy owls in Britain. The finder was Bobbie Tulloch, pictured with the nest on Fetlar, Shetland.

Yell and gave me a first-hand account of how he had found the nest. 'I'll never forget that June day as long as I live. I walked slowly over the place and saw nothing at first, then something that looked like a few feathers, and inside the rough cup of the nest three eggs. I felt the hairs on my neck rising. What I had always hoped had happened. The thing now was to keep the nest a secret until I could get news to George Waterston and organize a night and day guard to make sure the snowy owls had every chance? The precautions paid off, and the watchers recorded much that was fascinating in the breeding biology of the snowy owl. Breeding has continued since then, and snowy owls are being seen in Orkney, on Foula and on St Kilda.

Lying in our tent at night we could hear the Manx shearwaters screaming on their way to the headland of the Lamb Hoga where storm petrels too have their burrows. Walking across to these cliff-haunts in daylight we passed little peat lochans on the skua ground, an occasional one harbouring red-throated divers and their young. In other places on the island we got to know the wet flows where red-necked phalaropes hid their chicks – little balls of yellow fluff, well described as 'bumble bees on stilts'. A fearless parent, the dainty cock bird would fly round our heads and come to our feet if we seemed to be too close. Then it would desist and, taking to the water, swim and pirouette to create a vortex thus swirling insects into easy catching range.

Having explored from the Wick of Gruting to the Horn of Ramsness in eight days we felt George Waterston could not be very wrong when he claimed that there was no better bird island than

The adult snowy owl with chicks.

Fetlar in the 110 km of the Shetlands. Some would have Unst as a rival, with its superior cliffs and great gannetry where the waves crash on Muckle Flugga, but it is hard to compare one superlative with another. Some figures from a survey of Unst in 1974 by Mike Harris put the puffin colony in the same class as that of St Kilda, with guillemots at 18,228 birds, razorbills 110 birds, kittiwake nests 3952, arctic skua pairs 70, great skua pairs 800, and gannet nests 5225 – yet until 1917 there were no gannets at all there.

Shetland needs a whole book to itself, but particular homage must be paid to the island of Noss near Lerwick, hardly more than a simple hill rising gently from the sea on one side, but from its highest point cut clean down to the sea. Compressed into 2 km² is the greatest variety of seabirds in Shetland – 14 species, excluding the commonly found eider. The 'hang-lip' edge of the Noup is the focal point. From there you are eye-to-eye with the 4000 pairs of gannets thronging the ledges, which until 1914 were unknown here. The stack known as the Cradle Holm carries the biggest greater black-backed gullery in Shetland, and on the ledges below the throng of kittiwakes and guillemots is overpowering. Fulmars nest. Skuas wheel about. The hill loch has red-throated divers. Today Noss is inhabited only in summer by a shepherd, but in 1874 it carried twenty-four inhabitants, and before that, according to old records, its pastures yielded butter and milk of superb quality.

The one and only Fair Isle lies midway between the Shetlands and the Orkneys, but it can be passed over briefly here since justice has been done to it by Kenneth Williamson in his *Fair Isle and Its Birds* and by the annual reports of the Fair Isle Bird Observatory Trust. Take note of just some of its migrants recorded in one season: Leach's petrel, honey buzzard, gyr falcon, marsh harrier, spotted crake, red-necked phalarope, long-tailed skua, hoopoe, short-toed lark, golden oriole, nightingale, yellow-breasted bunting, little bunting – just a few from an island that can produce 190 species in a single season.

Fair Isle has been known as an exceptional island for bird migration since the days of Eagle Clarke, but not until a former Naval camp became a bird observatory with the late Kenneth Williamson as its first warden did its true worth become known. Even the setting up of the Observatory is a remarkable story, for its concept was dreamed up by two prisoners of war in Bavaria in 1943. One was George Waterston. The other was Ian Pitman.

George was to see Fair Isle sooner than he thought, for due to ill health he was repatriated, and his voyage home was by way of Sweden and along the east coast of Norway, then west across the North Sea. It took him past Fair Isle. Talking about it with me he said: 'I think the most emotional moment of my life was when somebody shouted "Land ahead", and there only two or three miles off was the Sheep Rock and Fair Isle standing in the sunshine. The tears ran down my cheeks – I knew the island so well, and it had been in my thoughts so often.' George had been to Fair Isle on pre-war visits. He had found the islanders really keen and knowledgeable about birds, great fun to be with and always good for a laugh. Back from the war he planned a campaign to buy the island, better the lot of its isolated community, and attract people to Fair Isle for bird study.

The plan was sound, but with a limited amount of funds there was a better way of aiding the islanders, and that was to pass it over to the National Trust for Scotland, keeping the Fair Isle Bird

Observatory as an independent trust. The modern building with its 24-bed hostel was built in 1969. But alas, as on other remote islands, the human population of Fair Isle was falling to a dangerously low level, with too many elderly and too few young able-bodied islanders. Peter Davies, one of the Bird Observatory wardens, had written in 1963: 'the Observatory will sink or swim with the island community for in the event of evacuation the Observatory could only be continued by occasional expeditions, mounted at considerable expense. Meantime the work has steadily gone forward.'

The situation has improved since then. The school roll has risen and the average age of the adults has gone down. The island is in good heart. Much work has been done to improve the houses and provide electricity. The Observatory is a focal point of island life. The future looks good, and the National Trust for Scotland and the Fair Isle Observatory Trust are to be congratulated.

Bird island enthusiasts tend to keep meeting each other in remote places. In this case the place was Scrabster in 1962, the ornithologist was Dr Sandy Anderson of Aberdeen University, and we were both catching the Orkney boat to Stromness. The last time we had been together was on St Kilda when he was studying fulmars, and twenty years later here he was heading for Eynhallow on the same quest. One of the objects of his study is to determine the life-span of the fulmar by colour ringing, which is difficult because the birds last longer than the rings: their length of life may prove to be thirty years or more.

Sailing from Scrabster one's first sight of the Orkneys are the dramatic 300-metre cliffs of St John's Head and the slender chimney-stack pinnacle of the Old Man of Hoy. The Orkney Field Club have a hut there available to all bona-fide naturalists, and there is plenty of challenging study on a cliff-girt island thronged with nesting seabirds such as golden eagles, hen harriers, peregrine falcons, buzzards, merlins, bonxies and arctic skuas. But Hoy is not typical of the Orkneys – it is much higher and wilder, whereas the norm is agricultural.

Farming is the mainstay of Orkney, which has a sandstone soil that breaks down easily and produces good grass able to sustain one cow to 2 hectares. Modern machinery is changing its land surface: wet places are drained, rough hill land is reclaimed, and the status of birds is constantly changing, however imperceptibly. Writing of Orkney in 1968, RSPB watcher Eddie Balfour recorded increases of the red-throated diver, hen harrier, kestrel, oystercatcher, curlew, great skua, arctic skua, great black-backed gull, stonechat, sedge warbler and reed bunting. Notable decreases he listed are Manx shearwater, corncrake, coot, lapwing, common sandpiper, red-necked phalarope, lesser black-backed gull, mistle thrush, pied wagtail and corn bunting. The total bird list is impressive, with breeding redwings and fieldfares in recent years.

But the big success story of Orkney is the hen harrier, for Orkney was its British stronghold before its remarkable spread to the mainland of Scotland in the 1940s. Homage should be paid to two outstanding local ornithologists now deceased, George Arthur and Eddie Balfour, especially the latter who studied the breeding biology of the hen harrier for 43 years and saw numbers build up to over 60 pairs.

Orkney is the most northerly base in the world of sandwich terns, and on one of its islands – Westray – is the second biggest seabird colony in Britain. The comparative list in *Birds and Mammals of Shetland* shows Orkney to have 88 regular breeding birds compared to 64 for

Leach's petrel

Shetland – the difference being made up almost entirely of inland species, as a result of the wider variety of habitat available. The nearest gannetry to the Orkney mainland is Sula Stack, with 4000 breeding pairs on a 40 metre high rock. Neighbouring Sula Skerry is the home of 50–60,000 puffins, and at night it purrs with storm petrels. Leach's petrels occur here and probably breed, as has now been proved on Foula.

It is a long way from the Orkneys to the populous shores of the Firth of Forth, but that is the distance we have to travel down the east coast to reach the next island – the Isle of May – 10 km south of Fifeness. A bare rock platform only 3 km long by 1 km wide, more seaward than the Bass Rock, it is not only a great seabird island but one of the most exciting migration stations in Britain.

Blackbirds from Norway, meadow pipits from France, pied wagtails from Cardiff, wood warblers from Algiers, redwings from the Frisian Islands, a wheatear from Sweden, robins from south Norway and Portugal, sandwich terns from the Gold Coast, lesser black-backed gulls from Morocco and Lisbon – these are just a few returns from the Isle of May Bird Observatory. Uncommon migrants such as red-spotted bluethroats, red-backed shrikes, wrynecks, rustic buntings, woodlarks and ortolan buntings turn up here regularly, but are rare on the mainland.

Season after season the May proves itself to the ornithologists who go there to man the traps. Ideal conditions for the bird ringer are the drizzle and south-easterly winds which drive down the migrants; in good clear weather the birds would pass on. Observers may begin to despair when wind and visibility favours the birds and not them – as shown amusingly by this extract from the Observatory Log for 27 September 1974 by the late Professor M. F. M. Meiklejohn, a frequent visitor in the migration season:

> *There was an old man on the May*
> *Who knelt on the North Ness to pray*
> *'Oh, Lord, I have sinned –*
> *But why need the wind*
> *Blow westerly day after day?'*

We sympathized with the professor on one fruitless visit, for on the day we should have left the island the sea was too rough for us to do so. Providence must have been on our side, however, for a wet drizzle soon enveloped the island, the wind shifted east, and as we looked out to sea we noticed small birds fluttering at wave-top level, fighting their way towards where we stood. They were using the troughs of the waves to get some relief from the headwind, and making definite progress. Little parties tired with the struggle were dropping around us, mostly blackbirds, with some redwings and fieldfares, then a few woodcock and snipe. We were looking at some bramblings when we noticed a stout rusty-coloured finch which we thought at first was a crossbill. It was a pine grosbeak, a November bird, and the first to be taken at any British Observatory. We were lucky to get it into the trap next day, and to photograph and ring this bird of the northern forests of Europe.

I have no personal experience of a really gigantic rush of birds lasting a week, as occurs when the winds are continually south-easterly with drizzle. One autumn observer who had the luck to be on the May at the right time described it thus: 'Out of low clouds the black specks

Top: A fulmar nests in a ruined croft on Foula.
Bottom: The first snowy owl chicks found in Scotland.

Above : An islander of Foula with a short-eared owl.
Above right : The St Kilda wren at its nest. This subspecies, the largest of the wrens, does not appear ever to leave the island.
Right : The unmistakable markings of the puffin are particularly vivid in summer.

Left : The great skua has a distinctive cry when guarding its nest.

of the birds kept falling until the island was alive with birds, not all of them blackbirds. There were also redwings, fieldfares, continental song thrushes, skylarks, flocks of chaffinches, bramblings – a host of birds that kept two observers busy trapping, weighing, measuring, ringing, sexing and recording – six days of hard going.'

The Isle of May has been a National Nature Reserve since 1956, but the Bird Observatory has been in operation since 1934, and the story of how this first co-operatively manned migration station was founded is an interesting one. It begins in 1907 at a time when John Harvie-Brown and Eagle Clark were the two outstanding names in Scottish ornithology. Clark was famous for his work on Fair Isle and for his theories of routes followed by migrating birds.

Clark credited northern birds with having the ability to follow established routes and use various islands as stepping stones. This theory was to be challenged by two very remarkable ladies who were later to become the joint authors of *The Birds of Scotland*, Dr E. V. Baxter and Miss L. J. Rintoul. By making spring and autumn visits to the Isle of May from 1907 to 1933, staying for as long as six weeks at a time, they discovered that this island was a second Fair Isle. From a study of the birds in relation to the weather that brought them, they posed a new and revolutionary proposition – now widely accepted in the world of ornithology though discredited by experts at the time – that migration routes are not predetermined, that what causes birds to land on coasts and islands is not choice, but the consequence of down-wind drift.

An ornithologist on the Isle of May inspects the catching box of the Gully Trap. In this instance the catch was a new bird for any British observatory, a pine grosbeak (above).

Top: The dizzy heights of Barrahead cliffs, a nesting site of peregrines. Bottom: Gannets thronging the Bass Rock: the birds are spaced only a beak's length apart.

It was the observation of these two distinguished ornithologists that inspired an Edinburgh schoolboy by the name of George Waterston to originate the Isle of May Bird Observatory, with the help of a few close friends who had formed themselves into a body they called the Midlothian Ornithological Club. (Waterston later founded the Fair Isle Observatory, as has been told.)

We pass now to the Bass Rock which rises beyond the May and near the Lothian shore like a rock stack escaped from St Kilda. Even if you cannot arrange a landing on it, you may sail round it on one of the tourist excursion trips from North Berwick. The poet William Dunbar described the thrilling experience as you come under mighty crags milling with white birds:

> *The air was dirkit with fowlis*
> *That cam with jammeris and with youlis*
> *With shrykking, skrieking, skyrmming scowlis*
> *And meikle noyis and showtes.*

The Low Light on the Isle of May, a dwelling place and library for visiting ornithologists. The coast of Fife lies in the background, and in the middle distance is the North Foghorn.

The Bass was the last fragment of Scotland to surrender to the Union of the Crowns when a handful of determined Scots held out for three years against the might of King William III. The staircase that leads to the tight pack of nesting gannets goes through the ruins of the old fortress where puffins squint out at you from prison cells that once housed Covenanters.

On top of the rock you are eye-to-eye with the gannets and able to watch their comings and goings. Masters of the slip-stream, they can

hang like kestrels and drift tail-first into the rock, steadying themselves with steering movements of their big webbed feet. Rich buff on the head, tipped black on the wings, and dazzling white all over, they bemuse you by their sheer number. The *Atlas* shows 10,500 pairs in 1974.

Dr Brian Nelson, a research scientist from Aberdeen University, spent three seasons on the Bass studying gannets from February to November, living in a prefabricated hut built into the ruins of the eighth-century St Baldred's Chapel. His two hides overlooked 250 nests and sites, and at one of them he talked to me about his work. I liked his story of how one day when he was watching some of the gannets in a shower of rain he noticed some tiny black specks suddenly appear on their heads. Later on he experimented by catching a gannet and sprinkling its head with water; sure enough out came the feather lice again. How true was his remark that parasites of all kinds have life histories as complex and fascinating as their hosts. As he said: 'The gannet plunging headlong into the sea is wonderfully adapted, but no more so than the louse clinging to its head.'

Dr Nelson grew to understand the signalling system of the gannets. Each posture had a meaning – welcome to a mate, reaction against an intruder, response to a chick – none of them obvious at a superficial glance, when something always seems to be happening to excite the birds. The twisting and jabbing of the head, the growling noise, is mostly play-acting to warn off other birds, as when a gannet pitches down from the air to feed its young and is met with a forest of open bills making stabbing movements.

A young gannet howls protest at an intruder on the Bass Rock, while a younger chick crouches quietly beside it.

The Bass gets an interesting share of passing migrants, but the density of other seabirds does not compare with Ailsa Craig. This is the Clyde's rival to the gannetry of the Bass, although, soaring up like a haystack to 35 metres, it is more than three times higher than the Bass and twice as much in circumference. But although the Craig supports about 4000 pairs of guillemots and twice that number of kittiwakes, and has a gannetry larger than the Bass Rock (16,000 pairs in 1976), it fails to make the visual impact of the smaller rock, despite the verticality and scale of the crags. The precipitous nature of the Craig and the impossibility of traversing it except at safe low tide makes it an awkward place for studying its thronging bird population – less now than it was at the beginning of the century when it held an enormous puffinry, estimated at three quarters of a million in 1860. The decline seems to have set in with the arrival of some rats from a wrecked ship, and at the time of writing in 1978 there are very few puffins.

In continuation of the work done by Dr Brian Nelson on the Bass Rock, a three-year study of gannets was carried out by a research student, Sarah Wanless, who noted a fair amount of injury to birds. This was my own impression when I traversed below the sheerest bit of the cliff and found a number of adults with broken wings – no doubt the result of collisions with the rock. In 1971–4 the gannet population was estimated at 9500 pairs. Operation Seafarer figures for 1969–70 were as follows: guillemots 4200 pairs, razorbills 2300 pairs, puffins 20 pairs, kittiwakes 7700 pairs, and a surprisingly low figure for fulmars, only 32 pairs.

An ornithological party sails in to the Bass Rock to undertake the formidable task of ringing gannets.

According to J. A. Harvie-Brown there is one small island off the Sutherland coast that has more birds than the Bass Rock and Ailsa Craig put together: the island of Handa. This looks unimpressive when seen from the land because it is hardly more than a sloping grass shelf, but, like Noss in Shetland, it is all cliff on its seaward side. One's sudden arrival on that edge has a dizzying effect, not just because of the verticality, but in the swirl and rush of wings and their noise in a confined space above the plunging sea. One is on the edge of a chasm of pink Torridonian sandstone, in the throat of a plunging gully, but instead of looking out on the open ocean the way is blocked by a rock stack 100 metres high, a tenement of birds from sea to ceiling. By walking out along the edge of the two headlands which hem it in you can enjoy the verticality of three sides of the stack, on ledges packed tight with auks. Only on Dun Cruit on the Treshnish is there a comparable grandstand view, but the birds are more numerous here.

Local people will tell you about the bird fowlers from Lewis who saw a way of raiding the stack for birds; they stretched a long rope from one side of the gully to the other, to enable a man to climb the 15 metres, hand over hand, and drop on to the top of the stack like a spider from its strand. That feat was repeated by the late Dr Tom Patey in 1967, and he wrote of it: 'Additional excitement was provided by the numerous seabirds cannoning into the taut nylon and by two of the Guillemots on the Stac who started pecking the rope which had invaded their territory. The appalling 350 ft chasm underneath made this a most impressive occasion.'

The Bass Rock, 104 metres high and the core of an ancient volcano. The gannets for which it is renowned take their name, Sula bassana, *from the rock.*

In 1969–70 the Operation Seafarer census figure was 30,790 guillemot and 8370 razorbill pairs. Roy Dennis in his Handa census of 1962 made kittiwake numbers 7032 pairs and fulmars 2000 pairs. The great skua has colonized the island, and there is a fine range of other species from waders to red-throated divers and peregrine falcons.

Perhaps nowhere else in Scotland is there another bird island with such a setting as Handa: open sea stretching to the Butt of Lewis and North Rona, to the east the Cambrian quartzite peaks of the Reay Forest, changing colour with every trick of light, and up the bare coast the red rocks of Cape Wrath indented by a hundred lagoons, humanized only by the specks of the crofting town of Oldshore Beg.

From that far north coast the wintering barnacle geese stream away westwards in spring for Iceland and Greenland. Islay in the Inner Hebrides is the best island to see them when they come back again in October. In 1978 a count of the barnacle geese in March gave a figure of 21,500, which is a quarter of the world population and 65 per cent of the Greenland population. Of Greenland whitefronts I have seen 3000 in February, thought to be 15 per cent of the world population and 40 per cent of the British population. The Gruinard Flats is their main haunt, and I have a memory of the greensward covered as with a gigantic grey mat becoming mobile as we drew the car slowly to a halt to observe them. Then a few of the thousands began to yelp, and the chorus was taken up to become a great wave against a thunder of wings as the whole body took to the air. Alas, pressure from farmers against the geese has resulted in an extension of the shooting season, and foreign sportsmen are being attracted. Islay, with an airfield and only one hour's flying time from Glasgow, is no longer remote.

Islay has every kind of habitat. Agriculturally it is the Queen of the Hebrides. It has moors, lochs, marshes fresh and salt, woods, hedges, high hills and seabird cliffs. A flock of scaup duck winters there, enjoying the effluent from the distilleries. Islay has 110 species of breeding birds, and 224 species recorded in the period up to the mid-seventies. It is the Scottish stronghold of the chough, and the great cliffs of the Mull of Oa is one of the best places to see them, cavorting more erratically than any jackdaw, darting and diving with piercing voice. One day I watched one put its wings back high above me and, diving down the cliff-face like a peregrine, swoop on to a ledge. As I framed its red legs and red bill in the glass out darted another chough, snatched something from its bill and shot back into the cliff. Another time I watched one on a steep grass shelf peppered with stones; with a flick of the curved bill it would send a stone rolling, and jab at the hollow where the stone had been. No bug underneath stood a chance.

And there I must leave you, with a great deal untouched: the volcanic platforms of the magic Shiants, set in the sea between Lewis and Skye, with their massive columnar rock architecture where the last white-tailed sea eagle in the Outer Hebrides nested; Lunga of Tresnish and the stack called Dun Cruit, a pinnacle packed with birds from sea to summit, all within easy eye-range; the greensward of Canna and the mountainous Rhum, where the Manx shearwaters gather in their thousands on the sea, waiting for darkness before flying into their burrows. Experiments to re-establish the sea eagle are going on now, and in 1977 I had the thrill of seeing an immature bird hunting the great rock stacks of Mingulay at the tail end of the Outer Hebrides. It has been my good fortune to stand on the cliff edges of Barrahead and

the Butt of Lewis, to climb the highest hills in Harris and walk the marvellous machairs of South Uist whose lochans are a haunt of red phalaropes and where the greylag geese have their greatest breeding stronghold in Britain.

Razorbills on the island of Handa. The horizontally stratified cliffs rise to a height of 120 metres.

    To have tried to deal with it all would have been to write a catalogue, and this has been splendidly done in the massive *Nature Conservation Review* edited by Derek Ratcliffe. I leave you, I hope, with an impression of one of our greatest biological treasures in the twentieth century, these magical bird islands of which we know so little. Their future for the birds will depend on what we do to the ocean. Too many of the birds of which I have been writing are threatened by man the exploiter.

Chapter 8
The Hebrides

Scatter of islands

Dr Johnson was this morning for going to see as many islands as he could; not recollecting the uncertainty of the season, which might detain us in one place for many weeks. He said to me, 'I have more the spirit of adventure than you'. For my part, I was anxious to get to Mull . . . James Boswell, 1773

The high path to Dibidil crosses the Rhum Cuillin. Emerging from the seaside plantation of Kinloch, full of songbirds and deep quiet shade, it strikes steeply uphill beside the Corrie Dubh Burn with its crystal water and sandstone cisterns. In July days, meadow pipits are feeding their young on craneflies in the shaggy heather, and among the purple-flowered butterworts on the damp flushes there is the rarer pink species. The track becomes lost on the high shoulders of Hallival with its summit tower of banded ultrabasic rocks and green mantle. Does this seem strange? Such green pastures on grey wind-blasted mountain tops are unique to Rhum, where thousands of Manx shearwaters have their nesting burrows among the tumbled rocks on the cuillin tops; by day the place is peaceful with not a bird in sight but at night it is alive with flying and calling shearwaters.

The highest point on the path is the summit of Askival, also the highest of the Norse-named peaks of Rhum. Far below can be seen a tiny cottage in the profound glen of Dibidil. Ranged around, touching the clouds coming in from the ocean, are the tight cluster of peaks; once – some 50 million years ago – the core of a great volcano, they now lie gouged by the ice ages and shattered by the weather. Beyond them, scattered as far as the eye can see, are on the one hand the peaks of the Western Highlands and on the other, the Hebrides.

For the naturalist no more fitting introduction to the Hebrides can be obtained than from the high path to Dibidil. From the immediate surroundings of Rhum itself, there radiates to the horizon in every direction the grand relationship of land, sea and atmosphere. The geographical differences between the Inner and Outer Hebrides can be seen instantly: the Inner merge into the mainland landscape, while the Outer stand clear as a distant line of hills on the western horizon. Looking westward into the wind one is given a chill reminder of how much more exposed to weather and sea are the Outer Hebrides, Coll and Tiree than the Inner, and of the importance of such exposure in the moulding of the ecological character of the islands.

The rock tower at Cleadale, Eigg.

Those who have an eye for country will see in this scatter of islands all the signs of a great field of exploration. Each island has its own individuality, determined by such factors as its size, rock base, glaciation, coastline, exposure to weather and sea, and settlement and use by man. Each island is within itself a case-study which attracts the naturalist in search of simple ecosystems comparatively free from human influences, or within which man's impact can be readily assessed. Many islands, such as Rhum with its red deer and Manx shearwaters, have outstanding features, and many of these are in the western, inaccessible outliers of the Outer Hebrides. St Kilda, the Monach Islands and North Rona are all National Nature Reserves holding large breeding assemblies of seabirds and grey seals, which have importance in science and culture far beyond their tiny size.

The Hebrides are the peaks of a drowned platform which is part of the Continental Shelf, a feature which became established in the parting of the New and Old Worlds in the 'drift' of the continents and the settlement of the earth's crust. Rocks in the Hebrides are similar to those across the ocean in Labrador.

The platform is not uniform. The rocks range in age and type from Lewisian gneiss and Scourian-Laxfordian (Sutherland) granite in the Outer Hebrides, which are over 1500 million years old, to the lavas, gabbros and granites of the Inner Hebrides and St Kilda which are less than 100 million years old. The islands contain few emplacements of sedimentary rock. The ancient Torridonian sandstone laid down over 600 million years ago outcrops on a front from Raasay to Islay including South Skye, Rhum, Iona and Colonsay. Limestones are scarce and restricted to Lismore and localities in south Skye and Islay. There are, however, great depths of sedimentary rock filling trenches in the ancient substrates of the Sea of the Hebrides, the Minches and areas of the shelf to the west of the Outer Hebrides, Tiree and Colonsay. Such sedimentary rocks may also be present in the vicinity of the granitic peak of Rockall, some 368 km to the west of the Outer Hebrides. It is these sandstones and shales which form the exploration blocks for oil and gas which are now being planned and which, upfaulted in sandstones and conglomerates at Broad Bay in Lewis, are the only sedimentary rocks in the Outer Hebrides.

The different rocks contribute to the diverse landforms of the islands. Gneiss responds in a different way to ice, weather and sea than lavas do; granite shatters differently from gabbro. Take the differences in the skyline of Skye: the Red Cuillin are smooth elegant paps of granite, while the nearby Black Cuillin are serrated ridges and peaks of gabbro. Again, in the north and west of Skye the lavas are fashioned into angular, terraced landscapes with great stratified scarps, towers and tablelands which are characteristic of the Small Isles and Mull but in contrast to the undulating gneiss and granite country of Harris and the Lews.

The Inner Hebrides are rich in deep lava fields which provide fertile soil and a good living for man and wildlife. Indeed, from the high track to Dibidil a wonderful view is obtained of the remnants of lavas outpoured from the great volcanoes of Skye, Rhum and Mull; almost all of Canna, Eigg, Muck and most of Mull and the Treshnish Isles are piles of floes and ashbeds. The pillared architecture of Staffa, Ardmeanach and many localities northwards to the Shiant Islands provides fascination and wonder to all who see them. Embedded in the lavas immediately above the shore at the Burg in Mull is the 12-metre

The harsh outline of the Sgurr nam Gillein massif of gabbro in the Black Cuillins (top) contrasts with the gently rounded granite paps of the Red Cuillins (bottom).

135

trunk of MacCulloch's tree which is of outstanding interest, as are the Ardtun leaf beds in the lavas of the Ross of Mull.

Here, as elsewhere in Scotland, the ice ages have left a deep impression upon the landscape. It is thought that the Quaternary ice-sheet covered the entire Hebridean platform except for St Kilda. Ice travelling westwards from the Caledonian plateau swept round and over the islands, planing and engraving them and leaving behind moraines and fields of boulder clay. The summits of Skye, Rhum, Harris and South Uist may have been *nunataks* (peaks entirely surrounded by ice), on which some organisms may have survived the last ice age – somewhat as they do today within the polar ice fields.

An interesting feature related to the ice is the raised beach system seen best in the southern Inner Hebrides: Islay, Jura, Colonsay and Mull. There are two such beaches caused by the resilience of the earth's crust following the uplifting of the huge load of ice when, between 6000 and 10,000 years ago, it melted in two episodes; the first lifted the land some 22 metres and the second 8 metres further, resulting in beaches, cliffs, stacks and sea caves perched above present-day sea levels. Castle Duart in Mull is raised about 30 metres on top of a cliff which descends to the 8-metre wave-cut beach, and a perched sea cave at the base of the castle cliff is now about 100 metres from the sea. The 8-metre beach provides the excellent esplanade at Oban and the waterfronts at Tobermory and Port Askaig in Islay.

The mountain cores of the Hebrides have been deeply trenched by glaciers, and this is well seen on the high path to Dibidil as well as on Clisham in Harris and on the Paps of Jura. The most famous glaciated

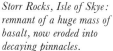

Storr Rocks, Isle of Skye: remnant of a huge mass of basalt, now eroded into decaying pinnacles.

valley in the Hebrides, however, is undoubtedly that which contains Loch Coruisk in the horseshoe range of the Black Cuillin of Skye. Many classical glacial features are present in the corries, spurs, moraines, striated pavements and the loch itself, perched in the narrow-necked basin provides a short torrential river with cascades to the sea. Within the Hebridean glens can be seen some of the features of an episode in the last ice age known as the 'Loch Lomond Readvance' – in other words, the ice sheet did not disappear in one continuous retreat. Present also on many of the slopes and broad ridges are soil-effluction terraces, frost polygons and stony fjellfields.

At the Dibidil bothy there are superb pools in which to cool off after the sweat of the high traverse from Kinloch. Hatches of northern eggars and drinker moths distract the mind from the grandeur of the scenery; they are but minute stitching in the fine embroidery of the wild and beautiful tapestry of wildlife which is stretched across the ancient islands. The moths among the *Calluna* and *Molinia* help to focus the mind on the detailed structure of the island habitats, and on the great natural processes of weather, sea, land and of biological decay and regeneration which are going on within them.

The stormy frontier

Sky lies open to the west and north to a vast extent of ocean, and is cooled in the summer by perpetual ventilation, but by the same blasts is kept warm in winter. Their weather is not pleasing. Half the year it is deluged with rain. From the autumnal to the vernal equinox, a dry day is hardly known ...

James Boswell, 1773

The weather of the Hebrides has probably changed little since Dr Johnson's tour in 1773. It is dominated by strong south-westerly winds generated by a pressure distribution in the north Atlantic and north-west Europe in which the Hebrides is often a no-man's-land between strongly differing types of air. The boundary between cold, dry, continental air and moist, warm, oceanic air often passes through the Hebrides carrying successions of depressions. These are heralded in the Hebridean skyscape by 'mare's tails' (cirrus), followed by the 'watery sun' (alto-stratus) and finally with the downpour (nimbo-stratus) and strong winds. Following the warm fronts comes the cold with its squalls; the islands are again bathed in sunshine but the wind persists with high breaking seas and gushing streams.

Sometimes the winds are from the north, bringing billowing anvil-headed clouds discharging slanting veils of rain and sleet so characteristic of the Hebridean winter seascape. Easterly winds are usually associated with anticyclonic weather – long periods of breezes with warm sunshine in summer and of clear frosty weather in winter, all the result of dry continental air from central Europe, Scandinavia and Siberia flowing north-west on the Continental Shelf. During easterly winds brilliant displays of spindrift are obtained when, before the storm beaches and against the wind, the ocean breakers have brilliant streaming veils over which fly flocks of sanderling, dunlin, turnstones and oystercatchers.

The weather from the west often overshoots the nether islands on the western rim, which remain sunny when the high islands are in the 'rain shadow'. Tiree and Coll often enjoy sunshine while Mull is hidden in rain, and the annual rainfall at Harris on the west of Rhum is about 110 mm compared with 230 at Kinloch 8 km away on the east of the island. The storm coasts are therefore drier and more windy than the sheltered areas, and this has a profound effect on the habitat, the accumulation of beach sands, effects of salt spray, formation of peat, tree growth and distribution of the fauna.

Professor Gordon Manley has given the following data for Stornoway, which lies on the sheltered side of Lewis. The mean daily temperatures range from 1.4°C (Jan/Feb) to 12.9° (July/Aug); relative humidity, 80 per cent (May) to 88 per cent (Dec/Jan); average monthly rainfall, 131 mm (Dec) to 65.6 mm (May/June); average monthly sunshine, 186 hours (May) to 25 hours (Dec); days with snow, 35 per annum; days with gales, 1 (May/Aug) to 9 (Dec). Average annual windspeeds compared with more exposed stations are Stornoway 31.8 knots; Benbecula 14.0; Tiree 15.6 knots. Maximum windspeeds occasionally exceed 100 knots, and the Butt of Lewis in January has had as many as 378 hours of gales (33 knots or above).

Though the Hebrides are bathed by waters which sweep north-westwards in the comparatively warm North Atlantic Drift and are mild and maritime, they are nevertheless very rigorous due to consistently high windspeeds. Shelter can provide great changes, as is well seen in the different character both of the intertidal zones on the storm and sheltered coasts of most islands and also of the growth of woodlands at Raasay, Stornoway, Rhum, Canna, Colonsay and Gigha. The comparatively high relative humidity reduces the transpiration rate but not significantly enough to allow growth of tall natural-type woodlands. Such are indeed rare in the Hebrides; some examples are mixed oak, ash, birch, rowan, hazel and alder in sheltered areas at Thocabaig Wood (Skye), Ardura (Mull) and Colonsay, with birch, hazel, rowan, willow, juniper and aspen at Garvellachs (Argyll), Allt Volagair and the islands of Loch Druidibeg.

Water reaches the Hebrides from two directions: some floods in from the ocean and some comes through the North Channel and around the west coast of Ireland into the southern Hebrides. The two waters meet in the Sea of the Hebrides. The stream which enters the area through the North Channel brings the pollutants which are discharged from the industries of North Wales, north-west England, Strathclyde and Northern Ireland, and this may result in unusually large concentrations of pollutants in the Sound of Jura, Firth of Lorne, Tiree Passage and the Sounds of the Small Isles, which have concentrations of breeding seabirds and commercial fisheries such as that at the Skerryvore Bank.

The Hebridean Shelf is for the most part 50–100 metres deep but extends to about 150 metres towards the edge. Sea temperatures in the northern Hebrides range from the minimum of 7.5°C in March to a maximum of about 13° in August. From November to April the temperature gradient from the surface to the sea-bed at 120 metres is negligible, but from April to November it is very steep, easing off to a fairly constant temperature below 100 metres. This temperature pattern affects the distribution of plankton and fish populations and is one of the basic features governing the distribution of fish and seabirds – and possibly also the degradation of pollutants.

The strong tidal races which characterize the narrow sounds between the islands and the entrances to many of the sea lochs can be as much as 6 knots and have a great effect on the nature of the sea-bed and its populations of plants and animals. The upwelling, swirling waters of the Gulf of Corryvreckan between Scarba and Jura provide a rich feeding ground for seabirds in search of titbits swept to the surface and spun in the whirlpools. Herring and mackerel often shoal on the surface in the approaches to these tidal races, attracting gannets, cormorants, shags, gulls, razorbills and guillemots. The food of the seabirds also includes such bottom species as codling, haddock, whiting, coalfish and lythe.

The tapestry of nature

Shell-sand, sea-shaped
In strands, sickle-shaped
Knits sea and land.
A rough but friendly hand
Puts gifts upon the winds;
Shell-sand – strewn mellower – finds
The peaty places, silent, dark
And beckons to the singing lark
To nest among white clovers.
                  J.M.B.

The tidal pool contains the secrets of the birth and being of the Hebrides. The rock basin in which the water is caught is often fashioned in some of the oldest rocks of the world; baked in the earth's

The Monach Isles National Nature Reserve, rich in flora and fauna, is noted especially for its wintering barnacle geese and the grey seals which pup there.

crust near the beginning of geological time it has been sculpted by ice and sea until it provides a smooth bowl. Sanded and washed by the storms of the ages it has the shape and texture of monumental stone. Within the pool there is the life of the sea, the blending of sunlight and living creatures in the crystal setting of pure seawater. Seaweeds, limpets, periwinkles, mussels, sea anemones and sponges are all put together by nature in seeming chaos – yet everything is fitted into place in a way which transmits strength, stability and visual beauty. The immense physical strength and biological resource of the sea is incalculable, but within the tiny pool the great generative principles of the sea are in full display. The pool is a battery in which the sun's energy becomes trapped and converted by plants and animals, the hard skeletons of which fall into the grinding mill of the surf and are cast up on the shore. What happens in the pool happens throughout the great ocean itself, which continuously offers up its huge load of animal and plant debris. As if by magic the substance which is invisible is suddenly there; the tissues of marine creatures have extracted the chemicals from solution in the sea, and the destiny of their small bodies is the enrichment of both sea and soil. Vast populations of marine life in the fertile seas to the south-west of the Hebrides and upon the shores have engendered enormous drifts of creamy white shell-sand. These form the great *traighs* of Tiree, Barra, the Uists, Benbecula and Harris, and the countless small, idyllic beaches throughout the isles,

The Isle of Eigg, on which the Scottish Wildlife Trust has recently established a new nature reserve. The picture shows Dalmisdale, landing point for the island, with the rock fang of the Scuir rising in the distance.

wave-rippled as with finger prints at low tide. The sand on most Hebridean beaches usually has over 80 per cent carbonate content.

The sublittoral zone off-shore has a forest of kelps which possesses a rich fauna of tube worms, hydrozoa, polyzoa, sponges, sea-squirts and the large sea urchin. Seaweeds of the genus *Laminaria* washed up after winter storms provide 'the tangle' which is collected and dried by crofters for the alginate industry. The exposed beaches have a poor fauna often restricted to a single species of isopod; sheltered beaches have varied populations of bivalves and worms.

Plant communities of the foredunes take hold of the drifting sand, and the fixing process begins. Above high-water mark there are large areas of free-blowing sand, as can be seen in the great banks at Luskentyre in Harris and Eoligarry in Barra. Landward, the walk from the shore into the dunes is one from desert to sea-meadows rich with herbs, through ranges of sand hills which become gradually clothed with an ever-thickening community of plants in which marram grass plays a dominant part in company with sand couch-grass, sea rocket, sea sandwort, ragwort, curled dock, orache and bird's-foot trefoil. It is, however, the deep-rooting marram grass which is the key to dune formation; without it the other plants would find it very difficult to obtain a hold.

Within the dune system proper the marram grass grows in profusion, and the community thickens with red fescue grass, meadow grass, lady's bedstraw, wild white clover and ribwort. The increasing frequencies of clover and trefoil provide the necessary nitrogen fixation for the development of skeletal soils. Further inland from the dunes these are transformed by the denser plant and animal communities into a sandy loam, enriched also by grazing stocks.

On the back slope of the dunes the marram grass gradually disappears. Beyond, the machair has no marram, and in June it is a riot of colour with buttercups, daisies, eyebright, common storksbill, dove's foot and bloody cranesbills, primrose, sea pansy, buckthorn and sea plantains. Sometimes the machairs have dense floral mosaics arising from recolonized cultivated land – great ragged blankets of trefoil, clover or cranesbill can be found in full bloom. With the sand fixed and the loam developed, there is a secure basis for agriculture; from the fertile sea to the poor peaty land there is passed on the wind a gift of soil-enriching chemicals.

The machair is an exhilarating place: it provides a marvellous sense of freedom, its flowery carpet giving a spring to one's step, heightened in summer by the songs of skylarks, lapwings, ringed plovers and oystercatchers and in winter by the plaintive call of golden plover and the wild music of whooper swans from nearby lochs. The scene is made yet more colourful by the butterflies – common blue, small tortoiseshell, meadow brown – and the bumble bees. On this back pasture the cross-bred cattle produce their calves which are fattened for export to the mainland. In most parts, however, the machair has been cultivated. Often the cultivation is very patchy, but in South Uist the 'run rig' system of cultivation provides wide continuous stretches of cereals in summer and stubble grazing in winter. Large dung beetles dig under the cow-pats, and snails abound.

The machair is a paradise for rabbits – indeed, the rabbit has been responsible for the destruction of many machairs and of their return to dune conditions. Rabbit burrows can provide a grip for the wind, and often a throat is developed in the sand and great acreages of rabbit-infested dunes and machairs are overblown by sand in winter gales. Islands such as Tiree and Bernera (Harris) have miraculously escaped rabbits, and these islands have distinctly more stable, fertile and floristically richer machair and dune systems than most other islands. Most machairs possess the fieldmouse and the pygmy shrew, and fall within the hunting range of the kestrel, peregrine, buzzard, hen harrier and golden eagle, which breed on nearby moorlands or sea cliffs.

Between the machair and the 'black ground' of inland and eastern areas there is a chain of lochs. These have the machair on one side and on the other the fertilized 'in-bye' ground of crofts, usually enclosed and cultivated. These lochs are, in their own way, like the machair: very fertile with excellent stocks of brown trout and sea trout, and at all seasons fine stocks of wildfowl, particularly mallard, teal, wigeon, shoveler, pochard, tufted duck and coot. In South Uist the lochs provide a nursery for the largest native population of greylag geese, and also in these areas between the machair and the moorland there nest dunlin, redshank, snipe, and much more rarely the red-necked phalarope.

So our walk continues across the island. We are now through the machair lochs and among the croft houses built on the swelling landscape beyond the sandy fringe. Both in the machair and the in-bye ground there are fine beds of iris, stands of ragged robin, and several types of orchid. The corncrake and lapwing still flourish in the absence of the combine-harvester, and the corn bunting is a dominant songbird. The green-veined white butterfly is common in this area.

The road from Lochboisdale to Lochmaddy following the west coast all the way runs roughly between the 'light' and the 'dark' ground. Across the road to the east you are out of the in-bye of the crofts and on to the peat moorland, with many dark sour lochs possessing low scrub-covered islands and characterized by ling, the blue moor grass, deer's hare grass, bog cotton, mat grass, black bog rush, sedges and mosses. Also within this area is to be found the tormentil and the little insectivorous sundew – an exceedingly shy and delicate flower which emerges only on the brightest and calmest days, and shares the same habitat with the blue milkwort, the delicate pink lousewort, and the bog asphodel with its golden florets standing proud on the bare peaty ground. Among the scraggy heather and moor grass of the dark ground there are meadow pipits, skylarks, twites, stonechats and wheatears, and many attractive insects including the dark green fritillary, small pearl-bordered fritillary, peacock, marsh fritillary, emperor moth, garden tiger, magpie moth, transparent burnet and the ghost swift.

Many hundreds of hectares of moorland are ribbed by the 'lazy-beds' (*feannagan*) of a vanished race, but today large areas have been improved by fertilization with shell-sand at about 25 tonnes per hectare with a compound fertilizer and a mixture of clover and grass seed. Man is now transporting the chemical enrichment from the sea to ameliorate areas of barren moorland which are out of reach of windblown sand, thus creating new permanent pastures.

The high heaths are generally poor in species, but they are richer on the gabbro, ultrabasic and lava hills of Rhum, Skye and Mull than on the quartzites of Jura or the gneiss and granite of the Outer Hebrides. In the former the moss-grass heaths have thrift, moss campion, purple saxifrage, mountain avens, mossy cyphel, alpine

Left : An osprey flies in with a fish (top) and (bottom) devours it on a fence post.

Right : A female golden eagle feeds her already large chick.
Below : A damselfly is caught in the sticky embrace of the sundew.

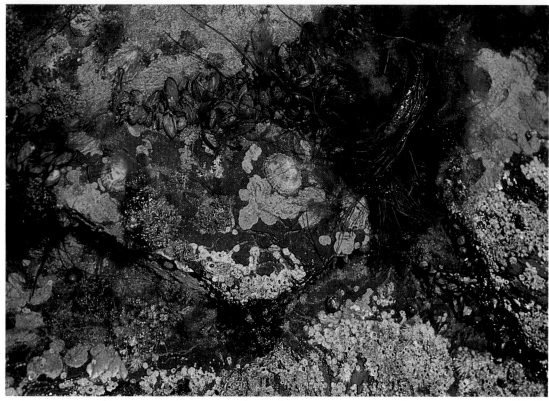

meadow rue, northern rock cress, alpine lady's mantle, least willow and alpine club moss.

The walk across the islands from west to east finishes on the edge of the weedy inlets from which, in the Outer Hebrides, are gathered harvests of 'wrack' as fertilizer for potatoes locally and for export to the alginate industry. Dense growths of fucoids grow in very clear zones according to length of immersion and exposure to both air and surf: prominent are bladder wrack, flat wrack and knotted wrack in broad bands on the mid-shore.

At low tide the laminarian forest in the deeper water becomes exposed, and on the more exposed headlands and in caves the rocks become encrusted with pink *Lithothamnion* and, in pools, *Corallina*. A distinct barnacle line is developed on the surf zone. It is from these sheltered shores that the crofters gather winkles and offshore fish for the market. This is the habitat favoured by the common seal, the otter, and the red-throated and black-throated divers.

Islands for science

The Land, and the Sea that encompasses it, produce many things useful and curious in their kind, several of which have not hitherto been mentioned by the Learned. This may afford the Theorist Subject of Contemplation, since every Plant of the Field, every Fibre of each Plant, and each Particle of the smallest Insect carries with it the Impress of its Maker and if rightly considered may read us Lecture of Divinity and Morals . . . Martin Martin, 1703

Dean Munro provides the first account of the Hebrides in 1549, but Martin's *Description* of 1703 provides the basis for historical record. In the eighteenth and nineteenth centuries individual travellers left accounts which contained glimpses of natural history and natural resources: Pennant's *Voyage* in 1774; the *Old Statistical Account* in the 1790s; MacCulloch's *Description* in 1824; Macgillivray's *Account* in 1830; the *New Statistical Account* in 1845; Harvie-Brown and Buckley's *Faunas* in 1888 and 1892. The first scientific work was MacCulloch's *Geology* in 1819. Little was done thereafter until the Darwinian period at the end of last century, when an abiding and growing interest in the natural history of the Hebrides began often with patronage of landowners like Lord Dunmore, Sir John Ord, Lady Gordon Cathcart and Lady Matheson of the Lews. Today, a century later, it is still extended by Lord Granville in North Uist, Colonel David Greig and his partners in South Uist and Benbecula, and others.

The first editions of the one-inch and six-inch to the mile Ordnance Survey maps in the 1880s were followed by the *Bathymetrical Survey of Freshwater Lochs in Scotland* by Sir John Murray and Lawrence Pullar in 1910, improved on in the brackish reaches by Edith Nicol in 1936. The 1930s saw the beginning of the scientific expedition era. The Oxford and Cambridge expedition to the newly evacuated St Kilda in 1931 provided a set of key scientific papers. There followed expeditions from Edinburgh University to Barra in 1935, Glasgow University to Canna in 1936, the Garvellachs in 1948, St Kilda in 1952 and 1956, and North Rona in 1958. In the past twenty years there have been many more to Rhum, the Monach Islands, the Shiants and Mingulay, with published results.

Top: A sea urchin.
Bottom: A rock pool with mussels, limpets and barnacles above the water level.

143

In the 1930s Fraser Darling (later Sir Frank) brought a new approach to natural history, making it a way of island life. He was touched with a sense of challenge, both intellectual and physical, and he saw in small remote islands a clear expression of ecological interdependence and basic life-processes. He had an unswerving conviction that man and animal were parts of the same system, and that man's morals and politics were ecologically as important as rocks and rainfall in fashioning the natural environment. He expounded this view in the *West Highland Survey* in 1955.

The Hebrides lie on the extreme edge of the great Eurasian continent. Their position on the edge of the world, as it were, makes them of outstanding interest to science; they contain the extreme western representatives of the Palaearctic flora and fauna which change genetically through such great ranges of latitude, longitude and altitude. By the same token, they are on the edge of the Atlantic Ocean, the pasturage of countless seabirds which, though ranging far throughout the year, come to breed in the Hebrides. That is one of the reasons why in the Hebrides there are six National Nature Reserves (NNRs), one RSPB Reserve, one SWT Reserve, 98 Sites of Special Scientific Interest (SSSI), two Biosphere Reserves of UNESCO and one 'Ramsar' wetland of IWRB (Ramsar is a conference centre in Iran which gave its name to an international agreement).

The NNRs are at Rhum, St Kilda, North Rona, Monach Islands, Thocabaig Wood in Skye and Loch Druidibeg in South Uist (the Ramsar site). The RSPB Reserve is at Balranald, North Uist, and the SWT Reserve is on Eigg. Important among the SSSI are the tidal flats and lochs at Gruinart, Islay and Loch an Duin, North Uist; the saltings at Tong and Gress, Lewis; shores and dunes at Luskentyre, Harris and Kilchomen, Islay; machair at Balevullin, Tiree and Eoligarry, Barra; heaths and bogs near North Tolsta, Lewis; freshwater lochs at Loch Hallan, South Uist, Lochs nam Feithean and Scadavay, North Uist; mountain habitats in North Harris; geological sites at the Gribun, Mull (Triassic, Rhaetic, Cretaceous) and many others westward to Rockall (Rockallite). Chief among the physiographical sites are Fingal's Cave on Staffa, The Storr and Quirang north of Portree, and the raised beaches at Kiloran, Colonsay. SSSI devoted to a single species are now restricted to the grey seal breeding islands of Haskeir, Shillay, Coppay and Gasker which are additional to seal sites on the North Rona, Monach Islands and St Kilda NNRs. Many SSSI have 'compound' interest – for example, the entire islands of Colonsay, Coll, Canna, Mingulay and Berneray (Barra), Shiant and Treshnish Islands.

Since the early 1950s the Nature Conservancy and others have done research on the NNRs and SSSI. Many of the projects are long term, with baseline studies already completed; NNR inventories of plants and animals, for example, have been done with studies on ecological processes including structure and dynamics of plant and animal populations.

In Rhum a long-term study is in progress on red deer. Between 1959 and 1969 the structure and response of the population to a one-sixth cull, a 12-month study of seasonal nutritional requirements, and physiological response in stags and hinds was investigated by the Nature Conservancy. Detailed studies of breeding biology of stags and hinds are still in progress under Dr Tim Clutton-Brock of Cambridge University.

The late Sir Frank Fraser Darling, pioneer of nature conservation. Sir Frank died soon after this book was published.

Dr Roland Randall in 1976 studied the structure and development of the sand dune–machair system in the Monach Islands NNR. His work is coupled with that of Dr Bill Ritchie, who has described the generation and decay of these coastal systems. Dr Randall examined 54 quadrats of 1 square metre in the machair of the Monach Islands and recorded 105 species of plant, of which 71 occurred in less than 10 per cent and the following 15 in more than 50 per cent of the quadrats: daisy, red fescue, ribwort, yarrow, sand sedge, eyebright, lady's bedstraw, buttercup, bird's-foot trefoil, self-heal, white clover, ragwort, cathartic flax, moss and lichen. This is a herb-rich grassland with only one grass (red fescue) in the first 15 species.

St Kilda possesses much that is of scientific interest. The Soay sheep are the most primitive sheep in Europe, closely resembling the original wild species still found in the mountainous recesses of Sardinia, Cyprus and Central Asia, and bearing some resemblance to the domesticated sheep of the neolithic farmers in Britain some 5000 years ago. The population on Hirta, the main island, was established by a transplant of 107 sheep from the Isle of Soay when the St Kildans left the islands in 1930. Since then the population has grown within the confines of Hirta's 607 hectares, with its exposed climate and maritime heaths and grasslands. Apart from ravens, hooded crows and greater black-backed gulls taking lambs, there are no predators. Professor Peter Jewell, myself and others have studied the mechanism of natural control of the population, and of the underlying factors of nutrition, reproduction, social organization and parasitism.

Soay ewe and lamb. This unique and primitive breed, resembling the wild species still found in remote parts of Europe and Asia, remains pure to this day.

The population has fluctuated between 600 and 1800 during the years 1952–77, but may still be increasing to a steady state in relationship to its resources of pasture and shelter. In 1960, 1964 and 1967 the population was subject to crashes caused by malnutrition and the draw-down by heavy intestinal parasite burdens. Rams are more severely hit by this than ewes, due to the tendency of rams to cease feeding during the rut, thereby failing to achieve the necessary intake of food to see them successfully through the winter. In times of high numbers, a late spring followed by a cold wet summer and a hard winter will cause high mortality in both sexes, with pregnant ewes at great risk. Lambs are born in April; the adults shed their fleeces in June and by August they have made good much of their 50 per cent loss in body weight of the winter.

The North Rona NNR has been a focus of research on the grey seal, started by Fraser Darling in 1938, continued by the author and others in 1959–69 and later by the Seals Research Division of NERC. The population of the breeding assembly at North Rona has probably fluctuated between 1750 to 2700 pups annually in the period 1961–76. In sharp contrast, however, the assembly at the Monach Islands NNR has steadily increased from 50 pups annually to 2575 in 1976, a 51.5-fold increase.

The grey seal congregates at long-established breeding sites in the Hebrides in September and October. Bulls arrive first and take up territories on the islands, into which cows come to deliver their white pups. The lactation period lasts about 17 days, during which the pup increases in weight from about 14 kg to 40 kg and loses its white coat. Soon afterwards the dam mates and departs to sea, leaving the pup to fend for itself. Pup mortality is high: 20 per cent die before leaving the islands, and about 80 per cent perish long before reaching breeding age – 3 or 4 years for females and 5 or 6 years for males. The status of the grey seal given by its pup production in 1976 is as follows: Monach, 2575; North Rona, 2500; Gasker, 2340; Shillay, 690; Coppay, 515; Haskeir, 385; Causamul, 270; Treshnish, 246; Oronsay, 140; Gunna, 79; Deasker, 75; Nave Island, 13.

The common seal haunts sheltered sea lochs, and breeds in June in tidal rocks in the Sounds of Gigha, Jura, Islay, Mull, Barra and Harris, and Lochs Linnhe, Scridain, na Keal and Sunart. Both species now have close seasons and are hunted only by licence.

The machair lochs lying close to the sea are affected by salt spray; they are rich in crustacea and molluscs and also have many brackish species such as *Neomysis integer*, *Gammarus duebeni*, *Diaptonus wierzejskii* and *Potamopyrgus jenkensi*. *P. jenkensi* penetrates into the mesotrophic lochs and *G. duebeni* is the only shrimp penetrating to the oligotrophic, replacing *G. pulex* and *G. lacustris*. No sponges were found in the machair lochs, nor any triclads or planarians in any of the lochs. The fish found are salmon, sea-brown trout, eel, common goby, black goby, three-spined stickleback, ten-spined stickleback and flounder.

Many other important scientific studies have been done in the last 25 years. These include the invertebrate survey of the Outer Hebrides by A. R. Waterston; the flora of the Outer Hebrides by Miss M. S. Campbell and the ornithology by her late brother Dr J. W. Campbell, W. A. J. Cunningham and others; the entomological study of Rhum by Peter Wormell and others; the *Lepidoptera Cannae* by Dr John L. Campbell; the status of the huge wintering populations of barnacle, white-fronted and greylag geese on Islay by the Wildfowl

Trust; and at St Kilda, North Rona, Sula Sgeir and Rhum attempts to measure the size of the breeding assemblies of seabirds particularly gannets, puffins and shearwaters. The Tertiary Volcanic centres in Rhum, Skye, Mull and St Kilda continue to attract geologists in quest of finer details of already well-documented rocks. The establishment of the Scottish Marine Biological Association at Dunstaffnage has resulted in a much increased research effort on Hebridean shores and seas.

In 1948 the late James Fisher said of research in the Hebrides: '... everybody must hope that soon a new synthesis will be made, and new targets set by a united band of scientists on the threshold of new discoveries'. His hopes are now being realized.

Strongholds of wildlife

> *... we shall try to perpetuate forest, moor, sand dunes, salt marsh, Hebridean islands and the denizens and vegetation of all these places but the national ethos has changed towards a greater respect for the natural world around us and a sense of our trusteeship ...*
>
> Sir Frank Fraser Darling, 1964

The Hebrides still remain the stormy frontier, yet with modern travel and social services – not to mention the pervasive effects of tourism, recreational pursuits and pollution of air and sea – the frontier is changing. Remote outliers such as St Kilda, North Rona and Sula Sgeir, not long ago the *ultima Thule* of only the most determined and

Grey seal pup. The grey (or Atlantic) seal has increased rapidly since it began to colonize islands deserted by man.

enterprising, can now be reached by plane and helicopter in two hours from Glasgow. Gone is the notion of pure air and sea, when the load of pollutants from the industrial mainland – carried by drift from the Irish Sea through the North Channel to the Inner Hebrides – is measured, or when the Hebridean sunsets are enriched by pollutants in the atmosphere. The dunes and machairs, though providing favourable settings for caravans, are most fragile, brought already to the verge of collapse by over-intensive agriculture and rabbit damage.

Despite the changes of modernity, however, the Hebrides is still a wildlife area of world importance and the stronghold of 'oceanic' species and communities. Though certain dangers exist to predatory birds from marine pollution, the present populations of golden eagles, peregrines, kestrels, buzzards, hen harriers and short-eared and long-eared owls are encouraging at a time when in other parts of Britain and Europe such species are in decline. The sea-eagle bred in the Hebrides until about the end of the last century, when persecution is thought to have exterminated it there; its last British breeding record is from Shetland in 1912. John Harvie Brown saw a pair at a breeding site on the Shiant Islands in 1887. Today it breeds in such numbers in Norway that eaglets have been provided for a reintroduction project by the Nature Conservancy Council on Rhum. The young eagles are reared until they are fully fledged, and then released in favourable weather when they are about one year old. It is hoped to continue the project as long as young Scandinavian birds (which would otherwise probably by shot in Norway or come from captive breeding projects) are available, with a view to re-establishing the sea-eagle as a breeding species in Britain.

Again, the grey seal has increased greatly in the Hebrides during the past century due, it is thought, to many remote islands such as North Rona, St Kilda and Monach becoming annexed by seals following the departure of the human community, as well as to a decline in demand for seal oil, meat and skins and to protective laws. Now indeed efforts are being made by the Department of Agriculture and Fisheries for Scotland to reduce numbers.

The status of the otter is unknown, but in the Hebrides there is a marine species which visits the freshwater systems of the islands. Holts are usually placed on inaccessible and seldom-visited islets. The otter has always been hunted and shot by local gamekeepers and is capable of sustaining such losses. Recently, however, hunters from outside have been trapping them alive, and there is a distinct danger that in the Hebrides, which is possibly the last stronghold of the otter in Britain, the species could become extinct within this century unless the protective law is applied in Scotland.

The Hebrides, in particular St Kilda, Mingulay and Berneray (Barra), Flannan Islands, North Rona and Sula Sgeir, Shiant Islands, Rhum and the Treshnish Islands, are a stronghold of seabirds. St Kilda boasts 17 species: fulmar, Leach's petrel, storm petrel, Manx shearwater, gannet, shag, eider, red-necked phalarope, great skua, greater black-backed gull, lesser black-backed gull, herring gull, kittiwake, razorbill, guillemot, black guillemot and puffin. There are thought to be the following pairs of main species at St Kilda: puffin, over 100,000; gannet, 59,000; fulmar, 40,000; guillemot, 20,000; kittiwake, 11,000.

These large assemblies of seabirds are agencies for the concentrations of pollutants in the sea. Traces of heavy metals and polychlorinated biphenyls (PCBs) picked up from planktonic or fish food become concentrated in the tissue of the seabirds. Such substances become even more concentrated in seabird predators such as coastal peregrines and golden eagles; the eagles on Rhum, for example, feed on shearwaters and gulls and have low breeding success. The situation requires careful monitoring, and research is already under way at St Kilda and elsewhere on the concentrations of pollutants in puffins and other species. The large seabird stations could be essential monitoring points of the cleanliness of the sea.

The prospect of isles as far as the eye could see must have awed and challenged Mesolithic man when he first saw the Hebrides – a feeling still shared, almost 6000 years later, by visitors today, not only the first time but again and again. For here the roots of Gaelic culture go down with those of the plants into the shellsand and peat, and the tenacity of the people to their islands may be likened to the holdfasts of seaweeds and shellfish on their stormy shores. Within the Hebridean mind there is an awareness of the strength of nature: man and wildlife share in the ritual of survival on what has been called 'the edge of the world'.

Rhum ponies at Kilmory, Isle of Rhum. They are thought to be of Arab sire and West Highland mare lineage, the sires having escaped from a galleon of the Spanish Armada, wrecked off the coast.

Chapter 9
Scottish Mammals

Scotland has lost many mammal species over the ages. The last to go was the polecat, although there is some doubt about this as there are today many feral polecat–ferrets that closely resemble the ancestral type, not to mention some full-blooded polecats that have been released in many parts of the country.

The brown bear disappeared in the ninth or tenth century, probably exterminated by man. The reindeer was likewise exterminated in about the twelfth century, but it has since been reintroduced and can be seen today in the Cairngorms.

The elk – the deer of shambling gait known to the Romans – was still around when Wallace marched to Stirling, and may have lasted until Bannockburn in the early fourteenth century. The beaver probably lasted into the sixteenth century. The wild boar seems to have disappeared about the same time as James VI: the one to extinction, the other to London. The wolf outlasted them all, remaining until 1743, when the last one (which might have been a wolfdog) was killed on the Findhorn.

In the nineteenth and twentieth centuries there were massive killings of wildcats, foxes, martens, polecats, otters, badgers, stoats and weasels. Yet, as we shall see, Scotland today has a mammal fauna that can compare with anywhere in Europe.

Wildcat
The popular image of the Scottish wildcat is of a bristling, snarling, flat-eared demon, with all its weaponry of teeth and claws set for war. This is a myth, often perpetuated by artists and photographers portraying as the norm a cat at bay, cornered, caged, or so terrified that it has to unleash its total armoury in self-defence. Of course, wildcats do bristle and snarl and flatten their ears and hiss explosively, but most of the time they pad around like any other cat, with their ears unglued from their skulls and their teeth locked away.

The contrived portrait becomes living truth when you see a big cat bayed on a crag by terriers or a mountain fox. Then you will see explosive cattiness, with moon eyes slitted, back arched, tail bottle-brushed, and teeth bared to the gums. And to hear the wild pibroch of him – scream, sob and skelloch – is to know the spirit of the wild places, which he shares with the eagle and the mountain fox, the raven and the red deer.

There are many cats running wild in many parts of Scotland, but they are deserters from the fireside of man, which are not, and can

A red deer stag bellows defiance at a rival.

never become, wildcats however long they may lead the free life. The true wildcat is a species, not a way of life.

The wildcat, like the pine marten, took heavy punishment from the game ascendancy in the nineteenth and twentieth centuries, and by the time of the First World War it was not to be seen south of the Great Glen. Since the Second World War it has been spreading, and is now found well south of the Great Glen: it is common in Banff, Angus, Moray, Nairn, Argyll, Perth and west Aberdeen.

The wildcat inhabits forests and rocky hillsides up to 450 metres. It dens in rock cairns, under tree roots, sometimes even in the disused eyrie of a golden eagle. The kittens, usually four, are born in May, and are self-supporting at the age of five months. Second litters are not unusual. The male wildcat holds a territory which he defends against other males, but his hunting range extends far beyond that area.

From time to time there is interbreeding between wild and domestic cats, and known records indicate that this is usually wild tom to domestic female. It has long been said that the wildcat is untamable, but although this is true of adults or well-grown young it does not apply to hand-reared kittens taken before their eyes have opened, or shortly afterwards.

Wildcats prey mainly on small animals, particularly voles and woodmice, but they also kill rabbits and mountain hares, especially leverets. From mouse to hare is the normal range of prey, but a big wildcat can kill roe deer fawns, and sometimes even does. Wildcat kittens, in turn, are sometimes taken by the golden eagle and the mountain fox, and there is strong presumptive evidence that mountain badgers occasionally take them too.

Badger

Scotland's native members of the weasel family (mustelids) are the weasel and stoat, pine marten and polecat, otter and badger. Now there is also the American mink – naturalized, breeding wild, and clearly here to stay.

The badger is the least weasel-like of the clan. More bear-like, he is powerful, squat, hand-footed and sheathed in muscle: a shambler and a plodder, with almost a bear's gait. But he can move fast when he has to, and when he does so he is all weasel. Although shy and retiring, dedicated to minding his own business, he can nevertheless become a terrible fighting machine when roused to action; then he can cut a terrier to pieces, kill a fox, or cripple a collie.

Badgers like rolling, hillocky country, in or out of agricultural areas, and shun marshes, bogs and low-lying ground liable to flooding. Wooded knolls, copses, woods on hillsides, rabbit warrens and coastal cliffs are all suitable habitats, and they are found in mountain cairns up to and even over 450 metres. Mountain badgers, when not in burrows or cairns, sometimes den out among rocks or stands of bracken.

An adult badger will weigh up to 16 kg, but animals over 18 kg are not uncommon. Individuals go much heavier even than that, but weight varies according to the season and the beasts are much heavier at the beginning of winter than in the spring; boars are heavier than sows. There is one moult a year, lasting most of the summer.

In Scotland badger cubs are born mostly in March, but births occur in April and even May. The size of the litter varies between one and four. The sow mates again soon after the birth of her cubs, and most matings take place between March and May. But breeding in

A wildcat kitten (top), and an adult hunting (bottom).

this species is more complicated than that; matings may take place any time up to October, and due to the phenomenon of delayed implantation there is no way of knowing which is the successful one. Implantation of the fertile egg is delayed in the case of the badger until December/January, but it has to be earlier or later than that for earlier or later born cubs, because the time between implantation and birth has to be constant within a small margin.

Cubs stay below ground for about 8 weeks, and they are weaned after 12 weeks, when the sow regurgitates food for them, as vixens do for their cubs. Soon after that the cubs forage for themselves. They may leave the parents in autumn and find new quarters, or remain in the set through the winter.

Although a carnivore, the badger is really omnivorous. Animal food includes rabbits, leverets, voles, mice, hedgehogs, beetles, wasp grubs, earthworms, snails, frogs and newts. Few badgers kill poultry, and lamb-killing is exceptional. Earthworms are a main part of the diet and badgers will gorge on them whenever possible, but their actual intake must vary with the nature of the terrain. Vegetable food includes pig nuts, bulbs and other underground storage organs, acorns, beech mast, blackberries, blaeberries, hips and windfall fruits.

Badgers are distributed widely on the Scottish mainland but are absent from all the islands. They are more thinly spread in the Highlands than in the south and west.

Attitudes to the badger vary from neutrality or welcome to outright hostility. Sheep farmers and poultrymen are suspicious of them, with little solid reason. Foresters welcome them because they prey on rodents and wasp grubs. On balance it would be fair to say that the badger is not economically important one way or the other.

Otter

The otter is the water weasel, yet in many ways it resembles a seal. It has the seal's streamlining, the powerful nose and ear muscles that snap shut before a dive, and the heavy bush of sensitive whiskers set in a swollen upper lip. It is supremely adapted for its dual role of land and water hunter.

The coat of the otter is darker in winter than in summer. The guard hairs are long, strong and sheened; the underfur has the quality of eider down. In water the beast is insulated against the cold by air bubbles trapped under the waterproof layer of outer fur. Out of the water this quills up, giving him a spikey appearance until he shakes himself dry.

There has been a decline in otter numbers in recent years, as notable over much of mainland Scotland as most of England. Its strongholds today are in the west, north-west and the islands – Orkney, Shetland and the Inner and Outer Hebrides – and at the head of the Great Glen, round the Cromarty and Moray Firths. Elsewhere it is thinly spread, and from many former haunts it is absent altogether.

The otter shuns polluted rivers and heavily built-up or industrialized areas: where pollution invades the otter retreats. But pollution is not the main reason for the general decline in numbers. There is a dangerous complacency in Scotland about the otter's status in the West Highlands and Islands, where it is thought to be safe and thriving, but with a shy, elusive beast like the otter, which is mainly nocturnal, assumptions about population density and stability can be very wide of the mark.

Otters are found from the headwaters of rivers down to the sea, and on lochs on mountain and moorland. They live by rocky shores and in sea caves. Clean water, salt or fresh, is the otter's world, and its holt is rarely far from either.

There is no peak breeding season, and cubs, usually two or three, may be born in any month. The breeding holt is usually away from the main stream, and as often as not has an entrance under water; others are screened by washed-out tree roots or other vegetation. Sea caves and rock holes are used by the marine otters of the islands. One litter a year is the general rule.

Evidence from Wester Ross and the Western Isles suggests that otters hold a stretch of about 8 kilometres along the best river and shore habitats. If they really hold territories, as stoats and weasels do, the so-called wandering otters could be mainly dispersing juveniles, or nomadic adults in search of a territory of their own. But this is speculation.

Whatever the explanation, otters do wander, travelling down to the sea, from sea to headwater, and from one watershed to another. They can be tracked in snow over the contours, up to 370 metres; they will cross wide moorlands and other open country by way of lochs, ponds and streams. They will desert a stretch of river for a while, for no obvious reasons, and fail to settle in a habitat that appears to have everything they require. In fact the one sure thing known about the otter is that very little is known.

Anglers are divided in their opinions about otters, some

The favourite food of the badger is earthworms, but it is omnivorous and will eat anything from rabbits to bluebell bulbs.

considering them a menace on a salmon river, others looking upon them as an asset in broad terms. The belief that they are a menace to game fish is not supported by the facts, and if game fish become scarce it will not be because of predation by otters. The other charge against the otter is wastefulness – that it takes a bite out of the shoulder of a big fish and leaves the rest. Like other mustelids the otter can be choosey when food is abundant, but it will eat every scrap when it is scarce. Sporting man is all too ready to assume that a competing predator is as wasteful as he. In the life-cycle of the salmon the otter is probably the least significant predator.

Its range of prey is wide: eels, coarse fish, trout, salmon, crayfish, water birds, rats, water voles, field voles, frogs and newts. On rocky coasts it preys on crabs, other crustaceans, mussels, and probably saithe, lythe and other rock fish. But it is a versatile hunter and, when pressed, will take gulls and their eggs, poultry, ducks, rabbits, leverets and even carrion.

The part played by the dog otter in the life of the family is always under debate. What seems clear is that he provides food for the bitch when she is lying up with cubs. There is also plenty of evidence to indicate that at least some dog otters stay with the family for some time after the cubs are in the water. In Mull such parties are regularly observed.

Stoat

The stoat is likely to be seen anywhere on the Scottish mainland and on the islands of Mull, Jura, Islay and Skye. It has been introduced to the mainland of Shetland. It is not found in the Outer Isles, nor on most of the smaller islands. The stoats of Islay and Jura are treated as a separate race.

Woodland, young plantations with plenty of undergrowth, rabbit warrens, agricultural land and sand dunes are typical habitats, but stoats range through the contours – from sea-level to the tops of mountains. In winter they may be seen on the same ground as the ptarmigan. Even on treeless deer forests they can find ample cover, for they are small enough to hide easily in heather, scree and rocks.

The summer coat of the stoat is brown above and white below, with a clean line of demarcation. The change to complete white in winter is common in Scotland, and the rule in the Highlands. There are two moults a year: brown to white in winter, and white to brown in spring. The change from brown to white may take place in three days but usually takes much longer – in fact it may not be completed, so one can find white and brown-and-white animals on the same ground at the same time.

Dog stoats hold a territory of up to 20 hectares although ground hunted by the bitch is usually much smaller. The sexes live amicably together during the breeding season, when the male helps to feed the kits; outside this season there is no hostility although the pair do not share a den. The mating period is July/August, but kits are not born until the following April/May, implantation of fertile eggs being delayed until March. Young females become fertile at three months, but young males take longer to reach maturity, despite being as big as their mothers at the age of eight weeks.

Before myxomatosis the stoat preyed largely on rabbits, but in fact its prey range is wide. Young forestry plantations, with plenty of grass and therefore plenty of voles, provide an ideal habitat for stoats, and in such a place they will kill mainly voles. They need almost a quarter of their own body weight in food every day, which means that dog stoats require about three voles a day and bitches two.

The stoat climbs well and swims well, and is playful at any age. Both young and adults play, singly or in a party.

Stoat and weasel can occupy the same ground at the same time, with the weasel's territory within that of the stoat. There is no evidence that the larger animal excludes the smaller, or that there is direct competition on vole ground when vole numbers are high.

Man is probably the main predator on the stoat, since it has been labelled 'vermin'. Dogs and cats also kill stoats, but do not eat them; foxes kill them at different times, but eat them only occasionally. Small stoats are sometimes taken by buzzards, owls and kestrels, but apart from man, foxes and terriers probably account for most of the killings.

Weasel

The weasel is found over most of mainland Scotland, but is absent from all the islands except Skye and Raasay. It is found on much the same ground as the stoat, but is not so common on mountains or high moorland. In recent years it has become much scarcer in many parts, which could be due to a variety of causes, including variable food supply, destruction of habitat, changing agricultural practices, perhaps even toxic chemicals used on farmlands and in gardens.

Dog weasels are bigger than bitches, often strikingly so. Males weigh up to 200 grammes (which puts them in the weight bracket of a female stoat), females up to 85 grammes. But there are many exceptions to this weight range; one dog weasel was weighed at just over 255 grammes. Scottish weasels consistently weigh heavier, on average, than English ones.

Like the stoat, the weasel is territorial. The male holds a territory of 1–4 hectares, and defends it against neighbouring males. Territorial chases are often to be seen, with the pursuing animal breaking off at a limit point and then returning to his starting point. Females hunt within the male's territory, or adjoining it. The sexes only come together during the period of mating.

Female weasels probably breed twice in most years, although some will have only a single litter, while a few, in a good year, will breed three times. One captive female had three litters of 7, 8 and 8, and reared them all. The kits grow quickly with a steady food supply, and the young males at eight weeks old are as big as their mother, or bigger. The disparity in size between dog and bitch weasels has given rise to the belief that there are two species: the common weasel and the so-called mouse weasel. In fact, the mouse weasels are all bitches.

Weasels are specialist predators on voles and mice, especially on field voles, which often make up almost their entire prey for long periods. But they are also opportunists, killing small rats, birds, nestlings, young rabbits and water voles. Prey is killed by a bite on the neck, and is held by the forepaws while being scratched by the hindfeet. A weasel with a small prey will often roll over and over with it, as though playing with it. Many weasels store surplus food, and usually return to it, unless there is an abundance of available live prey.

Young forestry plantations are optimum habitats for weasel and stoat, where both prey on voles. When the vole population crashes the stoat has to get out, or enlarge its territory to find a living; the weasel can last much longer at low vole densities, probably because, being so small, it can follow the prey down the burrows. It is a known fact that a weasel, stirring up voles underground and forcing them to surface, inadvertently helps the stoat, which is too big to enter the burrows.

Although the weasel has the eyeshine of the night hunter it is often active by day, when it hunts hedge bottoms, ditches, tussocks, ratholes and vole creeps. By using mole tunnels and hidden runways it can move from point to point without surfacing and showing itself. When it surfaces it will sit up in listening pose, with nostrils twitching, and is not readily put off by the mere proximity of a human being.

Polecat

The polecat is the stink weasel, the foumart – so called to distinguish it from the sweet mart, or pine marten. It is supposed to be extinct in Scotland, but this is dubious for two reasons. The first is that a number of Welsh polecats have been released, or escaped, here and there. The second is that there are a lot of ersatz polecats in the form of polecat ferrets. The island of Mull has long had such a population, and many individuals from there look so like the real thing that they are indistinguishable.

So there are polecats in Scotland, and what it comes down to is a question of 'right' polecats and 'wrong' polecats. The purist will say that all Scottish polecats are wrong ones; but the purist would be wrong. Anyway, right polecat or wrong, real or ersatz, if one gets into a henhouse the result is the same and the argument is academic.

There is no certainty about any method of telling the right from the wrong, and facial markings are no reliable guide to identity. If, as is now widely accepted, the British polecat is the ancestral type of the polecat ferret the problem becomes even more complex. Polecat ferrets have gone wild and bred with polecats ever since man has kept ferrets, so it is a reasonable assumption that no wild polecat has escaped this admixture, and unreasonable to suppose that Welsh polecats have somehow managed to keep themselves in splendid isolation. Any polecat that looks like a polecat, acts like a polecat, and breeds polecats that look and act like polecats, may surely be considered a polecat.

Pine marten

The pine marten is the giant weasel of the trees, and was a common species in the old Caledonian forest. The destruction of the forest, followed by intensive game preservation, drove it to the verge of extinction, but it managed to survive in the wildest country of rock and scree, often treeless. Today it is found in coniferous forest, birch scrub, rocky gorges, open hillsides and cliffs – habitats sufficiently diverse to indicate that it is inherently an adaptable species.

In recent years it has been spreading north, north-east and east on a three-pronged front, and is now regularly recorded far from its old strongholds in Wester Ross, in south Ayrshire and the Cheviots.

The fur of the marten is dense and smooth, chocolate brown in colour, and darkest on the legs and tail. There is a creamy-yellow throat patch, often bright orange when the fur is prime, which is a distinguishing but variable feature. The soles of the feet are hairy, and give the animal grip when it is running along an icy branch. Male martens are bigger than females. A fully grown adult measures more than 76 cm in overall length, and weighs from 1134 to 1360 grammes.

The breeding season is in July and August, but implantation is delayed until January, so the young are not born until March or April of the following year. They become independent at about five months and fully grown in the first year, but do not breed until their second.

Marten dens in Scotland are most often in cairns, crags or holes in trees, but breeding has been recorded in the old nests of buzzard and crow, in river banks, in peat hags, and in the peat cap of a large boulder. Like the fox, the marten has a number of dens apart from the main one which it uses from time to time, leaving the signs of its presence. Such sites include the unused eyries of golden eagles, inside moss cushions on old tree stumps, and in nesting boxes.

Research into the food of Scottish martens has shown that, for most of the year, small rodents and small birds make up the bulk of its prey, the short-tailed vole being the commonest mammal taken. Birds preyed upon are mainly tits, wrens and tree creepers. The marten also eats beetles, caterpillars, carrion, fish, wasp grubs and berries.

The marten sleeps by day, and comes out around sunset to hunt. It is an excellent climber and jumper and moves in trees with the agility of a squirrel. It can leap a distance of 3.5 metres from branch to branch or from one tree to another.

The marten's fur, which is valuable, was once an important Scottish export, and there is no doubt at all that animals are still being killed today for the money their pelts will bring. Contrary to widely held belief the pine marten has no statutory protection; its only sanctuaries are the Ben Eighe Nature Reserve and those provided by the goodwill of individual landowners, including the Forestry Commission.

The pine marten often makes its den in unused nests, and has secondary dens which it visits intermittently.

Mink

The American mink, now widespread in Scotland and breeding successfully, appears to be here to stay. The wild population consists either of recent escapees, or the descendants of earlier escapees.

The banks of rivers, streams, ponds and lochs are the habitat of the wild population. When a feral mink raids a poultry house, or decimates ornamental waterfowl, we hear about it at once; but the actual prey range must be as wide as it is in North America, although little work has so far been done on this in Scotland. Fish are a big item, as are probably water voles. It remains to be seen if there is any clash between the otter and the mink in terms of coexistence.

Wild mink are dark brown, almost black, with a white spot on chin and lower lip. Prized mutants, such as sapphires and blues, also appear in feral populations.

Fox

The most anathematized mammal in Scotland, in both Highlands and Lowlands, is undoubtedly the fox, and it is almost impossible, especially in hill sheep areas, to have a serious discussion on foxes this side of hysteria. Considering its wide distribution and abundance, and its standing with the game preserver and sheep farmer, it is surprising how little serious work has been done on the fox until now, and the results of recent research will not be available for some time. As a general statement it could be said that in Highland sheep-farming areas the fox is a symptom of wrong land-use more than anything else.

No animal is more adaptable or resourceful. Its main requirements are cover and food supply, and so long as it has these it will live almost anywhere – on mountains, on low ground, in forest or woodland, beside lochs and ponds, on the seashore, even in cities. It is no longer news that foxes live in Edinburgh and Glasgow.

The weight of foxes varies in different habitats, according to food supply and season, and probably for other reasons. Weights usually given as average are 7 kg for dog foxes and 5.5 kg for vixens, but many foxes come much heavier than that – up to 10.5 kg.

In lowland Scotland the fox's den (the term earth is not widely used) is often no more than an enlarged rabbit burrow. According to locality the fox will den in shrubberies, reed beds, gorse brakes, old quarries, cairns and screes, or on sea cliffs. Vixens will often use an unoccupied part of a badger set. In the Highlands a fox den among rocks can be a veritable fortress, with holes reaching a depth of 12 metres. On its hunting ground, apart from the main den, the fox has several lying-up places which it uses from time to time. Not uncommonly a fox will spend a great part of the day in a tree 4–6 metres from the ground. Disturbance or threat of danger will drive a vixen from one den to another and a hill vixen will move cubs without hesitation. (She will move them at least once anyway during their period of dependence.) Hill foxes, in fact, sometimes split the family and hide them in different places after the style of the wolf.

The mating period is February onwards, and during it several dog foxes may be seen following one vixen, and fighting over her. Once a pair has been mated they stay together, and the dog fox carries food for the vixen and family. This is the time when Highland foxhunters do most of their work, putting terriers to ground to bolt the vixen and kill the cubs. Snaring, trapping, shooting, gassing and poisoning are other methods used, without noticeable effect on the population of foxes.

A fox at bay.

*Above : A weasel has killed
and tows away a vole, its
commonest prey.
Left : A stoat in ermine.*

*Right : Soay sheep scratching
themselves on dead juniper
branches ; they shed their
coats in early summer.*

Red deer

Thrice the age of a dog the age of a horse;
Thrice the age of a horse the age of a man;
Thrice the age of a man the age of a stag;
Thrice the age of a stag the age of an eagle;
Thrice the age of an eagle the age of an oak tree.

The old Gaelic rhyme has a lot of truth in it, but is a long way out with the age of a stag. The milk-white hind of Loch Treig who lived for a hundred and sixty years in the wilds of Lochaber, and Damh Mor – the Great Stag of legend – who lived for two hundred years in Badenoch, were mythical beasts, the creations of wishful thinking and poetic fancy. The life of a stag can in fact be measured by the rise and decline of his antlers, as a tree's by its rings of growth. At twelve the stag is in his prime, if he lives that long; thereafter he goes quickly downhill, and is aged before boys have attained to manhood.

The red deer is the biggest land mammal in Britain. It occurs in some numbers in the Southern Uplands of Scotland, but the biggest concentrations are in the Highlands and Islands. The present Scottish population is over 200,000, of which up to 35,000 are culled each year. Red deer are stalked with the rifle, stags and hinds each in their proper season. The close season in Scotland is 21 October to 30 June for stags, 16 February to 20 October for hinds.

The red deer society is a matriarchy, and the sexes live apart in separate herds for most of the year, hinds and stags keeping to their traditional ground. The breeding season (called the rut) takes place in September/October, sometimes dragging on into November. The onset of the rut is heralded by the roaring of the stags when they break into the hind ground to collect their harems. The gestation period is eight months, so most calves are born in June, the peak period being in the first half of the month. Single calves are the rule.

Only stags grow antlers. Size and weight vary with feeding and geography, and there is no such animal as an average stag. Highland heavyweights are in the order of 125–150 kg; more usually they are 95 or 100, up to 115 kg. Hinds are smaller and lighter, standing less than a metre tall at the withers against the stag's 1.2–1.3 metres. Both sexes are spotted white at birth, but the spots disappear in late summer.

Although naturally a forest animal the red deer is adaptable, and exists in great numbers on the almost treeless Highland hills. There it moves up and down through the contours, coming low in winter or during storms. Mortality among calves can be high in such a shriving environment, and a calf born late in the season will seldom survive.

The main food of Highland red deer is grass, heather, blaeberries, lichens and mosses, with the addition of rowans and other browse when they are on low ground. Marauding deer may be a serious problem to low ground graziers and farmers. Cast antlers are chewed and eaten, by both sexes; deer near the sea will eat seaweed.

Roe deer

Roe deer are widely distributed on the Scottish mainland, and are found on the islands of Skye, Islay, Seil and Bute. They appear to thrive in a variety of habitats, from mature forest to the open hill. They like open woodland, young plantations, scrubland, and the birch thickets that take over where a forest has been cleared. They need cool shade in summer, and good cover in winter to lie up in.

Top: A roe deer buck scrapes its antlers on a tree.
Bottom: A sika deer in summer coat, with antlers in velvet.

159

A browser and grazer, the roe has catholic tastes. It eats leaves, buds and twigs of hazel, alder, elder, ash, oak, chestnut, beech, birch and thorn, as well as crab, pear, sloe, dogrose, holly, broom and pine. In a young planting it will nip out the leader shoots of small trees. In autumn it eats beech mast, chestnuts, hips and haws, rowans, blackberries, juniper, raspberries and blaeberries. Grass and a variety of plants are also eaten. Hill roe, not having such a wide choice, eat more grass, and heather tips as well.

The summer coat of the roe is foxy red; the winter coat, which grows in during October and November, is thick, springy and brittle, and varies through many shades of grey and grey-brown. In winter, there is a grey-white patch on the throat and gullet. The rump patch is buff or creamy buff in summer, white in winter.

The rut is in July and August, when the bucks chase the does in rings. The fawns, usually twins, infrequently triplets, are born in late May or early June of the following year. The length of pregnancy is the result of delayed implantation, which takes place late in December.

Roe are territorial. The buck holds ground which he defends against other bucks, and the doe will drive other does from her ground. During the rut there is much chasing, some fighting, and occasional casualties. Bucks bark at any time, but their deep 'bough-bough' is a common sound during the rut. The doe calls 'whee-yoo' to her fawns, who 'peep' to her in reply.

The fawns do not run with the doe until they are strong on their legs and able to keep up with her; before that she hides them and leaves them alone for long periods. This is when people pick up fawns thinking they have been deserted, but one should not move a fawn for this reason. A doe, dying of wounds, will go to her fawns who are alive; unwounded and fit, she will tryst with fawns who are dead, and stay with them for a day or more.

With the wolf gone, man is the roe deer's main enemy. Big dogs are opportunist predators, but a buck in hard antler is a match for most. Foxes and eagles can, and do, kill fawns, and sometimes weakly adults. An adult roebuck will fight off an assaulting eagle.

Roe are a problem mainly to foresters by damaging young trees. But the Forestry Commission, once the roe's greatest enemy, now has a management programme for roe that gets the best of both worlds.

Fallow deer

There are wild fallow deer in many parts of Scotland, especially in the Border area, Perth, Argyll and Ross. They are found on the islands of Islay, Mull and Scarba.

Fallow deer are widely kept in parks, from which numbers escape to form small feral herds. They prefer mixed, or deciduous, woodland, with plenty of thickets and ground cover, although at times they will live in the open with red deer, sharing the same ground. Fallow on more open ground will lie up in bracken, and drop their fawns there.

There are two main colour phases in fallow deer: the dark type with hardly any visible spotting, and the brown or fawn type, with white spots in summer. A mature buck will stand nearly a metre tall at the withers; does are smaller. The rut is in October, kindling up when the red stags are already roaring, and lasts about four weeks. The gestation period is eight months, and the fawns are born in late May or early June. Singles are the rule, but twins are reported from time to time.

Sika deer

Several species of sika have been kept in deer parks, but the one that has become settled in Scotland is the Japanese, which is now found in Argyll, Caithness, Fife, Inverness-shire, Peebles, Ross and Sutherland.

The sika is a smaller edition of the red deer and might easily be mistaken for one. But size means little in the field, and coat colour is not a certain guide because many red deer are as red as sika. The velvet on the antlers is a better guide. In the sika stag this is red, tipped with black, so he is easily identified from May to August. During the rut he whistles, and this whistle, followed by a grunt, is a sound uttered by no other Scottish deer. The white tail of both sexes is distinctive.

In this species the rut begins in September and goes on into November. Like red deer stags, the defeated sika retire after the rut and may be seen singly, or in twos and threes. The hinds live in small units of up to a dozen during much of the year, but hive off to give birth to their calves. Hinds with a calf at foot, or perhaps with a calf and a yearling, are a common sight in June and July. A hind with a calf at foot will scream in alarm, and the sound can be heard a long way off.

Reindeer

The only free reindeer in Britain are in the Cairngorms in Scotland, where they were introduced by Mikel Utsi from Sweden in 1952. Earlier attempts had been made to reintroduce this species, extinct since the twelfth century, notably at Dunkeld in the eighteenth century and in Orkney and the Forest of Mar. But all these attempts failed, and it was left to Utsi to create the nucleus of the herd that can be seen today.

Reindeer stand 90–106 cm at the withers. Both sexes are antlered. Calves are chestnut at birth, and unspotted. They are born in early summer, and single births are the norm. The food of reindeer is mainly mosses and lichens, and Scottish reindeer eat the so-called reindeer moss wherever they find it. They also eat herbage more typical of the red deer.

The only predator in Scotland is man.

Voles

The field vole is found throughout the Scottish mainland, and on the islands except Lewis, Barra, South Rona, Raasay, Rum, Orkney and Shetland. In Orkney it is replaced by the Orkney vole.

This vole is brown above and grey below, less red than the bank vole which it otherwise resembles. Its tail is barely a third of its body length; it is blunt-faced and beady-eyed, and the ears are almost hidden in the fur.

Field voles like rough grassland, for grass is their food and their cover. Young forestry plantations are ideal habitats, and there the vole numbers can be high. Fair numbers are found on sheep walks and moorland, and they have been recorded on the alpine plateau of the Cairngorms.

The breeding season extends from March to September or October, sometimes even later, and occasionally goes on right through the winter. Young voles can breed from the age of three weeks, but this depends on the stage of the population cycle. In ideal habitats vole numbers fluctuate on a four-year cycle, rising from a low number to a high, then crashing back to a low again. In a year of peak numbers the young voles stay small, or grow slowly, and may not breed at all.

Weight varies not only with the season, but with the number of voles on the ground. In winter, adults weigh about 21 grammes, increasing to 28 grammes in spring. Some big males reach a weight of 42 grammes. The tendency is for voles in the north to weigh heavier than those in the south. A great many mammals and birds prey on the field vole, which could be called the bread and butter of the hunters.

The bank vole is also widely distributed on the mainland, but is absent from Orkney, Shetland, the Outer Hebrides and some of the Inner Hebrides.

Bank voles are blunt-faced, but more mouse-like in profile than the field vole. Their upper fur is chestnut brown, the underparts light grey or buff. They have small eyes and their ears can be clearly seen. The tail is fully half the length of the body, dark above and light below, and often carried high.

This species prefers deciduous woodland and scrub areas with plenty of ground cover. It also likes hedgerows, and banks where brambles and other trailing plants grow thickly. Provided there is cover of some sort, bank voles will often be found far from trees. They have been recorded in scree at 760 metres. Besides the leaves and stems of plants, the bank voles eats berries, seeds, fungi, roots, insects and their larvae. They take fewer insects than woodmice, but otherwise their food is very similar.

The bank vole's nest is made of grass, moss and bark, all finely shredded, and may be built above or below ground. Nests above ground are built in thick cover or in mossy tree stumps.

The Orkney vole, similar to the field vole of the mainland, is closely related to the Continental vole, and weighs 50–64 grammes.

The biggest vole is the water vole, which is found on the mainland from the Clyde–Forth line south to the Border and north to Inverness in the eastern half. From most of the rest of the country it is absent, or scarce. The race of water voles in the north has been given sub-specific status, but the justification for this is doubtful.

In general appearance the water vole is an outsize field vole, with something of the porcupine and beaver about it. It has the field vole's blunt muzzle and hidden ears. Males will measure up to 35.5 cm, including nearly 13 cm of tail; females are noticeably smaller. The most usual habitats are slow-moving rivers and streams, but water voles are also found on mountain streams up to 600 metres. The main foods are grasses and reeds that grow by the waterside.

The normal territory of the water vole is about a hundred metres along both banks of a river or stream. On this stretch there are many burrows but no other voles, because the resident male defends his territory fiercely and allows only his mate and offspring within it. Upstream and down he marks this territory from his flank glands, and with droppings strategically placed so that no intruding vole could possibly miss them. Yet the vole will lose his territory in the autumn and his life before the winter: the first to one of his growing family, the second because he will be aged. Although so much bigger than the field vole his life span is about the same, and few of his kind survive a second winter.

Goats and sheep

Feral goats are found in the Highlands, Islands, and Southern Uplands of Scotland. Although usually referred to as wild goats, they are no more than the wild-bred descendants of domestic animals that became feral a very long time ago. The Persian wild goat is the ancestor of the domestic breeds, and feral animals revert in time to this ancestral type, with variations resulting from more recent admixtures of domestic blood. Feral goats may be black-and-white, brown-and-white, black, brown, white, or cream.

Feral goats move about in small herds and travel up and down through the contours. When they are alarmed they give an explosive hiss that can be heard a long way off, and which will alert any deer within earshot. Where the goats are not being disturbed or harassed they may be tolerant of human beings down to about 90 metres, but on ground where they are being shot at they become as shy and wild as the wildest deer, and have to be stalked just as carefully.

The mating season is October/November, and kids are born the following February/March. As this is often when the weather is most severe, mortality among the kids can be high. Eagles and mountain foxes prey upon goat kids; apart from these, the main predator is man. In a few areas feral goats have been exterminated.

Nowadays Soay sheep can be seen in many parts of the Highlands and Lowlands, on exhibition in parks. Small flocks have been established on several islands, but Soay is the ancestral home, and there the sheep lived in association with man for a thousand years or more. The breed remains pure to this day, despite the fact that the St Kildans introduced a number of other breeds and crosses over the centuries. Segregated on Soay it has survived as a type, and no other sheep like it exists today. It was introduced to Hirta in 1932.

Feral goats have a wide range of coat colours.

Bats

The pipistrelle is the most common bat in Scotland, being found over most of the mainland and on most offshore islands. It is the smallest bat, with a wingspan of under 20 cm. The colour is usually some shade of brown, and the sexes look alike.

Pipistrelles haunt buildings, but also occur where there are none, and may be found in trees and rock clefts, whether near human habitation or not. The flying season is from March to October; but pipistrelles can be seen in any month of the year, on fine days, even when the hills are blanketed in snow. They take most of their prey on the wing, but carry larger insects to a resting place to be dismembered.

In the flying season and during hibernation pipistrelles are gregarious, and large numbers can be found roosting together. Barn and tawny owls are occasional predators, and rats take a few from rafters. Many people put up with bats; others clean them out because of the accumulation of droppings.

Daubenton's bat is found as far north as Elgin. Although it is bigger than the pipistrelle the difference in size is not easily noticed in the field, so the two can be easily confused. This is especially so when the bats are hunting over water, as Daubenton's does all the time and pipistrelle some of the time. Daubenton's is the one most usually caught on the fisherman's fly.

Daubenton's bat feeds almost exclusively on aquatic insects, which it catches in flight and eats on the wing; larger insects are pouched. Recorded prey includes dragonflies and large moths. During the summer months Daubenton's bat roosts in holes in trees and rocks as well as in caves and buildings. On warm, humid nights numbers of them can be seen hawking low over the water like swallows, lightly breaking the surface at intervals to drink on the wing. The female gives birth to a single young, born in June or July.

The long-eared bat is widely distributed on the Scottish mainland, except in the far north, and is found on the less exposed offshore islands. The enormous ears of this species are its most distinctive feature, being almost as long as head and body together.

Mating takes place in October/November and April/May, the first mating being of mature animals and the second of those too young to mate in the autumn. But it is not known if the spring mating is

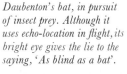

Daubenton's bat, in pursuit of insect prey. Although it uses echo-location in flight, its bright eye gives the lie to the saying, 'As blind as a bat'.

confined to young animals. A single young is born in June or July.

The principal food of the long-eared bat is moths, and butterflies of the tortoiseshell and peacock family; but beetles and a variety of other insects are also taken. Prey is captured mostly on the foliage and trunks of trees, but some insects are caught and eaten in flight. Large prey is pouched and carried to a resting place to be eaten.

Although the whiskered bat is common over much of England, it is extremely rare in Scotland, and confined to the area between the Border and the Clyde–Forth line. This bat comes out early, sometimes in daylight, and hunts on and off throughout the night. It hibernates from October to March, mostly singly but sometimes in small colonies. In summer, outside the breeding season, it is unsociable and usually roosts alone.

Natterer's bat is found on the mainland from the Central Belt to the Border. It frequents woodland and timbered parkland, often in the vicinity of water. The wingspan is 26.5–28 cm. The usual colour is greyish brown on the upper side and dirty white underneath, with a line between the zones from the base of the ear to the shoulder.

The noctule, a large bat with a wingspan of 33–35.5 cm, has been recorded in Scotland, but not in recent years.

Mole

The mole is found in every county of the Scottish mainland, and on the islands of Mull and Skye. It needs a good humus soil to burrow and find its food in, so is most numerous on arable ground and in deciduous woodland. But it is also abundant on reclaimed hill pastures, and has been recorded at 460 metres on flush grassland. It avoids peaty moorland (except where it has been broken up and reseeded), coniferous forest, and saltings liable to flooding.

Moles are preyed upon by foxes, badgers, stoats, weasels, herons, owls, buzzards and kestrels; but man is the main predator and the one who can make the greatest inroads on their numbers. The old-style trapper hardly exists now; the modern style is to kill moles with worms doctored with strychnine, and strychnine is made available for this purpose, and only this purpose. It is, however, an open secret that the poison is used to kill foxes, badgers, eagles, buzzards, crows and ravens.

Shrews

The common shrew is an abundant species which is widely distributed on the Scottish mainland and on the islands of Islay, Jura, Gigha, Arran, Bute, Mull, Ulva, Skye, Colonsay, Raasay, South Rona and Scalpay.

Common shrews have pinhead eyes, long whiskers and a flexible snout like a short trunk. The upper fur is dark, varying from sandy brown to dark chocolate; the underparts are greyish white. The tail is dark above and light below, and never exceeds half the body length. Young animals have paler coats. The teeth have red pigment.

Wherever there is good ground cover this shrew will be found, from sea-level to mountain tops. It is a hunter of the undergrowth and ground litter.

Dogs, cats, foxes, martens, stoats and weasels kill shrews, but rarely eat them. Dogs and cats that swallow them usually vomit them soon afterwards. Foxes, stoats and weasels can digest them, but appear only to eat them when there is no alternative. Bird predators, on the other hand, eat shrews readily and carry them to their young.

Shrews live at high pressure and age quickly; most of them die before their second autumn. They require great quantities of food, and sleep literally between bouts of eating. They die if deprived of food for more than a few hours.

The pygmy shrew is the most widely distributed species in Scotland, being found throughout the mainland and on the islands, except Shetland, North Rona and St Kilda. Tail length helps to distinguish the pygmy from the common shrew which it otherwise closely resembles: the pygmy's tail is two-thirds of its body length.

The water shrew is patchily distributed in Scotland, and absent from the islands of Skye, Islay and Arran.

Pools and streams of clear, unpolluted water are the habitat of this species, and pollution may account for the unevenness of its present distribution. But it will live, and breed, far from water. It is usually, but not always, black and white – black above and white below – with a clean line of demarcation between the zones. Melanism occurs, and water shrews in the north are often darker on the belly than those in the south, although dark- and light-bellied individuals can be found in the same litter. Albinos have been recorded.

This is the biggest and heaviest of the British shrews. It preys upon insects, crustaceans, snails, small fishes and frogs. It is preyed upon by cats, foxes, stoats, weasels and owls, and is certainly eaten by owls. The pike is also a predator.

An alert woodmouse, with sharp eyes, large, mobile ears and sensitive whiskers.

Rats and mice

The woodmouse and the house mouse are found all over Scotland, including the islands, the only qualification to this being that the house mouse disappeared from St Kilda soon after it was evacuated in 1930, and the woodmouse is not found on North Rona or Lunga.

On St Kilda the woodmouse took over the houses and byres formerly occupied by house mice, and is still there despite today's considerable human population. Frank Fraser Darling's experience with house mice on Lunga, of the Treshnish Isles, is equally interesting. The island had been uninhabited for eighty years, and the house mice had been living the open-air life of fieldmice (woodmice). Yet as soon as Fraser Darling's tent went up the mice were in again stealing the stores in the classical manner of commensal house mice.

The brown rat is also found everywhere, from sea-level to the tops of mountains. On many of the islands it lives on seabirds during the summer, and along the tideline in winter. Brown rats live on the Shiant Isles; on Eigg they raid the shearwater burrows; on Rhum they appear under any deer carcass that has been left lying for more than a few days.

The rat that cleared North Rona of its human population soon after 1685 must have been the ship rat (black rat) as the brown had not then arrived. The tradition is that the rats ate up the meal so the inhabitants starved to death, and the steward of St Kilda found the last woman dead on the shore with her child at her breast. Fraser Darling and Boyd have posed the question that the rats might have brought plague.

Red squirrel

The red squirrel is widely distributed on the Scottish mainland, except for a belt across the waist from Edinburgh to Glasgow which is mostly occupied by the American grey.

The ancestral home of the red squirrel is coniferous forest, and it is still most numerous where the old forests remain, or where new ones have been planted, as at Speyside or by the Forestry Commission. In Scotland the species has had a chequered history. Common all over the country up to the eighteenth century, it suffered from the widespread destruction of the forests into the 1800s, and may even have become extinct. Certainly red squirrels were reintroduced to several places from England, and became numerous because their arrival coincided with the maturing of replanted forests. At the turn of the next century they were destroyed because of the damage they were doing to 20-year-old trees. Thereafter there was a sharp decline in their numbers, which might partly have been due to disease and a succession of poor cone years. Their recovery was slow because of renewed felling in the First World War, and the squirrels had to adapt to mixed woodland.

In Scotland it appears that red squirrels have only one litter a year, but this cannot be taken as a rule. The young, at birth, have whiskers but no fur. They are weaned at 6 or 7 weeks. At two months of age they are independent, and active in the vicinity of the nest.

The build-up of red squirrels in the Highlands in recent years, and their colonizing, is in contrast to an otherwise general decline since the Second World War. The grey squirrel is often blamed for this, but the relationship between the bigger intruder and the native red is obscure. There could be other factors, not involving the grey at all. What is clear is that the grey has taken over ground once held in

Top: The pygmy shrew has a voracious appetite, its high level of activity burning up the food almost as soon as it is eaten.
Bottom: The St Kilda fieldmouse.

strength by reds, as well as ground the reds had never occupied. The red seems unable to recolonize ground that has been taken over by greys, whereas the grey can take over from the red wherever it moves in. This take-over implies competition of some kind, probably of a complex and subtle nature.

Predators on the red squirrel are fox, stoat, golden eagle, cat and pine marten. Very little is known of the relationship between the marten and the squirrel.

Grey squirrel

The grey squirrel, an American species introduced into Britain from 1876 onwards, occupies an area of Scotland mainly across the centre from Edinburgh to Glasgow: Fife, Stirlingshire and Clackmannanshire, the Loch Lomond area and parts of south Perthshire.

Grey squirrels are bigger and heavier than reds, measuring up to and over 50 cm in length, including tail. Their preferred habitat is mixed deciduous woodland, but they can and do breed in coniferous woodland where there are hardwoods close at hand. There are two breeding seasons, in spring and late summer. The average litter size is three, but up to seven have been recorded.

The staple food of the grey squirrel is the seed and nuts of deciduous trees – oak, beech, hazel, chestnut, maple, elm and sycamore – but it takes a great variety of other plants, fruits and grain, as well as eggs, birds and insects. It is a hustler and thruster, strong and knowing how to use its strength. An adult grey is a handful for anything less than its own size, including potential predators.

Brown hare

The brown hare is common in Scotland south of the Clyde–Forth line, north-eastwards through Fife and Perth to Aberdeen, Inverness and Easter Ross, then along the coastal strip to John o' Groats. Westwards it is thinner on the ground, and from Sutherland, Caithness and Wester Ross is absent almost entirely. It is found on the islands of Mull, Skye, Arran, Luing and Coll. It has been introduced to a number of other islands, including Orkney and Shetland, from the last of which it seems to have disappeared again.

Generally speaking brown hares like open, undulating country, up to 600 metres and down to sea-level. Most of them are found below 300 metres, on marginal farms, arable farms, moorland, aerodromes, salt marshes, dunes and woodland. There is some evidence that, in recent years, the beast has been pushing further into the glens, on traditional mountain hare territory.

Leverets are found in every month of the year, but most are born between February and August, with the peak season in May and June. The onset of the main breeding season is heralded by the gatherings in late February and March when hares, traditionally, go mad. At these ceremonies mating takes place, or pairs hive off to do so. The gestation period is 42–44 days, and there are probably three or four litters a year. The leverets are born fully furred and with their eyes open, and can run about within a few hours. They breed in their first year, but have smaller and fewer litters than older adults.

The hare is built for speed and is at its best uphill, which is the way it usually runs. When turned about, it will run a diagonal rather than a straight descent, for its long hindlegs put it at a disadvantage on a fast downhill chase. Depending on its age and condition, the hare is preyed upon by foxes, eagles, wildcats, dogs, stoats, weasels, ravens, crows and buzzards. But man is the main predator.

Mountain hare

This is the hare of the high ground, and it is found over most of the Highland mainland and in the Southern Uplands. It is present on Mull, Jura, Skye, Raasay, Scalpay and Eigg, and in the Outer Hebrides, Orkney and Shetland. But the biggest numbers are found in the central and north-eastern Highlands, especially on well-run grouse moors, where conditions suit it best.

A young mountain hare

The mountain hare is smaller and more thick-set than the brown. It has a bigger head, shorter legs and shorter ears, but none of these characteristics is obvious in the field, and the fur is not much guide despite its bluish bloom. Tail colour is, however, decisive: the tail is white, above and below. In winter coat the mountain hare can be mistaken for nothing else – it is the only British mammal (apart from the stoat, and an exceptional high-ground weasel) that turns white in winter.

The change from summer brown to winter white, and from white back to brown, is the result of a moult, as in the stoat. In addition to these changes the hare moults into a new brown coat in autumn. The white coat begins to come in as early as September, and is complete by mid-November to early December. In 1958, Ray Hewson defined the sequence of moults in this species, and disposed of the old notion that loss of pigment caused the change to white.

Mountains and high moorlands are the terrain of the mountain (or blue) hare, mainly from 300 to 750 metres, but it will range up to 1200 metres. The hares will move down during storms or prolonged, deep snow, when they may be found in forest and scrub. In many places the ranges of the brown and mountain hares overlap, especially at the 300–450 metre contours.

Unlike the brown hare the mountain hare will use burrows and other shelters. Like the brown it has its peak mating season in March, and these rowdy assemblies often take place when the snow is blanketing the hills. The gestation period is probably 50 days. Summer litters number two or three, occasionally four. The leverets are born fully furred, with their eyes open, and they go to ground readily from the beginning of their lives. The young do not breed until the year after their birth.

Rabbit

The rabbit is ubiquitous, and it would be more difficult to say where it is not found than where it is, despite the fact that myxomatosis has cut the population to pieces in many areas. It is not a native of Scotland, any more than it is of England or Wales: it was planted over a long period. The plantation of the rabbit in Scotland was as real an event as the Scots plantation of Ulster, and about as disastrous. Many people brought it to many places – according to Osgood Mackenzie it was being planted around Gareloch in about 1850. It is difficult today to realize that most of the men who marched to join The Prince at Glenfinnan in 1745 had never seen a rabbit, yet a few of them may have known the wolf.

Hedgehog

The hedgehog is found throughout the Scottish mainland, but is local and thinly spread in the Highlands. It occurs on Orkney, Shetland, Skye, Bute, Mull, Coll and Canna, to some of which it may have been introduced. It avoids very high ground, very wet ground, and tall closed forest.

A fully grown male hedgehog will come close to 30 cm in length, and a mature female is only slightly smaller. The weight range is 900–1245 grammes. Young hedgehogs have been recorded in every month from May to October, but the peak littering periods are May/June and August/September.

The motor car is now a major threat to hedgehogs, and there must be few people who have not remarked on the mounting casualties. Apart from this accidental slaughter, man is still a considerable killer by intent, mainly in the interests of game preservation. Gamekeepers are the chief offenders, and hedgehogs are still common corpses on their gibbets.

A modern hazard for the hedgehog is the cattlegrid. In its nocturnal wanderings the hedgehog falls through the bars and being unable to escape soon dies; if all cattlegrids had a built-in ramp the lives of many of these creatures would be saved.

The hedgehog feeds fat in autumn for the long, slow burn of hibernation. Once a beast is really bedded down for the winter its temperature falls, its breathing slows down, and its heartbeat becomes a tick-over. By this means the hedgehog ekes out its stored fat until the spring. In Scotland, hibernation usually begins early in November. March is the month of waking, although some animals are on foot in February and some sleep on until April. One hedgehog, weighing 1048 grammes at the beginning of hibernation, weighed 765.5 grammes on waking 132 days later.

Grey or Atlantic seal

By world standards the grey seal is a rare species. It is also a highly vulnerable one, because it has to come ashore to breed and modern transport has made its remote breeding stations readily accessible. Scotland, with a very large proportion of the total population in its waters, has therefore a special responsibility in terms of management and conservation.

All Scottish breeding stations are on islands or rocky coasts: North Rona, Orkney, Shetland, the Hebrides and Caithness. The largest breeding colonies are on North Rona and Orkney. Scottish pups are born from late September to November, the time varying from colony to colony. Pups weigh between 10 and 20 kg at birth, put on about 2 kg a day, and reach 30–45 kg a fortnight later. At three weeks they are weaned, and begin their first moult. The first teeth are shed before birth, the adult teeth appearing a day or two after. The cows mate as soon as their pups have been weaned, then leave for the sea. Neither the bulls nor the cows eat during the breeding period.

Mating takes place on land, in shore pools, or in the sea. Young cows breed in their fifth year, and give birth to their first pup in their sixth. Bulls are mature at the age of 6 years, but are not usually able to hold a territory until some years later.

Although this species has a statutory close season there has been an authorized cull of pups and adults for some years, in an attempt to reduce the overall population by 25 per cent. This has caused much controversy. That the grey seal damages salmon nets and marks salmon with its claws is not disputed; that it has any significant effect on salmon stocks is dubious. The other complaint against this species is that it is the host of a nematode whose final larval stage is in cod, and that an increase in codworm is correlated with the increase in the number of grey seals. The cull is an experiment which may or may not work; what has always to be borne in mind is that this seal is a rare species, a national heritage, whose future should not be endangered by hasty over-reaction.

Common seal

The common seal is found right round the Scottish coast, and on the Northern and Western Isles.

Both sexes are distinguishable from the grey seal at all times by their snub noses and slanted nostrils. This is an adaptable species, and although it likes mudbanks and sandbanks it will haul out on shingle, beaches of sand or shell, rocks, and the islets of sea lochs. It tends to remain in shallow coastal waters, or offshore waters, at all times.

In the north of Scotland common seal pups are born in late June and early July. They shed their white coats before birth or soon after. The cow suckles her pup mainly under water. Unlike grey seal pups, young common seals can swim and dive from birth, and are often born in the water. Because this species does not have to come ashore to breed there is no land-based assembly, and no territorial behaviour by bulls. There is however the well-known 'water play' in the month before the pups are born. Then the seals roll, and porpoise, and slap the water – behaviour that is a delight to watch. In Shetland they have been recorded mating on the sea bottom, at a depth of two to four fathoms.

Chapter 10
Plants and People

Life in Scotland in the sixteenth century and before was a stern affair, particularly in the hills and uplands. Dense forests and great bogs abounded, making communications difficult, and in the far north the Scots Parliament's hold was tenuous. In the Lowlands the land improvements of the eighteenth and nineteenth centuries, with their emphasis on drainage and liming, were still a long way off. Although the union of the crowns was expected, Border life was not always peaceful, and the stresses and strains of the Civil War and the rights of the Covenanters were still to rend the seventeenth century. At such a time wildlife was hardly a matter of interest or a subject for study – rather wild animals were a source of food and wild plants a source of medicine and of dyes. Birds of all kinds and their eggs, deer, rabbits and hares all found their way to the table. So important were these forms of food that the Scots Parliament in 1551 passed an Act regulating the prices of 'wilde' as well as 'tame' meat.

Wildlife contained enemies to be overcome. The killing of domestic animals by wolves is recorded from earliest times in Scotland. Places like the great forests of Rannoch and Lochaber were regarded, perhaps wrongly, as too dangerous to traverse because of wolves, and in spite of continued efforts to reduce their numbers these animals had reached almost pest levels in the sixteenth century. They were all exterminated by 1743, largely through the destruction of the great forests which had harboured them.

Before the second half of the seventeenth century nearly all travellers or explorers in Scotland were more interested in the standard of farming, the food supply and the condition of the people than wildlife for its own sake. Although Jean de Beaugue (a Frenchman and close friend of André de Moutalenbert, Sieur d'Esse, who led the French army which came to the assistance of the Scots after the disastrous battle at Pinkie in 1547) comments in his diary on the 'large white birds like swans' which made their nests on the Bass Rock, this was because he had discovered that the 100 to 120 men garrisoned there were expected to exist on the fish carried to the Rock by these birds, and to keep warm by burning the material the birds had collected for their nests. Sir Robert Sibbald, the famous seventeenth-century Scottish naturalist, devotes part of his discussion on the Bass Rock gannets to describing a method of killing them by attaching herrings to a board, so that when the birds dived their beaks became embedded in the wood and they were easily secured. He also notes that the young were captured and lowered in baskets over the cliff to boats

Salisbury Crags, for centuries the site of many interesting wild flowers.

below, to be sold in Edinburgh at two shillings apiece. A hundred years later, in 1769, Thomas Pennant, that inveterate traveller and observer, could not resist remarking that gannets were the only provision 'whose price has not been advanced' over the last century.

Although this interest by travellers in wildlife as a food supply was to persist into the nineteenth century, an appreciation of nature for its own sake began to be apparent during the seventeenth century.

In spite of the difficult days following the Restoration, when religious prejudice and persecution disrupted the proper filling of university chairs and the ancient incorporation of Surgeons and Barbers in Edinburgh dominated the medical scene, there appeared in Edinburgh at this time the science of botany and with it the notable Sir Robert Sibbald and his colleague and friend, Andrew Balfour. Both of these men were medical practitioners: Andrew Balfour studied at St Andrews and Robert Sibbald, after a general degree at Edinburgh, took his medical qualifications at Leiden. Balfour, the elder of the two, was strongly influenced by Robert Morison, an Aberdeen medical graduate who studied plants under the botanist to the French king until 1669 when he became physician and director of the Royal Garden to Charles II and the first Professor of Botany at Oxford. Sibbald and Balfour worked together in close harmony to improve medicine in Edinburgh and to acquire land for a physic garden. Sibbald took up the study of native Scottish plants partly to provide this garden with medicinal herbs.

Even in the troubled seventeenth century, friendship and shared interests flourished. A young man, Patrick Murray of Livingstone, had started a plant collection from seeds collected in Britain and elsewhere and had about a thousand plants in cultivation. Through this he became friendly with Balfour and Sibbald. Sadly, having taken Balfour's advice to travel abroad in search of new materials for his collection, he died of a fever at Avignon. After his death his collection became a major source of plants for Sibbald and Balfour's garden, established in 1670 at St Anne's Yard, near Holyrood, to be replaced five years later with a new garden where Waverley Station now stands.

Scottish asphodel

Sibbald published many works, the most important being *Scotia Illustrata*, which was commissioned by Charles II and published in 1684. In it he mentions two plants recorded for the first time in Britain – *Sibbaldia procumbens*, that familiar of base-rich highland hills, called after Sibbald, and *Ligusticum scoticum*, the lovage of so many Scottish sea cliffs. He makes reference too to red german catchfly and forked spleenwort, both discovered in 1670 by George Willisel, an official collector for the Royal Society on the Salisbury crags in Holyrood Park where, despite the pressure of centuries, the plants still remain.

Sibbald's interests went beyond collecting, and he made observations on the building of bogs, or 'mosses' as he called them, by fallen trees, impeded drainage and rainfall. He recognized the different colorations in peat, and observed that 'black is the best fire'. He also considered how the 'mosses' might be converted to useful and profitable ground, a thought never very far away in the Scotland of that time, a poor country dominated by mountain and bog.

Working with Sibbald and Balfour was James Sutherland, who in 1695 became the first Professor of Botany at Edinburgh. He took his students 'herbarising' round Edinburgh, as well as travelling around Scotland himself in his younger days. It is written that his personal examination of the shores and mountains of Annandale and Nithsdale 'amply discovered him the riches of his own country'.

The year before Robert Sibbald returned to Edinburgh to practise medicine, John Ray, the English naturalist, decided to visit Scotland. Ray was a clergyman, apparently a more common background for botany in England than medicine. He produced the first book on local flora in Britain, *Catalogus Plantarum Circh Cantabrigiam*, and also a list of British plants (*Synopsis Stirpium Britannicorum*). Like many travellers to Scotland before and since, he complained about the food and houses. 'They are not very cleanly in their houses and but sluttish in dressing their meat. They have neither good bread, cheese or drink; their butter is very indifferent and one would wonder how they could contrive to make it so bad.' He visited the Bass Rock, perhaps already recognized as of particular interest to the naturalist, where he saw gannets, guillemots, black guillemots, kittiwakes and shags, as well as wild beet, scurvy-grass, sea campion and tree mallow. On his return to England he went by the Lowther hills and saw alpine clubmoss. His second visit in 1671 was with Thomas Willisel. Together they found London rocket on the walls of Berwick, as well as Scottish asphodel and northern shorewort which had been seen by the indefatigable Willisel in the previous year. One wonders what tales of Scotland Ray told when he returned to the sunlit flatlands of Cambridge and to English food.

Although Scottish naturalists and visiting Englishmen had made a start in the discovery of Scottish plants and there was some continuing interest in botany, nearly a hundred years were to elapse before there was any significant exploring of the Scottish flora. Heading this exploration was John Hope, who became Professor of Botany at Edinburgh in 1761. Like many of his predecessors he had had a varied education, both in Europe and Scotland. He graduated in medicine in the University of Glasgow in 1750 but, again in common with many medical men, his main interest was in botany. Being of an influential family – his father was Lord Rankeillor – he was able to obtain agreement to divide the teaching of botany from medicine. His great interest was in field botany, and he encouraged his students to seek out the flora of Scotland and annually awarded a gold medal for the best herbarium.

Hope and his students have a special place as explorers of the Scottish countryside and its plants. His notebooks make it clear that he and his students travelled widely over the country, including the Northern Isles, Skye and Arran. In these notebooks can be found lists of plants and where they grew, before they had been recorded by others and sometimes published as new records. The first specimen of alpine speedwell from Scotland was lodged in Hope's herbarium in 1768, collected on Ben Nevis by his students. Alpine poa, creeping azalea, creeping spearwort, the spurge *Euphorbia esula*, pyramidal bugle, creeping lady's tresses and dwarf birch are often considered to have been discovered by the Reverend John Lightfoot during his Scottish tour in 1772. These were, however, all listed by Hope in 1768: alpine poa on Ben Cruachan, creeping azalea on Scaraben in Sutherland, *Euphorbia esula* near Edinburgh, creeping lady's tresses from a wood near Moy on the road to Inverness and dwarf birch on moors in Ross-shire. There is a specimen of the bog grass *Trichophorum alpinum* in Hope's herbarium from an unknown location. This was known in Britain from one locality only, Restennet Moss in Angus, where it was discovered by George Don and Robert Brown in 1791; it

Alpine speedwell

is now probably extinct through drainage. *Primula scotica* was found near Thurso by one of Hope's students, though recorded under the name of bird's-eye primrose. Even James Brebner's discovery of the bog rush *Schoenus ferrugineus* beside Loch Tummel in 1884 was not the first report of it in Britain, for the plant had been previously recorded by Hope's group in Skye, although it has not been seen there since.

This range of plants, some very scarce, others from a wide variety of places and habitats, gives an idea of the area covered by Hope's students. But there are many questions unanswered. How widespread were the plants, for example? Was dwarf birch a real constituent in the transition zone from scrub birch to high moorland, as in Iceland, or was it always scattered as it is in north-west Ross-shire today? Perhaps fire had already modified its habitat – as it has so many others.

We know little about Hope's students as people, or how they found their way around Scotland. Travel was not easy, particularly in the Highlands, and places like Ben Cruachan or the moors of Ross-shire must have seemed fairly inaccessible. No doubt this intrepid band suffered many a cold wet night in their pursuit of knowledge.

When Thomas Pennant made his second tour in Scotland he invited the Reverend John Lightfoot to come with him as botanist. Lightfoot was librarian and domestic chaplain to the Duchess of Portland, herself a great English plant collector, and one hopes she gained some specimens after the tour. We know little about Lightfoot's reactions to Scotland, though the conditions, as he rode through cold and wet countryside, must have contrasted with the comfort of his life in the employment of the Duchess. No doubt Thomas Pennant's numerous contacts, and his knowledge of Scotland, eased some of Lightfoot's hardships. Certainly the publication of the *Flora Scotica* in the 1770s was another milestone in Scottish botany. The tour, recorded by Pennant in three volumes, gives us a mass of information concerning wildlife, the state of the country, superstitions, industry and much else besides. It lacks the usual comments about bad food and bad inns, and was largely carried out on horseback to avoid the nauseous swing of the stagecoach on badly surfaced roads and tracks. Pennant was much impressed with the great pinewoods of north-east Scotland and the large size to which the pines grew, and wrote in high praise of the beauty of Loch Lomond. He must have been one of the last to comment on the native capercailzie, by then confined to the pine forest north of Loch Ness. It was reintroduced from Scandinavia in the early nineteenth century at Taymouth near Kenmore and has since spread widely.

In the last quarter of the eighteenth century material conditions improved in Scotland. The 'new town' of Edinburgh was being built, the University was filled with a brilliant generation hot in the pursuit of learning; questioning was in the air. Hope's numerous students were scattered throughout the world – as for instance Alexander Menzies, born in Aberfeldy in 1754. He had made a botanical tour of the Highlands and the Hebrides, with particular attention to grasses and sedges, and having gained a high reputation he was appointed as naturalist on the *Discovery* during Captain George Vancouver's voyage round the world from 1790 to 1795. But interest in natural history was not just confined to Edinburgh or to Hope's students. There are references to a Mr Gibb of Inverness, to the Reverend Dr Burgess of Kirkmichael, John McKay from Kirkcaldy, and to George Don, the famous botanist and clockmaker from Forfar. Don's explorations in Glen Clova and the surrounding Angus glens, and also on Ben Lawers, are still mentioned today. In 1779 he was considered to be the only botanist who had explored the high mountains of the Cairngorms and the central Grampians; he was a man of character who liked to be alone and who lived frugally. During his frequent visits to Ben Lawers he collected alpine sandwort, alpine forget-me-not and *Carex atrofusca*, all new to the British flora. He saw *Woodsia alpina*, two-flowered rush and chestnut rush, and located alpine bartsia on Ben Lui and curved woodrush on the great mass of Ben Macdui. The Angus glens were always his favourites, and here he found yellow oxytropis and red alpine catchfly. In 1812 he published *An Account of the Native Plants in the County of Forfar and the Animals to be found there*. How he responded to the beauty of his finds or whether he was struck with the brilliance of the blue of alpine forget-me-not on a sunlit day, we can only speculate.

The general interest in local plants was not limited to naturalists. A number of working gardeners from the Botanic Garden and from Dickson's nurseries in Edinburgh formed themselves into a society for mutual instruction called the Leith Walk Glencairn Society. They possessed one copy of Lightfoot's *Flora Scotica* which had to be shared, emphasizing that books were both expensive and hard to come by.

In spite of the difficulties of communication and the non-existence of a postal service, naturalists and scientists carried on correspondence with each other and, as the nineteenth century progressed, managed to exchange as well as to collect specimens. Sending things by stagecoach was, however, both time-consuming and hazardous, for they were often lost or stolen.

Two very different people of that time were William MacGillivray, born in Aberdeen in 1796, and Sir William Jardine who was born in 1800. MacGillivray, of humble background, qualified in Aberdeen to lecture on anatomy, and then came south to Edinburgh to act as secretary to Professor Robert Jameson. Jameson, who became Regius Professor of Natural History at Edinburgh, influenced both MacGillivray and Jardine, as well as many others including Charles Darwin. Like many of his contemporaries MacGillivray climbed the hills, existing on oatcake and a bite of cheese. He also visited the Hebrides. His hardiness was proverbial, and until nearly the end of his life he walked his students off their feet. (His own death was considered to be due to exposure.) In 1819 he was so anxious to see the bird collection in the British Museum that he walked to London and back, eating very little and finding that his few precious Scottish pound notes were unacceptable in England. In later life he became Professor of Civil and Natural History at Aberdeen University until his health deteriorated in 1841. An outstanding naturalist of his day, he had begun to consider plants in relation to the conditions in which they grew – an approach that was quite new and a pointer to the future. His *Remarks on the Phenogamic Vegetation of the River Dee*, published in 1832, follows the changes that take place in vegetation from the alpine zone down to the valley flora.

Sir William Jardine (1800–74) grew up in very different circumstances, for his family owned the then recently improved estate of Applegarth in Dumfriesshire. His own interest in natural history, as with William MacGillivray and others, started with the study of medicine at Edinburgh University, but in his case the course was never completed. Because of his independent means he was able to develop

Red alpine catchfly

his interest in natural history from Applegarth, and he became one of the outstanding figures in the natural history world. He is best known for his *Naturalist Library*, which was priced at a modest figure and was therefore more easily available than previous publications. In 1820 he married Jean Lizars, described as a talented watercolour painter, and this brought about the fruitful connection with her brother, W. H. Lizars, the publisher, in the production of the *Library*. Jardine and his wife, with two of their daughters, provided many of the illustrations in these volumes; Jardine shared the Victorian capacity for deploying many talents, and could also draw and paint as well as shoot and collect.

An unpublished manuscript about Sir William Jardine gives a fascinating picture of his life as a naturalist, a writer of natural history books, an avid collector, a correspondent, an estate-owner and a sportsman. He was in constant correspondence with other naturalists of the day, exchanging information, advice and sometimes specimens. There is an intriguing description by J. J. Audubon of how, when Audubon visited Edinburgh in 1826 before he became famous, he gave Jardine and P. J. Selby (the Northumberland naturalist) drawing lessons: 'I showed these gentlemen how I set up my specimens, squared my paper, and soon had them both at work drawing a squirrel.' Selby worked the faster but at the end Audubon regarded the results as equally good.

In 1832 Jardine and his family took a house at Holmes on the Tweed, letting Jardine Hall for three years. At Holmes he became interested in entomology and joined too the Berwickshire Naturalist Club, the first such club of its kind in Britain, to which he was elected on its first anniversary in September 1832. He had a sharp eye for the birds and plants around him, and his notebooks are filled with observations in a singularly 'crabbit' hand. In 1833 he notes that grouse were less plentiful than previously and that some thought that blackgame would oust the grouse – this last a view not shared by Sir William. Though specimens were sent to him from all over the world, he did not travel widely himself. He visited Holland and France and there is a description of him journeying to London by train, a novel experience 'with excellent service'.

In 1834 he went on a tour of Sutherland, accompanied by his youngest brother John, P. J. Selby, R. K. Greville and James Wilson (a naturalist born in Edinburgh in 1795, originally destined as a Writer to the Signet, and at that time working on the natural history of fishes). Having reached Tain by stagecoach they arranged for a special conveyance for the rest of their expedition. This was a boat upon wheels drawn by two highland ponies, a contraption which was both novel and multi-purpose. It could be used for fishing the lochs and visiting the nesting places of birds. It also served as a sleeping place when turned upside down. As Sir William writes, 'It was found to answer most admirably, containing all our luggage with sufficient room for ourselves.'

Sutherland at that time was described as a country less well known to naturalists than Lapland. Jardine's diary is full of interest, and although his handwriting is somewhat obscure, everything is recorded. He comments that greenshank were for the first time found nesting in Britain. Ospreys, white-tailed eagles and black-throated divers are all mentioned. The noise of the curlew is noted as incessant on the Sutherland moors, the ground apparently too wooded for this bird south of the Dornoch Firth. He refers to bogrush and dwarf birch, the latter seen by him for the first time. On 23 June, setting off south from Scourie, he remarked: 'Royal ferns were seen on many parts of the road and lochsides, and *Cladium mariscum* (saw sedge) was observed a short way beyond Badcall Bay. A very northern station for a plant which is very abundant in the Cambridgeshire fens.' Saw sedge is still there in that site, but most of the royal fern has disappeared with burning and grazing.

MacGillivray and Jardine, both outstanding naturalists, had demonstrated how common interests could overcome very different backgrounds, and indeed MacGillivray contributed one of the volumes (*British Quadrupeds*) to Jardine's *Naturalist Library*. In later years something went wrong with their relationship, for reasons that are not known to us.

The nineteenth century was a period when collecting reached its zenith: insects, plants, birds, birds' eggs and many other things. In 1836 Dr John Hutton Balfour, an Edinburgh physician who was later to hold the chair of Botany and Regius Keepership of the Botanic Garden, formed with eleven others the Botanical Society of Edinburgh. The founding members included R. K. Greville, who had discovered alpine milk vetch in Glen Clova in 1831 and who had joined Jardine's Sutherland tour in 1834. The objects of the society were to forward the advancement of botanical knowledge in Scotland, and to create a plant collection to include representatives of the mountain flora. Collecting continued to be a major activity until the end of the century, as it was regarded as the main tool for the increase of information – indeed, knowing the single-mindedness of the

The alpine milk vetch, first discovered by the nineteenth-century botanist R. K. Greville in Glen Clova. This plant was reputed to increase the secretion of milk in goats.

Victorians, Scotland is perhaps fortunate to retain as much of its flora as it does today.

Birds too were threatened by collecting. Naturalists' houses were full of stuffed birds in glass cases and cabinets with tiny drawers to hold eggs. Charles St John toured Sutherland in 1849. This Englishman, on his own admission, found difficulty with the Scottish place names, and certainly his spelling is more than variable. He travelled from London to Edinburgh in 13 hours, and then from Granton to Invergordon in 36 hours by steamer, which he regarded as quick and easy. From Invergordon he followed William Jardine's example of fifteen years earlier and moved in a boat on wheels. St John is a supreme example of the Victorian ornithologist with a gun. He manages to bemoan the reduction in numbers of ospreys and white-tailed eagles while at the same time shooting them. He is critical of egg collecting for sale by the local foresters and shepherds, yet he arranges to remove peregrine and osprey eggs from inaccessible places and scoops eggs from black-throated divers' nests. By the end of the nineteenth century this seemingly thoughtless predation by naturalists, whether by gun or vasculum, was having its effect on wildlife in Scotland.

In the latter part of the last century natural history societies flourished, and as with the societies of the eighteenth century there was a strong accent on field work. The Perthshire Society of Natural Science, of which Dr Buchanan White was founder member and first president in 1867, is a good example. It published proceedings and transactions and organized excursions. It authorized the issue of the *Scottish Naturalist* which, in 1892, merged into the *Annals of Scottish Natural History* under the editorship of Dr J. A. Harvie Brown. It also had an offshoot called the Perthshire Mountain Club which made excursions every year to one of the mountains in the county. With what appears to be great foresight, Dr White sought co-operation among the various Natural History Societies in part of Scotland at least and, in 1884, the first meeting of the East of Scotland Union of Naturalists' Societies was held.

From the mid-eighteenth century or earlier there has run a strong thread of interest in the Scottish mountain flora which still continues today. Naturalists in their search for alpine plants were able to cross the moors and climb the mountains without significant hindrance from owners or their employees, so long as sporting interests remained undisturbed. It is the exception to read of what became dubbed the Battle o'Glen Tilt in 1847 when James Hutton Balfour and his students found themselves in direct conflict with the Duke of Atholl and his retainers.

Shooting and ornithology continued to be linked, thus giving ornithology some sporting status. The collecting of plants continued, with ever more minute concern for differences, and even today attics will turn out dusty herbarium sheets collected by enthusiasts in days gone by. The widening of interest foreseen by MacGillivray began around the start of this century, when the brothers William and Robert Smith created a landmark in the plant world with their papers on vegetation, to be followed by the teaching in the University College of Dundee of D'Arcy Thompson and Patrick Geddes. Even in the late 1940s D'Arcy Thompson still retained a capacity to inspire the young: his venerable appearance with the then unusual beard, his enthusiasm, his belief in a broad education and his habit of referring to the Franco-

Prussian War of 1870 as 'The War' caught the interest of several young would-be scientists after the Second World War. Though interest in individual plants continued, the study of their geographical occurrence, the pattern of their existence and the make-up of their communities gradually gave botany a new and wider perspective. With this came recognition that plant communities were not static but had a dynamism of their own, and that there was an interdependence not only between plants themselves but between plants and animals. Such knowledge was in due course to lead to the concept of the ecosystem and the ideal of conservation.

It was in the twentieth century that the wider aspects of bird study grew, and the watcher took over from the shooter as field-glasses became more readily available. Watching without slaughter fostered interest in behaviour and habits. Dr Eagle Clarke, an Englishman who settled to work in Scotland, and Norman Kinnear, a Scot who later headed the British Museum (Natural History) in London, took to visiting Fair Isle. Eagle Clarke made arrangements with George Stout, a Fair Isle man whose family still lives there, to make records of birds, and from this grew his own work on migration. His interest was later taken up by Miss Rintoul and Miss (later Dr) Baxter who, in 1907, started regular trips to the Isle of May which led them to ideas on migrational drift related to the wind. Miss Rintoul and Miss Baxter lived in Fife with independent means and were able to devote much time to their work on birds. They belonged to a generation who withstood climate and terrain clad in tweed skirts, burberries and hats. Their other interests included judging home-made jam, oatcakes and shortbread, and the finer side of embroidery, but their kindly authority and high level of ornithological knowledge made them leading figures in Scottish wildlife. They belong perhaps to the last generation of those whose interest in wildlife was untrammelled by government intervention and the organized approach which was to become inevitable for the long-term wellbeing of wild life.

In the years between the wars the whole relationship of people and wildlife was changed by the motor car. Mobility without effort, and the desire of a people who had become urban-based to experience the countryside, gradually brought new pressures. Gone was the committed naturalist or the intrepid searcher after wildlife, prepared to tramp miles on a piece of oatcake or sleep overnight in some friendly cottage. The Scottish countryside was something to be seen and enjoyed easily, and its wildlife to be touched lightly rather than savoured, examined or collected. Fresh air was good and people were encouraged to visit the countryside. The whole approach became more organized, almost paternal. Professor G. M. Trevelyan, in his foreword to the pamphlet 'The Case For National Parks in Great Britain' (July 1938), wrote: 'It is no less essential for any national health scheme to preserve for the nation walking grounds and regions where young and old can enjoy the sight of unspoiled nature and it is not a question of physical exercise only, it is also a question of spiritual exercise and enjoyment'. This epitomizes the view, still held by many, that the countryside *per se* is good for people.

The Forestry Commission, set up in 1919, was anxious to offer national forest parks as a means of contributing to leisure in the countryside, and led the way with the creation of a park in Glentrool in Galloway in 1935. This was followed by the Argyll National Forest Park and the Queen's Forest in the Cairngorms. These areas were to have no restrictions on public access at any time of the year. The National Trust for Scotland was not far behind. At first, motor cars were not so numerous that the amount of visitors gave cause for concern, and indeed they were actively encouraged. The hill-walkers, of whom the more adventurous still followed in the traditions of Hope's students and George Don or the Mountain Club of the Perthshire Natural History Society, made their ways over the Scottish hills as before, generally unmolested except during the stalking and grouse shooting seasons. Early youth hostels and mountain bothies, both few in number, provided welcome staging posts and shelter.

Until after the Second World War there were only modest pressures by recreation-seeking man on much of the countryside and its wildlife. The work of naturalists in the field continued. Ruthless collecting was now on the decline. Herbaria and vascula were replaced by the poly-bag, the camera, field-glasses and the inevitable notebook, although the colour film was still to come into everyday use as the new tool for recording. Older botanists who still carried out their explorations included the late A. J. Wilmot and Miss M. S. Campbell who were working on the flora of Uig in Lewis. Expeditions to study the flora of certain parts of Scotland took place, such as that involving a small group of scientists and students which Miss Campbell led to Harris in the late forties. Even at that date crossing the Minch was still a fairly slow and stormy affair, the one car for the party (complete with petrol ration coupons) being battened down on the deck and covered with salt spray. The group explored parts of Harris in wayward weather. As well as discovering plants, they were happy to find in those days of shortages that Cadbury's milk chocolate, scarce on the mainland, abounded in Tarbert.

Rhum was still the closed preserve of the owner. Nearly all visitors were unwelcome, and some even shot at, except for a small group under the late Professor Heslop Harrison who visited the island regularly. Members of the group were expressly forbidden to appear in sight of Kinloch Castle, but could roam the rest of the island to find Norwegian sandwort and mountain avens on the mountains and pyramidal bugle on the raised beach, or listen to the Manx shearwaters in their nests at night, or discuss grazing pressures. Certain species allegedly found on the island caused a hotbed of comment and counter-comment which found its way into the plant folklore of its day. Meanwhile M. E. D. Poore and V. C. Robertson were following up the early survey of vegetation by G. C. P. Petch on St Kilda in the early thirties, and coining a new word – zooplethismic – to describe the interaction of seabird communities on the vegetation of the island. New sites of arctic-alpine plants such as drooping saxifrage were being discovered, and even new records established, such as that for *Diapensia lapponica*. With greater interest in habitats and communities, the deciduous forest fragments of the west were being investigated by Donald McVean, which led to discoveries such as that of Rassal ashwood on limestone near Loch Kishorn.

The old interests, evolving since the time of Sir Robert Sibbald, were still there, and amateurs and trained scientists worked together in the field. Changes were on the way, however: 1949 saw at last the recognition of wildlife by the state and the intervention of government in the naturalist's world. For eager students of the late forties came the new opportunity to continue the work of previous generations on the payroll of the government, in the form of the Nature Conservancy.

Top: The yellow mountain saxifrage growing amongst rocks beside a mountain stream.
Bottom left: The waxy flowers of the dwarf cornel.
Bottom right: The delicate starry saxifrage too flourishes in wet ground by mountain streams.

From that group, in England as well as Scotland, emerged some of the distinguished field botanists of the 1970s, outstanding among them being D. A. Ratcliffe.

Even during the Second World War talks had been taking place about national parks, recreation and wildlife conservation, with names such as Professor James Ritchie and Dr (later Sir) Frank Fraser Darling featuring in the discussions. In Scotland interest centred on fine scenery, wildlife protection, enjoyment by the people, and opportunities for rural improvement and development – this last a particular concern in Scotland down the years, to naturalists as well as others. Until then the need for measures to safeguard the countryside generally, rather than the concept of protecting special areas, had not become apparent. The ebb and flow of thought, the near achievement of proper National Parks, the inertia in certain quarters, resulted eventually in the setting up of the Nature Conservancy by the National Parks and Access to the Countryside Act 1949. This is now past history, but it is surely heartening to recall that, even in the dark days of war, thoughtful and far-sighted people were seeking new ways to safeguard our wildlife and scenery, and to improve the use and enjoyment of the countryside against the changes which they saw in the years that lay ahead. In the end, the government did take action in safeguarding wildlife. Safeguarding the countryside as a whole in Scotland was left to look after itself.

Until 1949 any protection of wildlife by Act of Parliament had involved the prohibition of certain activities, such as the taking of the St Kilda wren in 1904. Acts of this kind had usually been concerned with birds, and go back to the time of William the Lion (1165–1214) when the eyries of falcons were protected. By the time of James III in 1474 their eggs were also included. Legislation to protect woodlands existed too, and is amply dealt with in Chapter 3. The 1949 Act was quite different, in that it set up a government agency with a positive wildlife role.

The Nature Conservancy was charged with the establishment and management of nature reserves and the scheduling of sites of special scientific interest which dovetailed into the new far-reaching planning legislation – the Town and Country Planning (Scotland) Act 1947, for example. The Nature Conservancy supported the setting up of a biological records branch which, with the help of amateur naturalists, led to a much more detailed geographical recording and to production as a first step of the *Atlas of the British Flora*.

In the late sixties work started on the *Nature Conservation Review* which sought to identify habitats on a representative basis throughout Britain. The whole concept of gathering information about plants and animals had changed radically since the immense herbarium compilation sponsored by the Botanical Society of Edinburgh in 1836. But the objectives were different too. In 1836 not much was known about occurrence of plants in Scotland and the main thrust of activity was towards the acquisition of this knowledge. Safeguarding was not a consideration, although it perhaps should have been, as Victorian collectors could become quite serious predators – a fact demonstrated by the sad end of the Scottish sub-species *artaxerxes* of the brown argus butterfly on Arthur's Seat in Edinburgh in 1868, exterminated by over-collecting. The Nature Conservancy was set up with conservation as its prime objective, using specially protected areas, either reserves or sites, as reservoirs against the onward pressures of development and, later,

Top left: Alpine mouse-ear. Top right: Primula scotica, the Scottish primrose, is the emblem of the Scottish Wildlife Trust. Bottom: Purple saxifrage is common in the Highlands, where it forms dense carpets of flowers on stony ground.

of leisure. It was held then, and still is, that wildlife should be safeguarded not just for public enjoyment but for its own sake.

In Scotland the voluntary conservation movement followed the national lead – although stirrings of voluntary effort had been evident as early as 1831 in the Berwickshire Naturalist Society, but these were more concerned with the companionable pursuit of knowledge than with safeguarding wildlife. Although the National Trust for Scotland had done some early pioneering work on Ben Lawers, the voluntary body which became primarily concerned with conservation in Scotland was the Scottish Wildlife Trust which was founded in 1964.

There have been enormous changes in the pressures on the countryside during the last twenty years. Not only are there greater numbers of people interested in wildlife, particularly in birds, but the general interest in the countryside has increased with the rise in car ownership (266,000 in 1956 to 1,313,000 in 1976), the shorter working week and longer holidays. Much of this pressure is generated within Scotland itself, but there are increasing numbers of visitors from England and the Continent (the latter contributed about one-fifth of the visitors to the crofting counties in 1977).

The main pressure in the more remote districts is caused by holiday visitors during a short summer season. In areas within easy reach of the industrial belt, such as Loch Lomond or the Angus Glens, there are also large numbers of day and week-end visitors. Areas such as Speyside, with its increase in ski-ing facilities as well as in holiday provision generally, show the effects of high levels of pressure on both mountain and forest. Easy transportation by ski lift to near the summit of Cairngorm creates a new threat for the fragile mountain vegetation, demonstrating as well as anywhere in Scotland the impact of many human feet.

The National Parks and Access to the Countryside Act 1949 did not deal at all, as far as Scotland is concerned, with the conservation of natural beauty or make provision for public enjoyment, and it was not until the late 1960s that countryside legislation was given a more comprehensive form. The idea that the safeguarding of wildlife and natural beauty should be linked with the public's enjoyment of them grew into the notion of caring for the countryside as a whole. With this view came a recognition of activity in the countryside, and an awareness that much of its attraction depended on its being well used by those who tended its trees, crops and animals. In this wider thinking public enjoyment took on new aspects, too: informal recreation in the countryside was to be encouraged, but must be compatible with the productive uses of land and the conservation of wildlife. Urban life on its own was seen to lack an indefinable something. People had a right to the countryside, and the state would finance the consequences of their incursions into it. Within this comprehensive and sometimes conflicting package, called the Countryside (Scotland) Act 1967, the fundamental issues of how best to conserve natural beauty and wildlife remained unresolved. The new legislation had an innovation – it sought to designate countryside, and therefore to define areas in which the Act could operate and areas in which it could not. In practice it has jurisdiction on just over 98 per cent of the land and inland water surface of the country.

Whatever may be seen now as limitations in the Countryside (Scotland) Act 1967, it was a milestone in the relationship between people and wildlife. The Act recognized that the conservation of the natural beauty and amenity of the countryside is for the benefit of people, and in so far as amenity covers wildlife, this concept applies to it too. The Act set up a new government agency, the Countryside Commission for Scotland, to undertake (among other things) the increasingly difficult task of achieving greater public enjoyment of the countryside while still safeguarding wildlife and natural beauty.

During the ten years of its existence the Commission has given advice and financial assistance towards the creation of facilities in places where people – and this means their motor cars and caravans too – are encouraged to go. In these places picnic sites, camping and caravan sites, view points with car parks, and the inevitable but important 'loos' have been provided. But it can also mean the exclusion of vehicles from certain places and the maintenance of paths and tracks for walking only, the *non*-provision of stopping places in sensitive areas, the restoration of damaged sites such as beach machair and its flora, or the provision of boardwalks to prevent the pressure of feet on an interesting bog. Countryside conservation in the later twentieth century is largely concerned with vehicle control, since a high proportion of countryside visitors do not stray far from their cars.

A further aspect of this approach is the creation of areas designed to cater for large numbers of people in pleasant places with a variety of activities: country parks. These are usually near urban areas, in the countryside around towns; they are the green breathing spaces for those who live in 'deserts wi' windies' or whose lives are restricted by streets and small garden gates. There may also be a countryside ranger service operated by local authorities, voluntary bodies and some private estates. This service provides guidance, information and sometimes direction to countryside visitors in country parks or elsewhere in the countryside.

History and hindsight can be both enlightening and frustrating. The mistakes of our predecessors are always more obvious than our own, yet we are thankful to be able to build on their foresight and recognize the wisdom of days gone by. But we cannot today look to the future with the confidence of our predecessors, or say with the certainty of Evander MacIver in 1903 that he envied the young for what they might live to see and hear while he commented with approval that 'Cycles and motor cars will no doubt supplant horsepower on our roads'.

Though Scotland is still fortunate in having a population in scale with its size, it is in no way immune from its heavily over-populated southern neighbour. The ease of access which helps the flow of goods and services across the Border also increases the flow of visitors to the Scottish countryside. Even in Scotland itself the population is badly distributed: 80 per cent are crammed into the central belt, living in the untidy aftermath of the industrial revolution and dogged by chronic unemployment, while the other 20 per cent live mainly in small widely scattered communities with severe depopulation problems and a preponderance of older age groups. A perennially poor country which over two hundred years ago exchanged control of its own destiny for entry to United Kingdom markets, Scotland has always been concerned with development – which over the centuries has meant, and still in part does mean, better production from the land. From Robert Sibbald and his 'mosses' down the centuries to the Scottish National Parks Committee of 1947 this strand runs still and is enshrined in the Countryside (Scotland) Act 1967, taking its place alongside care of wildlife and scenery, and people's enjoyment.

Scotland has many clear needs: urban renewal, the expansion of productive agriculture and forestry, the better safeguarding of wildlife and natural beauty, and the development of leisure and recreation facilities both urban and rural. Nearly all these objectives require the injection of central government finance or encouragement; in varying degrees they require national oversight – especially those, such as wildlife and natural beauty, which are concerned with long-term objectives. These things are all possible to achieve in Scotland with proper planning, management, finance and willingness to proceed.

Our concern in this chapter has been with wildlife, mainly plants and people, and in these final paragraphs to think forward a little. In doing so it is necessary to keep in sight that continuing aim of our history to improve the land and create a more productive countryside. Agriculture today is concerned, among other things, with better grassland conservation and the relative value of livestock versus vegetable production in certain areas. Because an additional 1.7 million hectares of land in Scotland are capable of growing trees there is ample opportunity for the re-creation of forests and plantations for timber production, for wildlife, and for recreation. But how much land should be devoted to each of these purposes – and to agriculture – must depend on what is the best use of that land.

Much still needs to be done to increase the opportunities for recreation, both rural and urban, within and around the central belt. Green spaces are not enough on their own; they require to be linked with more 'natural' areas containing birds and animals and flowers so as to bring countryside characteristics nearer to the city centre. This would not only supply 'spiritual exercise and enjoyment' and a taste of adventure, but also create a more understanding visitor to the countryside.

However much we are concerned with the countryside as a whole and with the needs of people, wildlife and people are not everywhere compatible. It is necessary therefore that certain sites should continue to be specially safeguarded at national level to maintain their intrinsic value for wildlife and natural beauty, while others should be for the intensive use of people – and that these should coexist within the broad framework of a prosperous countryside. Future generations will be the judges of whether we succeed in carrying out these tasks.

Rock Formations in the Highlands

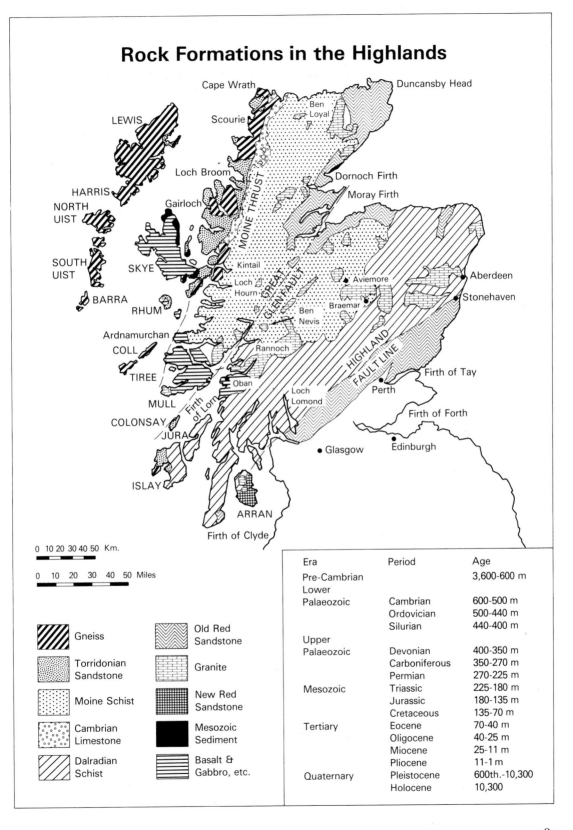

Cape Wrath
Duncansby Head
LEWIS
Scourie
Ben Loyal
HARRIS
Loch Broom
Dornoch Firth
NORTH UIST
Gairloch
Moray Firth
SOUTH UIST
SKYE
Kintail
Aviemore
Aberdeen
BARRA
Loch Hourn
Braemar
Stonehaven
RHUM
Ben Nevis
Ardnamurchan
COLL
Rannoch
TIREE
Oban
MULL
Loch Lomond
Perth
Firth of Tay
COLONSAY
Firth of Lorn
Firth of Forth
JURA
Glasgow
Edinburgh
ISLAY
ARRAN
Firth of Clyde
MOINE THRUST
GREAT GLEN FAULT
HIGHLAND FAULT LINE

Scale:
0 10 20 30 40 50 Km.
0 10 20 30 40 50 Miles

Gneiss	Old Red Sandstone
Torridonian Sandstone	Granite
Moine Schist	New Red Sandstone
Cambrian Limestone	Mesozoic Sediment
Dalradian Schist	Basalt & Gabbro, etc.

Era	Period	Age
Pre-Cambrian		3,600-600 m
Lower Palaeozoic	Cambrian	600-500 m
	Ordovician	500-440 m
	Silurian	440-400 m
Upper Palaeozoic	Devonian	400-350 m
	Carboniferous	350-270 m
	Permian	270-225 m
Mesozoic	Triassic	225-180 m
	Jurassic	180-135 m
	Cretaceous	135-70 m
Tertiary	Eocene	70-40 m
	Oligocene	40-25 m
	Miocene	25-11 m
	Pliocene	11-1 m
Quaternary	Pleistocene	600th.-10,300
	Holocene	10,300

187

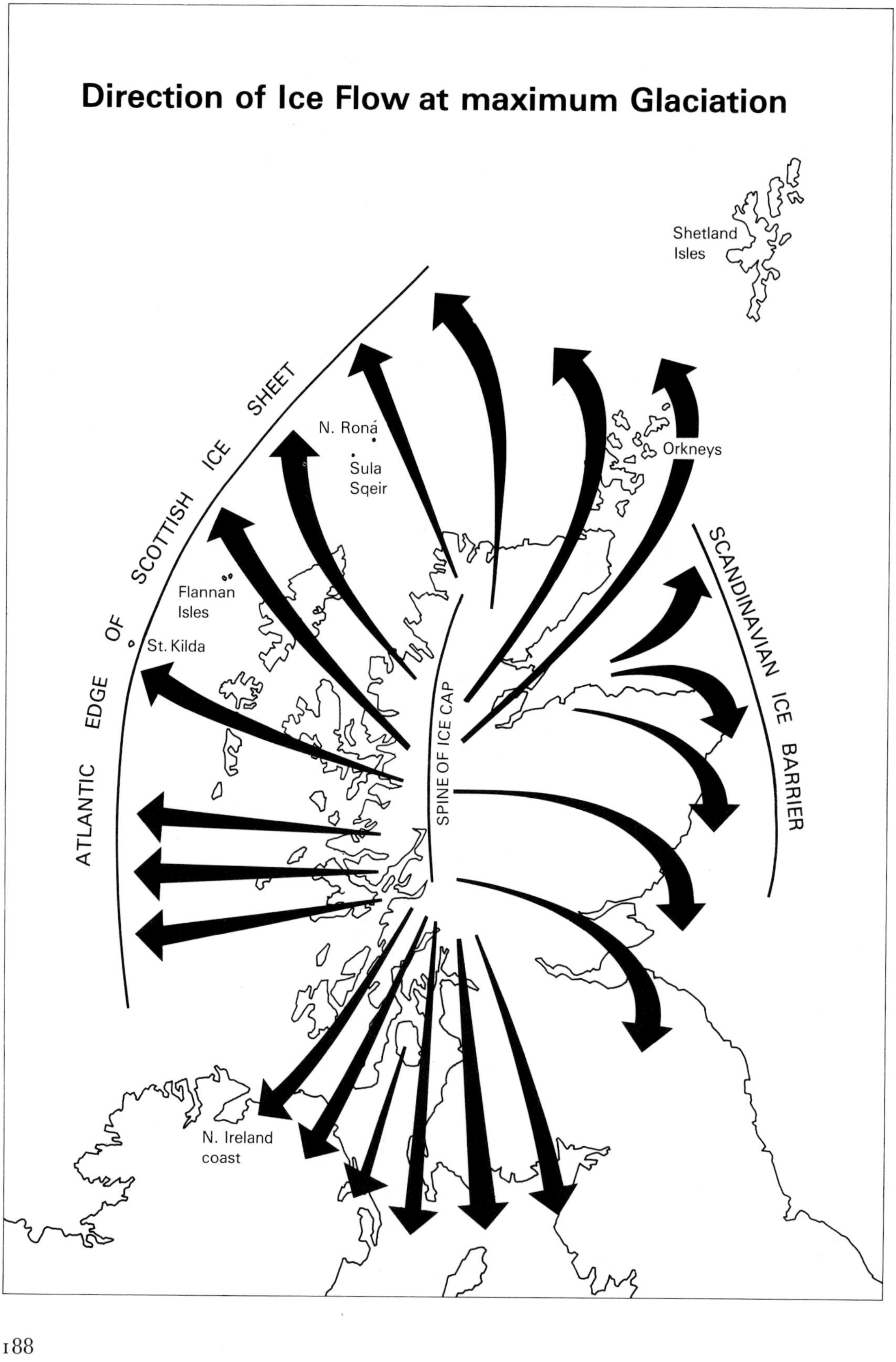

Direction of Ice Flow at maximum Glaciation

Shetland Isles

N. Roná

Sula Sqeir

Orkneys

SCOTTISH ICE SHEET

EDGE OF

ATLANTIC

Flannan Isles

St. Kilda

SPINE OF ICE CAP

SCANDINAVIAN ICE BARRIER

N. Ireland coast

Average Annual Rainfall

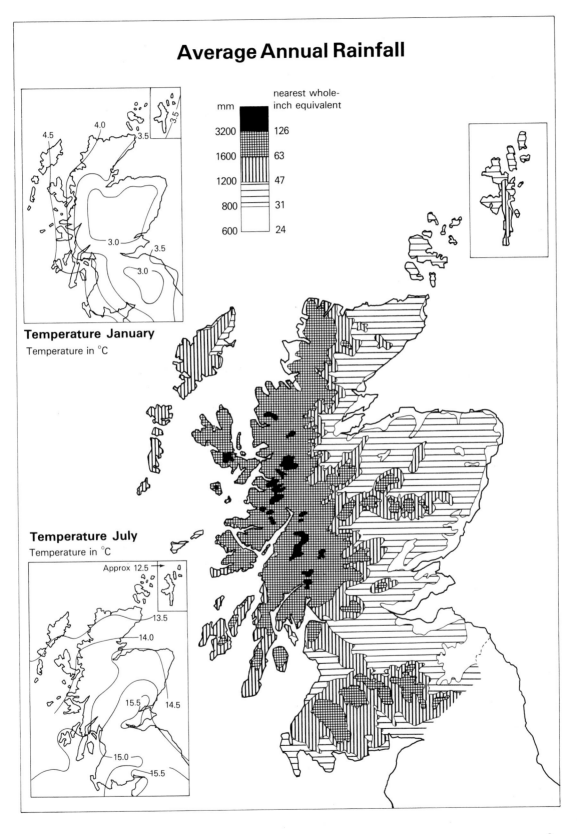

mm		nearest whole-inch equivalent
3200		126
1600		63
1200		47
800		31
600		24

Temperature January

Temperature in °C

Temperature July

Temperature in °C

Approx 12.5

Further Reading

Chapter One The High Tops
Burnett, J. H. (ed.), *Vegetation of Scotland*, Oliver and Boyd, 1964.
Charlesworth, J. D., 'Later Glacial History of the Highlands', *Transactions of the Royal Society of Edinburgh*, Vol. LXII, part iii, No. 19, 1954-5.
Craig, G. Y., *Geology of Scotland*, Oliver and Boyd, 1965.
Darling F. F. and Boyd, J. M., *The Highlands and Islands*, Collins, 1964.
Ford, E. B., *Butterflies*, Collins, 1977.
—— *Moths*, Collins, 1972.
Geikie, A., *Scenery of Scotland*, Macmillan, 1865.
Harvie-Brown, J. A. and Buckley, T. E., *The Vertebrate Fauna of Sutherland, Caithness and West Cromarty*, Edinburgh University Press, 1887.
——*The Vertebrate Fauna of the Outer Hebrides*, 1888.
——*The Vertebrate Fauna of Argyll and the Inner Hebrides*, 1892.
——*The Vertebrate Fauna of the Moray Basin*, 1895.
Hurley, P. M., 'Confirmation of Continental Drift', *Historical Geology* (Plate Tectonics), L. W. Mintz, Merrill, 1973.
Lamb, H. H., *Climate Present, Past and Future*, Methuen, 1972.
McVean, D. N. and Ratcliffe, D. A., *Plant Communities of the Scottish Highlands*, Monograph of the Nature Conservancy, HMSO, 1960.
Matthews, L. Harrison, *British Mammals*, Collins, 1960.
Nethersole-Thompson, D. and Watson, A., *The Cairngorms*, Collins, 1974.
Smith, M., *British Amphibians and Reptiles*, Collins, 1969.
Stephen, David, *Watching Wildlife*, Collins, 1978.

Chapter Two Wildlife on the Hill
Darling, F. F. and Boyd, J. M., *The Highlands and Islands*, Collins, 1964.
McVean, D. N. and Lockie, J. D., *Ecology and Land Use in Upland Scotland*, Edinburgh University Press, 1969.
Murray, W. H., *The Scottish Highlands*, Scottish Mountaineering Trust, 1976.
Nethersole-Thompson, D., *Highland Birds*, Highlands and Islands Development Board, 1971.
Nethersole-Thompson, D. and Watson, A., *The Cairngorms*, Collins, 1974.
Pearsall, W. H., *Mountains and Moorlands*, Collins, 1950.

Chapter Three Forests and Woodlands
Anderson, M. L., *A History of Scottish Forestry*, Nelson, 1967.
Peterken, G. F., 'General Management Principles for Nature Conservation in British Woodlands', *Forestry*, Vol. 50, No. 1, 1977.
Steele, R. C., *Wildlife Conservation on Woodlands*, Forestry Commission Booklet No. 29, 1972.

Chapter Four The Lowlands
Allison, A., Newton, I. and Campbell, C., *Loch Leven National Nature Reserve: A Study of Waterfowl Biology*, Wildfowlers Association of Great Britain and Ireland, 1974.
Arnold, H. R., *Provisional Atlas of the Amphibians and Reptiles of the British Isles*, Biological Records Centre, Monkswood Experimental Station, Huntingdon, 1973.
Biological Records Centre, Provisional Distribution Map: Lepidoptera, Nature Conservancy Council, Huntingdon, 1975 (unpublished).
Corbet, G. B. and Southern, H. N. (eds), *The Handbook of British Mammals*, 2nd ed., Blackwell Scientific Publications, 1977.
Fraser, Duncan, *The Flower People*, Standard Press, Montrose, 1977.
McCarthy, J., 'The Reserve Background', *Caerlaverock: Conservation and Wildfowling in Action*, ed. J. Harrison, WAGBI, 1974.
Mathews, S., 'The Agricultural Economy', *The Stirling Region*, ed. D. Timms, University of Stirling, 1974.
Ratcliffe, D. A. (ed.), *A Nature Conservation Review*, Cambridge University Press, 1977.
Sharrock, J. T. R., *Atlas of Breeding Birds in Britain and Ireland*, British Trust for Ornithology, Tring, 1976.

Chapter Five Lochs and Rivers
Burnett, J. H. (ed.), *Vegetation of Scotland*, Oliver and Boyd, 1964.
Maitland, P. S., *A Key to British Freshwater Fishes*, Scientific Publication No. 27, Freshwater Biological Association, 1972.
Mills, D. H., *Scotland's King of Fish*, Blackwoods, 1979.
Mills, D. H. and Graesser, H., *The Salmon Rivers of Scotland*, Cassell (in press).
Murray, J. and Pullar, L., *Bathymetrical Survey of the Fresh Water Lochs of Scotland*, Vols I to VI, Challenger Office, Edinburgh, 1910.

Chapter Six Estuaries and their Bird Life
Bourne, W. R. P., 'Seabirds and Pollution', *Marine Pollution*, ed. R. Johnston, 1976, pp. 403-502.
Campbell, L. H., *Report of Forth Ornithological Working Party*, Nature Conservancy Council, 1978.
Greenwood, J. J. D. and Keddie, J. P. F., 'Birds Killed by Oil in the Tay Estuary, March and April 1968', *Scottish Birds*, 5, 1968, pp. 189-96.
Milne, H., 'Breeding Numbers and Reproductive Rate of Eiders at the Sands of Forvie National Nature Reserve, Scotland', *Ibis*, 116, 1974, pp. 135-52.
Player, P. V., 'Food and Feeding Habits of the Common Eider at Seafield, Edinburgh, in Winter', *Wildfowl*, 22, 1971, pp. 100-6.
Prater, A. J., *The Birds of British and Irish Estuaries*, Poyser, 1974.
Swennen, C., 'Chlorinated Hydrocarbons Attacked the Eider Population in the Netherlands', *TNO-nieuws*, 27, 1972, pp. 556-60.
Thom, V. M., 'Wintering Duck in Scotland 1962-68', *Scottish Birds*, 5, 1969, pp. 417-66.

Chapter Seven The Bird Islands
Cramp, S., Bourne, W. R. P. and Saunders, David, *The Seabirds of Britain and Ireland*, Collins, 1974.
Darling, F. F., *Island Years*, Pan Books, 1973.
Darling, F. F. and Boyd, J. M. *The Highlands and Islands*, Collins, 1964.
Fair Isle Bird Observatory Reports.
Fisher, J. and Lockley, R. M., *Sea-Birds*, Collins, 1954.
Nelson, B., *The Gannet*, Poyser, 1979.
Nethersole-Thompson, D., *Highland Birds*, Highlands and Islands Development Board, 1971.
Scottish Birds, all volumes and special supplements.

Chapter Eight The Hebrides
Boyd, J. M. (ed.), 'The Natural Environment of the Outer Hebrides', *Proceedings of the Royal Society of Edinburgh*, B Vol. 77, 1979.
Darling, F. F., *West Highland Survey*, Oxford University Press, 1955.
Darling, F. F. and Boyd, J. M., *The Highlands and Islands*, Collins, 1964.
Jewell, P., Milner, C. and Boyd, J. M., *Island Survivors: the Ecology of the Soay Sheep of St. Kilda*, Athlone Press, 1974.
Murray, W. H., *The Islands of Western Scotland*, Eyre Methuen, 1973.
Randall, R. E., 'Machair Zonation of the Monach Isles NNR, Outer Hebrides', *Transactions of the Botanical Society of Edinburgh*, 42, 1976, pp. 441-62.
Ritchie, W., 'The Meaning and Definition of Machair', *Transactions of the Botanical Society of Edinburgh*, 42, 1976, pp. 431-40.

Chapter Nine Scottish Mammals
Corbet, G. B., and Southern, H. N., *The Handbook of British Mammals*, Blackwell Scientific Publications, 1977.
Matthews, L. Harrison, *British Mammals*, Collins, 1960.
Stephen, D., *Watching Wildlife*, Collins, 1978.

Chapter Ten Plants and People
Allen, D. E., *The Naturalist in Britain*, Allen Lane, 1976.
Fletcher, H. R. and Brown, W. H., *The Royal Botanic Garden Edinburgh 1670-1970*, HMSO Edinburgh, 1970.
Nicholson, M., *The Environmental Revolution*, Hodder, 1969.
Ratcliffe, D. A., *Highland Flora*, Highlands and Islands Development Board, 1977.
——(ed.), *A Nature Conservation Review*, Cambridge University Press, 1977.
Ritchie, W., Smith, J. S. and Rose, N., *The Beaches of North East Scotland*, commissioned by the Countryside Commission for Scotland and published by the Department of Geography, University of Aberdeen, 1978.

Index of Species

Plants

Animals

Index

Picture acknowledgements

Black and white

Crown Copyright by permission of the Controller of Her Majesty's Stationery Office facing p. ix; Aerofilms Ltd 57; Heather Angel 91; Forestry Commission 49, 52; M. P. Harris 119; Francis G. Howie 85; L. McNally 145, 153, 163; Derek Mills 74; C. E. Palmar 29, 33, 35, 45, 89, 96, 106; W. Ralston 92 (left); RSPB 99, 68 (Dennis Green), 98 (Jan Van de Kam), 109 (Richard T. Mills), 117 (Eric Hosking); Scottish Wildlife Trust 172; David Stephen 53, 166, 170; K. H. C. Taylor 51; John Topham Picture Agency 21, 157, 164; Bobbie Tulloch 18, 123; © Philip Wayre, The Otter Trust 61; Tom Weir ii–iii, 4, 8, 11, 13, 17, 25, 32, 36, 40, 43, 63, 72, 77, 80, 92 (right), 93, 112–13, 115, 118, 120, 122, 127, 128, 129, 130, 131, 133, 136, 139, 140, 144, 147, 149.

Colour

between pages viii and ix
I, II, III: University of Aberdeen, Dept. of Geography/NASA
between pages 6 and 7
I: Tom Weir; II: Tom Weir (top), BC/Jane Burton (bottom)
between pages 14 and 15
I, II: Tom Weir; III: BC/Charlie Ott; IV: S. C. Bisserot (bottom left), C. E. Palmar (top, bottom right)
between pages 22 and 23
I: Tom Weir; II: C. K. Mylne (top), Tom Weir (bottom)
between pages 30 and 31
I: David Stephen (top), Douglas Scott (bottom); II: Tom Weir (top), Adam Watson (bottom); III: Tom Weir; IV Tom Weir (top), BC/Pekka Helo (bottom)
between pages 38 and 39
I: C. E. Palmar; II: Tom Weir
between pages 46 and 47
I: Tom Weir (top), G. A. Dey (bottom); II: BC/Hans Reinhard (top), Tom Weir (bottom); III:BC/Hans Reinhard (top, bottom left), BC/L. R. Dawson (bottom right); IV: Tom Weir (top), Scottish Wildlife Trust (bottom)
between pages 54 and 55
I:BC/Leonard Lee Rue; II: Tom Weir
between pages 62 and 63
I:BC/Jane Burton (top), R. H. Bridson (bottom); II:BC/Hans

Reinhard; III: Tom Weir (top), Scottish Wildlife Trust (bottom); IV: Tom Weir
between pages 70 and 71
I: Tom Weir (top), BC/Jane Burton (bottom); H: C. E. Palmar (top), Scottish Wildlife Trust (bottom)
between pages 78 and 79
I: Scottish Wildlife Trust (top), Tom Weir (bottom); II: C. K. Mylne (top), C. E. Palmar (bottom); III: BC/Jane Burton (top), BC/Gunter Ziesler (bottom left), S. C. Bisserot (bottom right); IV: David Stephen (top), Tom Weir (bottom)
between pages 86 and 87
I: Tom Weir; II: Arthur Oglesby (top), BC/Jane Burton (bottom)
between pages 94 and 95
I: Tom Weir; II: BC/L. R. Dawson (top), BC/D. Middleton (bottom); III: BC/L. R. Dawson (top), Tom Weir (bottom); IV: David Stephen
between pages 110 and 111
I: C. E. Palmar; II: BC/L. R. Dawson (top), BC/D. and K. Urry (bottom); III: BC/Jane Burton (top), BC/Gordon Langsbury (bottom); IV: Tom Weir
between pages 126 and 127
I: Tom Weir; II: C. E. Palmar; III: Tom Weir (top left, bottom), C. K. Mylne (top right); IV: Tom Weir
between pages 134 and 135
I: Scottish Wildlife Trust; II: Tom Weir (top), C. E. Palmar (bottom)
between pages 142 and 143
I: BC/Barrie Thomas; II: BC/L. R. Dawson; III: BC/Pekka Helo (top), BC/S. C. Bisserot (bottom); IV: Heather Angel
between pages 150 and 151
I: BC/Hans Reinhard; II: David Stephen (top), BC/Jane Burton (bottom)
between pages 158 and 159
I: BC/Hans Reinhard; II: BC/John Markham (top), David Stephen (bottom); III: BC/Jane Burton; IV: BC/Jane Burton (top), BC/Hans Reinhard (bottom)
between pages 166 and 167
I: BC/Hans Reinhard (top), BC/S. C. Bisserot (bottom); II: BC/John Markham (top), C. K. Mylne (bottom)
between pages 182 and 183
I: C. E. Palmar; II: C. E. Palmar (top left, bottom); Scottish Wildlife Trust (top right)
BC = Bruce Coleman Ltd

198